SAGE was founded in 1965 by Sara Miller McCune to support the dissemination of usable knowledge by publishing innovative and high-quality research and teaching content. Today, we publish over 900 journals, including those of more than 400 learned societies, more than 800 new books per year, and a growing range of library products including archives, data, case studies, reports, and video. SAGE remains majority-owned by our founder, and after Sara's lifetime will become owned by a charitrust that secures our continued independence.

Los Angeles | London | New Delhi | Singapore | Washington DC | Melbourne

THE MUSEUM OF BROKEN TEA CUPS

THE MUSEUM OF BROKEN TEA CUPS

Postcards from India's Margins

GUNJAN VEDA

Los Angeles | London | New Delhi
Singapore | Washington DC | Melbourne

Copyright © Gunjan Veda, 2020

All rights reserved. No part of this book may be reproduced or utilized in any form or by any means, electronic or mechanical, including photocopying, recording or by any information storage or retrieval system, without permission in writing from the publisher.

First published in 2020 by

SAGE Publications India Pvt Ltd
B1/I-1 Mohan Cooperative Industrial Area
Mathura Road, New Delhi 110 044, India
www.sagepub.in

YODA Press
268 AC Vasant Kunj
New Delhi 110070
www.yodapress.co.in

SAGE Publications Inc
2455 Teller Road
Thousand Oaks, California 91320, USA

SAGE Publications Ltd
1 Oliver's Yard, 55 City Road
London EC1Y 1SP, United Kingdom

SAGE Publications Asia-Pacific Pte Ltd
18 Cross Street #10-10/11/12
China Square Central
Singapore 048423

Published by Vivek Mehra for SAGE Publications India Pvt Ltd. Typeset in 10/13.5 pt Avenir by Zaza Eunice, Hosur, Tamil Nadu, India.

Library of Congress Control Number: 2020931532

ISBN: 978-93-5388-338-6 (PB)

SAGE YODA Team: Arpita Das, Ishita Gupta, Tanya Singh, Amrita Dutta and Neena Ganjoo

*To Pragati, Aishwarya, Ganesh, Manjula and
all the people in this book who,
despite all odds, have not given up.*

*And to Salma, the little girl,
who once had stars in her eyes.
These stories I tell for her.*

Thank you for choosing a SAGE product!
If you have any comment, observation or feedback,
I would like to personally hear from you.

Please write to me at **contactceo@sagepub.in**

Vivek Mehra, Managing Director and CEO, SAGE India.

Bulk Sales

SAGE India offers special discounts
for purchase of books in bulk.
We also make available special imprints
and excerpts from our books on demand.

For orders and enquiries, write to us at

Marketing Department
SAGE Publications India Pvt Ltd
B1/I-1, Mohan Cooperative Industrial Area
Mathura Road, Post Bag 7
New Delhi 110044, India

E-mail us at **marketing@sagepub.in**

Subscribe to our mailing list
Write to **marketing@sagepub.in**

This book is also available as an e-book.

Contents

Acknowledgements	ix
Introduction	1
1. The Gallery of Portraits	23
2. Theatre of the Invisible	60
3. Budding Artists	124
4. The Unbroken	146
5. A Place to Remember	169
6. The Sacred Feminine	187
Epilogue: Confessions	260
Further Reading	**265**
Glossary	**268**
About the Author	**274**

Acknowledgements

No writing or author stands alone. This book is a reflection not just of the people whose stories it tells but of me, the storyteller. In the words of Chuck Palahnuik, 'There is nothing original about me. I am the combined effort of everyone I've ever known.' Starting with my parents who have always encouraged me to think for myself and follow my beliefs—wherever they might lead me—to my teachers, friends, colleagues and even strangers who have time and again shown me that humanity and hope continue to exist despite the mayhem of our times. I may not be able to thank everyone by name here, but I remain ever grateful for each and every one of you.

Dr Syeda Hameed, mentor, guide, friend, ammi. For your courage, your inspiration and your abiding faith in me. For teaching me that there is nothing embarrassing about getting up in a room full of people and saying, 'I don't know but I would like to. Will you help me understand?'

The Dalit Foundation for trusting me to do justice to this book and for being with me every step of the way. Martin for patiently expanding my horizons and Pradip for being my faithful companion, guide and translator during my travels, particularly in Maharashtra where this book first started to take shape. All the DF colleagues who travelled with me night and day as we went from village to village, collecting stories, music, culture and inspiration.

Arpita and Ishita, my editors, for believing in the book and for challenging me to step out of my comfort zone in order to be true to it.

Prashan Thalayasingam for being my first critic; for painstakingly reading the postcards from afar as they were written, for the skype discussions and long emails that helped me to always remember why I was writing this book. Siddhartha Gigoo and Prof Jacqueline Bhabha for their encouragement.

Mukta and Rajat for always being there—from whisking me off to the mountains when I was too disturbed after a trip to helping me find broken tea cups. You guys have been my rock!

Mom and Dad for your incredible patience and support. I know I am a nightmare when I write! Most importantly, Mom for showing me that real strength lies not in 'not making mistakes' but in having the courage to acknowledge them and to change, howsoever difficult that change may be. You are my strength!

And finally, the people without whom this Museum would not be. Thank you for opening your lives and homes to me—for sharing not just your aspirations, but your pain. For revisiting the darkest periods of your life just so that I and many others like me can gain strength and hope. For helping me confront my own biases. Thank you for your words, your talent and your actions. You bring light to this world!

Introduction

Heroism feels and never reasons, and therefore is always right.
—**Ralph Waldo Emerson**

I THE FIRST POSTCARD…

Dear Reader,

Welcome to the Museum of Broken Tea Cups. If you are here today, you are definitely the curious kind. Or are you just another museum enthusiast? A book lover, perhaps? Whatever the case, we, at the Museum, are very glad to make your acquaintance. By the end of this journey, we will be more than just acquaintants. We may even become fellow travellers, or in this case, co-workers. That, at least, is the hope with which we curated this museum.

What is this Museum about, you ask? Right now, I seek your indulgence. We have a long journey ahead. Along the way, I will answer all your whats, wheres and whys to the best of my ability. There will be many questions that remain. Perhaps we could explore those questions together? Seek out the experts; search the living libraries that are people's memories. Add new galleries, new collections, new stories?

But first the rules, or rather the rule, because there is just one here. As you walk through this museum, indulge your emotions. Let them roam free.

What we ask of you is not easy. In our world, emotions are seldom appreciated. All of us emote. Yet we seek to hide it, at least in our professional and public personas. No one wants to be an 'emotional fool'. A few emotions like sympathy or empathy are acceptable, perhaps even desirable in some small measure, but the rest we regard as the antithesis of rationality, of objectivity, even of spirituality; in short, of all the qualities that we, in this Age of Reason and Rationale, revere. We seek numbers; stories are not enough. Magnitude is important.

A couple of dead bodies—Sad, now where's my morning coffee?

A dozen. Tragic, did you pay the phone bill?

A hundred. Wait, what is happening? Turn on the news.

A thousand. I wish I could help; where do I donate money? This is unacceptable; let me float an online petition and tweet about it, tirelessly, ceaselessly.

Do not get me wrong. I do not seek to underestimate the power of online petitions or the succour provided by well-meaning donations. I am simply appalled that our well-intentioned anguish, sympathy and agitation need the persuasion of numbers to put in an appearance.

Somehow our agitation has become directly proportional to numbers; our admiration, inversely so.

One person has overcome all odds to make a difference. An icon, a role model. I wish I could meet her!

Two. We need more people like them.

A dozen. Admirable.

A hundred. Well really, many people seem to be able to rise above the situation. What's the big deal?

The tragedy of our age is that suffering is gauged by scale, achievement by the lack thereof. We as rational human beings seek comfort in numbers and science. But alas, rationality seems to be ephemeral. You may not remember specific equations from your Math textbook but a story from the Grade 5 Hindi or English Reader definitely rings a bell. That is why we use mnemonics—My Very Educated Mother Just Showed Us Nine Planets to remember the nine planets, or Idiotic Penguins Make Antarctica Too Cold to remember the life cycle of cells. Memorizing the infamous pi—3.1415926—was a nightmare, till you associated it with your favourite pep up drink! Just count the letters in every word of, 'May I have a large container of coffee?' and voila, you have pi! Mnemonics is a technique that uses acronyms, diagrams, rhymes, stories or acrostics—a poem or an invented sentence where the first letter of every line or word is the cue to an idea—to create associations that help us organize facts and remember them. And it is not a modern world phenomenon! Research in the field of psychology tells us that even in medieval Europe a good memory was considered a virtue. Mnemonic training was fundamental to medieval education and medieval lawyers used mnemonics to memorize entire sets of codes and laws.[1]

The fact—how we love them, facts, that is; the fact is that while we may shake our heads in despair at a horrific tragedy, vehemently state our point of view on Twitter or join a protest to express solidarity, we forget. As the numbers fade, so do our actions and reactions. We get busy with the business of living our lives, with our everyday wrinkles and laugh lines. Yet years later we remember that dialogue from our favourite book or movie. Life does not push it into oblivion. Perhaps the difference is of engagement. Reason makes us act or react, emotion makes us engage.

And what we seek here is your engagement. It is my sincere hope that you see these postcards with more than your head. Not that I don't have the deepest respect for that much-eulogized part of your anatomy. But in this Museum, we need your heart as well. We offer you not facts or figures, but faces. Real faces. Real stories. Real people, but without an arsenal of numbers and an armour of objectivity. This museum is personal, just like the postcards of yore when we always picked the card with the most interesting, inspiring and incredible picture for our loved ones and acquaintances. The message was simple—I am well. I saw this remarkable thing—remarkable because I have always wanted to see it, because it is unique or because I know you have a soft corner for it—and I thought of you. I want to share this moment, this story, this incredible find with you because I know you will appreciate it. If it excites you like I believe it would, you too can visit, find out more, experience it for yourself. Perhaps we could do it together someday.

And this, dear reader is exactly what I wish to say to you. Every broken tea cup in this Museum has a story attached to it. A story that is as true as yours and mine. A story that is remarkable. A story that needs to be heard, to be seen, to be known.

The first time I mentioned the Museum of Broken Tea Cups to a friend, she said it had a melancholic ring to it. Yet this museum isn't a melancholic place. If anything, it is magical because every painstakingly collected story in it has the power to fill the spectator with warmth, with hope and with energy. If you fail to feel its healing effects, the fault is entirely mine. Because sometimes breaking is a good thing. Sometimes breaking signifies a new dawn, a new hope and a new path. Sometimes breaking tea cups is the right thing to do.

Welcome to the Museum of Broken Tea Cups!

II WHERE IS THE MUSEUM OF BROKEN TEA CUPS?

It was on a sweltering summer afternoon in April 2015 that I first heard of the Museum of Broken Tea Cups. I was visiting schools in the Ahmedabad and Surendranagar districts of Gujarat, a state in Western India. Driving our air-conditioned Ford was Martin Mcwan, an unassuming 55 year old who has been leading the march against caste-based discrimination in India for several decades. Tall, slim and clean-shaven with bushy eyebrows and a swarthy complexion acquired from a lifetime of working tirelessly under the brutal sun, Martin was dressed in a simple cotton shirt. A recipient of the Robert F. Kennedy Human Rights award, he founded the Navsarjan Trust in 1988 to fight for the rights of the Dalits. The Trust runs schools in Gujarat where students from all castes and sub-castes not only study together, but also cook, clean and eat together. We were heading towards two of these schools.

Enroute, I heard Martin's story. His family had embraced Christianity and so despite the poverty and hardship of his early years, Martin never encountered caste-based discrimination. All this changed when he turned 18. 'The year was 1977. I was in my first year of college at St Xavier's, Ahmedabad. Two professors from the Behavioural Science Centre were undertaking research on the socio-economic conditions of Dalits in the Kheda district of Gujarat. I went with them to fill the survey forms. For the first time, I was confronted with the realities of untouchability, sexual exploitation of Dalit women and other forms of discrimination,' Martin recalled. The social and economic data collected during the survey may have been his first brush with the caste system in India, but young Martin soon forgot the details. The only thing that remained firmly entrenched in his memory were the *Rampatars.*

'As I walked through the streets of Vainaj, the first village we visited, I was intrigued to see a cup or a saucer lying outside the living areas of every house. These were either placed on the wooden pillar under the roof or on the courtyard fence. The village was like a veritable museum of tea cups!' Martin explained. He asked the Dalit residents of the village, who had been accompanying him, the significance of these cups.

'They are the Rampatars,' the villagers told him.

'Rampatars meaning the vessel of Lord Rama? Why are these holy objects in such poor condition and why are they kept outside the houses?' asked a perplexed young Martin. He was greeted with self-deprecating laughter. An elderly man, his tired, old eyes filled with decades of pain and resignation explained, 'These are not holy vessels. They are utensils used for people like us. Often, we go to their houses to do some work or to collect wages. If they are kind, they offer us tea in these cups.'

Eighteen-year-old Martin realized then that he had stumbled upon something significant. 'But it took me 25 long years to fully comprehend the role of the Rampatar and to break its symbolism,' Martin said.

Over the last few months, as I have travelled across the country, learning the stories of different communities and cultures, I have come to realize the significance of that cup of tea or glass of water, that many of us take for granted. For over 160 million people living in India, it is the difference between life and death, between acceptance and contempt. The so-called upper castes do not deign to pollute their utensils by letting the Dalits drink from them. Instead, they keep a separate set of utensils. When a Dalit labourer or worker comes calling, he or she picks up the Rampatar—often chipped and stained—and keeps it on the floor outside the house. The upper caste person pours water or tea into it from as far above as possible. After sitting outside the house and sipping his or her drink, the Dalit once again requests some water to clean the utensil and leaves it behind in its designated spot, outside the house. The 'pure' caste people are never 'tainted' by touching the vessels used by the 'impure'. The Dalits never touch any other utensils in the upper caste house. The fact that most of these utensils, at least till a few decades ago, were made by Dalit communities is conveniently forgotten by everyone.

As educated urbanites we often travel with our bottles of mineral water, wary of any glass that is offered to us, and oblivious of the environmental harm that we cause. In restaurants and hotels, we ask if the water is filtered with an 'Aquaguard' water purifier. If the establishment looks a little rundown or suspect, we quickly add bottled water to the tab. Here, I must confess that I am particularly fastidious about 'clean water'. Growing up, my water bottle and I were inseparable. I carried it on road trips, to school, college and subsequently, office, to meetings, to short trips in the neighbourhood and even to restaurants and five-star hotels. This was my quirk—unless it was treated water from a trusted source, I always needed my own water bottle or in the unlikely event of me being without it, a bottle of mineral water.

Yet I was collecting stories of people for whom water had always been a mark of social ostracism. Not only could Dalits not drink water from the utensils or wells of the upper castes—many a person has been killed for this—they were not allowed to offer them water in their own utensils. If I refused the glass of water that they offered me, I was rejecting them, their hospitality. My reasons notwithstanding, to them my refusal would always be a symbol of casteism. I quickly learnt to not say no. I would at least take one sip of the water, much to the discomfort of my fragile stomach, pampered by an almost lifetime of 'filtered water'. (Yes, I am ashamed to say I was one of the early adopters!). Yet sometimes taking that one sip became extremely difficult.

Once when we were travelling to Ahmednagar town in Maharashtra, we saw half a dozen makeshift tents by the roadside. They were little more than large sheets of plastic tied together. Old clothes were strewn over them to dry in the sun. Four men were squatting on the floor next to a rusty motorbike loaded with bundles of rags. Behind the tents were two small tempos with plastic sheets to cover their open backs. We stopped to speak to the people. The ground was uneven and covered with rocks. Two young boys, their faces streaked with dirt, clad only in shorts, were running around with sticks in their hand. A few more children peeked out of the tents on our arrival. Young girls who were busy mending clothes or gathering branches, looked up. They laid a few cement bags on the floor for us.

The group belonged to the Kudmude Joshi community who had till a few decades ago, lived off telling people's fortunes. They now collected old clothes, repaired and sold them. They had nothing except the torn, patched up clothes they wore, the plastic sheets that protected them from the harsh sun, a few bundles of rags that they intended to repair, some aluminium utensils and the rickety trucks in which they moved from one place to the next. As we crouched on the ground to speak with them, they sought to offer the only hospitality they could afford—water. Next to the tent, outside which we sat, there was an open aluminium tub—the one used to carry cement and soil at construction sites. In it lay some murky water. From where I sat, I could see sand, stones and a whole world in that tub. The tumbler, a well-worn and beaten down piece of aluminium, was lying in the dirt next to the tub. One of the girls picked it up, dipped it into the tub and offered it to us. To my utter shame, I froze. I could not make myself take that glass of water which she offered with so much respect on a sweltering day. My colleague from the Dalit Foundation quickly jumped to the rescue. He took the glass from her, saying he was parched and gulped down the water.

Even now, the memory of that day fills me with shame. I do not know if the girl or her family noticed my hesitation before my colleague stepped in. If they did, I had dealt one more blow to their already bruised souls.

But I digress. How easy it is to get lost in the labyrinth of one's own thoughts! After 25 years of seeing the Rampatars strewn all over the villages, not just in the upper caste neighbourhoods, but in the Dalit *mohallas* (colonies) as well, Martin realized that in them lay the genesis of the caste system and the reason for its continuity. The Rampatar denoted an act of co-operation between the 'pure' and 'impure' castes to honour and accept the caste system. It was not forced—remember, the elderly man felt that it was kept by kind-hearted 'touchables' to offer water and tea. Moreover, there was hierarchy within the Dalit communities as well. The lowest caste among the Dalits was treated by the upper caste Dalits in exactly the same manner as the touchables treated the untouchables. They too kept Rampatars for people below their caste rank.

Martin realized that the only way to break the caste system was to stop co-operating with it—to denounce the Rampatar, its biggest symbol. In 2003, the Navsarjan Trust, led by Martin, organized a foot rally that marched across villages with the slogan, 'Ram patar chodo, Bhim patar apnao' (abandon the Rampatar, accept the Bhimpatar). The Bhimpatar, named after Dr Bhimrao Ambedkar, the architect of India's constitution and the strongest crusader against untouchability, was the cup of equality. It forbade no one, denied no one. 'Around 200,000 people joined the 100-day foot march. In village after village, people across castes and sub-castes shared tea in the same cup. They pledged to never accept or offer anything in the Rampatar,' Martin recalled. It was a heady journey. As they passed through villages, the marchers removed any Rampatars that they saw. In some places, children would smash them. 'That's when I stopped them. Let's collect these Rampatars and create a Museum of Tea Cups, only this time the Museum would symbolize hope, not discrimination, I suggested,' Martin told me.

The idea stuck in my head. I knew then that I had the title of my book. A tea cup is perhaps the most ubiquitous and yet, the least noticed symbol of caste-based discrimination in India. A broken Rampatar represents a movement towards equality, a breaking of stereotypes, and each postcard in this book tells the story of someone who has broken a Rampatar or is likely to break one. So, what better title than The Museum of Broken Tea Cups, a museum that Martin still hopes to curate!

We began by asking where is the Museum of Broken Tea Cups? It is in that tiny village in Orissa where a woman defied tradition to take control of the looms. It is in the colony in Maharashtra where Babita, Ranjeeta and Prem managed to stop the tradition of brewing alcohol. In Manjula, the girl who refused her fate as a Devadasi and is training youth in Bangalore today. It is in every act of courage that a Dalit man, woman or child performs; it is in every moment of defiance; in every step towards equality that you and I take. Someday perhaps, it will have a physical location. A place where all the chipped and broken tea cups will lie together in a sunny courtyard, recounting these tales of valour. A place where people will celebrate equality, humanity and change. Till we come together to create this new space, the Museum will have to remain housed in its present location—your heart and mine!

III WHY DO WE NEED A MUSEUM FOR BROKEN TEA CUPS?

The Dalit Foundation is a non-governmental organization that works to empower Dalit communities in India by supporting individuals, community-based organizations and networks that promote social change. The year 2015 marked a decade of its existence, and the organization decided to celebrate it with a book on Dalits. In my previous avatar at the Planning Commission of India, I had often encountered the Foundation and its work, which I admired immensely. Yet, when in March 2015 they approached me with the idea of writing this book, I was surprised. Though I had worked with the government and with the social movements in India, I was not a part of the Dalit rights movement. In fact, I knew little about it apart from what I had read in the textbooks, in government and NGO reports. Having been born and raised in India, I was used to seeing the caste column in forms of all nature. As a child, whenever I encountered the caste column and asked my parents about it, I was told to leave it blank. Ditto the region column. My Dad loved to say, 'You are an Indian. Regional, caste and religious identities are irrelevant.' If ten- or twelve-year-old me insisted, he would name a new state each time. It took me a few attempts to catch on; then I stopped asking. A few times, people enquired about my caste, but generally they just assumed my caste identity based on my last name—Veda.

The Vedas are the oldest scriptures of Hinduism. Under the caste system only the priests or the Brahmins (upper caste) had the right to study them. Thus, it was assumed that I was a Brahmin. It was almost hilarious, this attribution of caste identity. Family names are normally used to trace the genesis of a person, his or her roots and in India, caste. Today, one could find anywhere between a few thousand to a million people sharing their last names; people they bear no relation to in the living memory of their extended families. Yet I can confidently say that any Veda (last name, not first) you encounter will be my kin. You see, Veda as a last name only came into existence a few decades ago. My grandfather decided that our family name Vedmehta was too long. Short names were more convenient in the sugar factory where he worked. So the common Vedmehta became the trendy Veda! Thus from childhood, caste was never a reality in my life. I read about it in school textbooks, just like the other kids my age did, but it never mattered to me. I was barely nine years old when the V.P. Singh government decided to implement caste-based reservations based on the report of the Mandal Commission.[2] I had little understanding of the violence that ensued. My first brush with the caste system was during my final years of schooling, when I often heard the anti-reservation rants of classmates who were preparing for the engineering and medical entrance exams.

It was in 2005 that I witnessed the ugly spectre of casteism. I had just entered the Planning Commission and one of my first field trips was to the state of Rajasthan in Western India. We were visiting the adjoining districts of Kota, Bundi and Baran. In Pinjna village in Baran district we visited a school where children were being served hot cooked meals prepared by Akshaya Patra, an NGO. The organization had begun operations in the village two months ago and was facing major challenges. 'Children from the upper caste refuse to have food cooked by women from the lower castes. Similarly, they refuse to eat with children from other castes. The caste lines are extremely strong here,' the local co-ordinator informed us. Before entering the village, we had passed a hamlet of rundown houses. These belonged to the Kherva community, a scheduled tribe that was extremely poor and lived outside the village. We discovered that no child from the hamlet was enrolled in a school. 'We are asked to pay a fee of ₹30 per child. We cannot afford it,' the people had complained. The District Collector, who is the chief administrator of a district in India, was travelling with us. He had been shocked to hear this. 'Education in government schools is free.' He had taken the children to register them in the school. This is where we met the Akshay Patra workers. Gradually, the story emerged. The villagers did not want their children to study with the Kherva children and those from the lower castes. By law, the school could not refuse admission to anyone on the basis of caste. Thus, they had come up with this ingenious solution. They knew that none of the lower caste families would be able to afford the fee. They could effectively segregate the children, without breaking the law.

In visit after visit from the Planning Commission, be it to Musahar *bastis* (habitations) in Uttar Pradesh and Bihar, to colonies of manual scavengers (people who lift the night soil) in Madhya Pradesh or to protest rallies organized by NGOs in Tumkur district of Karnataka, I learnt that caste-based discrimination continued to be a reality. Yet, at some level, I still believed that it was a problem of a few select pockets in rural India. Thus, when the Dalit Foundation asked me to write this book, my knowledge of the Dalit movement in India was limited to a few key names and events. 'Why me?' I wondered. But they were insistent. 'We are not looking for scholarly work on the subject. There are a lot of good academic books on the issue. What we want is a fresh look at the issue by someone who comes without prejudice.'

Thus, began my foray into the world of caste in India. I began by looking at what was available. I found my DF colleagues were right. There was no dearth of literature on untouchability, caste-based discrimination and the movement against it. The politics of reservation had been debated extensively. The last few decades had seen the emergence of Dalit voices telling their own stories, though most of these works are available in local languages only. Yet, I could not find a single book on Dalit cuisine.[3] Except for a couple of recent works on Dalit entrepreneurs, there was no volume mapping the impact of Dalit communities on our society. Their contribution as artists, weavers, musicians and dancers was neither recognized nor celebrated. I had found my book.

I spent the next year travelling across the country, meeting tattoo artists and *naqqara* players, *lavani* dancers and the makers of the famous *kolhapuri chappals*. The Dalit Foundation has, for over a decade now, been supporting not just emerging leaders from marginalized communities, but also Dalit artists and artisans, enabling them to use culture as a tool for liberation. They have an extensive network of people on the ground—people who became my guides, translators and in many cases, sources of inspiration on this journey. Their cups were the first broken pieces of crockery that I curated for this Museum.

Why is it important to document these broken tea cups? To hear these stories?

Ever since Independence, the Dalit question has grabbed headlines and eyeballs intermittently. Reactions to these news stories have oscillated between anger, disgust or sympathy, depending on which side of the political spectrum one is on. Consequently, there have been two parallel discourses that dominate mainstream thinking when it comes to Dalits: first, a discourse of deprivation and victimhood that laments the atrocities committed and seeks to make amends through reservations, political presence and empowerment. The second, a discourse that treats Dalits as interlopers, who seek to use their caste identity as a passport to positions that they do not merit. Seldom has any attempt been made to look at these communities as active contributors to our society and polity.

The Constitution of India, adopted on 26 January 1950, promises equal rights to all its citizens and prohibits the state from discriminating on the basis of religion, caste, region or sex. Article 17 specifically states that untouchability has been abolished and makes its practice a punishable offence. Over the years, a series of legislations have sought to address the different manifestations of caste-based discrimination in India: the Untouchability (Offences) Act 1955, the Protection of Civil Rights Act 1976, Bonded Labour System Abolition Act 1976, the Prevention of Atrocity Act 1989, The Employment of Manual Scavengers and Construction of Dry Latrines (Prohibition) Act 1993, and the Manual Scavenger Act 2013, to name a few.

Yet untouchability continues unabated. According to the National Crime Records Bureau, over 45,000 crimes against Scheduled Castes and Scheduled Tribes were reported in 2015. Simply put, in that year, a crime was committed against Dalits every 12 minutes. A 2016 report in *India Today* tried to put the various statistics on Dalits in perspective. Citing 2010 data, it noted that in India, a crime is committed against a Dalit every 18 minutes. Every day, on average, three Dalit women are raped, two Dalits murdered, and two Dalit houses burnt. More than one out of every three Dalits live below the poverty line, while one of every two is undernourished. 83 per 1,000 children born in a Dalit household die before their first birthday, 12 per cent before their fifth birthday, and 45 per cent remain illiterate. Dalits are prevented from entering the police station in 28 per cent of Indian villages. Dalit children are made to sit separately while eating in 39 per cent of government schools. Dalits do not get mail delivered to their homes in 24 per cent of villages. And they are denied access to water sources in 48 per cent of our villages.[4] In the last decade, not much has changed from what becomes evident in these statistics. In fact, the number of crimes against Dalits being reported has gone up. Is this because there is a greater backlash as Dalits try to claim the rights that have long been denied to them or is it simply a factor of better reporting? The question, while important, is not one this book seeks to address. Rather, it is based on a very simple premise.

Fear of law can limit overt acts of discrimination, but it does not weed out feelings of caste-based superiority or ingrained feelings of inferiority. In other words, it does not impact the social contract that is caste-based discrimination. It continues, albeit in more subtle forms and with more practical sounding rationale. The only way to remove this 'unequal' status is to recognize the contribution of Dalit communities, to give them the respect due as innovators, nurturers and artists. Traditionally in India, the performing arts have been the domain of Dalit communities. It is in their homes that these art forms have been fostered. It is their voices that have carried them. The intent behind the Museum of Broken Tea Cups is to celebrate the contribution of these unseen, unheard, unrecognized artists. To recognize the immense cultural contribution made by Dalit communities through the stories of individual artists who languish in the forgotten *gallis* (lanes) and *mohallas* (colonies) of our villages and towns. At the same time, it seeks to celebrate the everyday heroes who have, despite all odds, managed to change not just their own lives but the lives of those around them. These are students and teachers, artists and activists, storytellers and devadasis, daughters and mothers, sons and brothers—seemingly ordinary people whose faces get lost in the everyday, but whose stories have the potential to inspire admiration, action and change. Through their stories, this Museum seeks to expand the discourse around Caste in India.

IV WHO IS A DALIT?

The term Dalit was first used by Jyotiba Phule—a social reformer from Pune—in the late 19th century to describe the people who were outside the Varna system and were treated as untouchables. It is a political self-designation[5] that comes from the Sanskrit word 'dal' meaning oppressed, downtrodden, crushed or destroyed. In Marathi, the language in which the word was first used for social and political mobilization, it means broken.

To understand the meaning of the term Dalit, in the sense in which it is used in this book and by the Dalit Foundation, one needs to first look at the caste system in India. The subject has been extensively studied and explained in myriad works by sociologists, anthropologists and scholars.[6] This chapter uses these works to provide a brief overview of 'who is a Dalit' and the evolving meaning of the term.

The *Varna Vyavastha* (caste system) is a division of society based on occupation, whose origins can be traced back to the Rig Veda—the sacred text of Hinduism believed to have been compiled between 1500–1000 BC—and the Manusmriti. The latter is a treatise on human conduct, morality and sacred obligations, presumably drafted in the first century AD.

According to the Rig Veda, humans were created from *Purusha*, a being with a thousand heads, a thousand eyes, a thousand feet, and divided into four *varnas*. *Brahmins* were the priests and scholars who sat at the top of the social hierarchy and came out of the mouth of the Purusha. The rulers, warriors and the landed class were *Kshatriyas* who came of his arms, while the traders, producers and wealth creators were *Vaishyas* born of his thighs. The *Shudras* born out of the feet of the Purusha, were the toilers, peasants and labourers. The fifth category of people or the *Panchama*, were people who were *Avarna* (without varna) or outside this varna system. Some believe they were people born out of inter-caste marriages, while others claim they were the original inhabitants of India—the Dravidians. Over time, the division of society became hereditary. The people who worked with leather, those who swept the neighbourhood, or carried news of birth and death, and even musicians, performers and artisans who made utensils and idols began to be regarded as impure, so much so that mere contact with them would pollute the other castes. In short, they became untouchables and, in some cases, unseeables. This became an excuse to deny them their basic human rights. The cobblers manufactured shoes for everyone but were beaten to death if they dared to wear them. The potters who made utensils were not allowed to touch them after they entered the households of other caste persons. The sculptors who chiselled idols out of stone were denied entry into the very temples that housed those idols. Women from the 'untouchable' castes were sexually 'touched' and exploited. Men and women alike were flogged to death if they attempted to change their profession (like manual scavenging or drumming), if they drank water from a well belonging to another caste, or if they stepped into a neighbourhood belonging to the other caste. In some cases, the 'untouchables' had to tie a broom behind them, so that the earth was wiped clean of their footsteps. A spittoon around their neck ensured that their saliva did not touch the ground. In short, they were subjected to daily rituals of humiliation and violence.[7]

Many theories exist about the genesis of the caste system.[8] While some trace its existence to the Aryan conquest of India, others link it to notions of purity. According to sociologist Louis Dumont, '...the distinguishing characteristic of so-called untouchables is that they and only they must perform the tasks of ritual cleansing and pollution-removal...indispensable for the existence of Hindus as social beings. These are tasks which keep the "untouchable" in a permanently unclean state, but which thereby allow those of "clean" caste to maintain a state of ritual purity in a world which continually surrounds them with both tangible and intangible sources of defilement and pollution.'[9] The sanctity of the 'pollution line'[10] is heavily defended through a system of pain and penalties. Individual transgressions are collectively punished—sometimes, entire colonies of untouchables are denied water, food or excommunicated if one individual attempts to cross the line—in an exercise of social power designed to eliminate any threats to the hierarchy of privileges.

Ambedkar was one of the most vocal critics of the caste system. He strongly repudiated the theory of religious sanctity that traced the origins of the caste system to Manu (through the *Manusmriti*).

He also challenged claims that blamed it on notions of race or purity. Ambedkar believed that the caste system was born out of an original class system. The varnas were occupation-based classes and movement between them was open. However, at some point, this open-door policy of the classes underwent a change and class metamorphosed into caste—a hereditary occupational grouping, which did not permit inter-mingling or inter-marriage. Ambedkar defined caste as 'an artificial chopping off of the population into fixed and definite units, each one prevented from fusing into another through the custom of endogamy.'[11] He held the Brahmins responsible for the introduction of this endogamy and suggested that some classes simply imitated the practice followed by a higher social rank, while the rest were excommunicated in the process. The resulting system was one of graded inequalities wherein tasks were assigned prior to birth and were based on status, not merit, aptitude or capability.[12] Those at the base of this social hierarchy had no land or legal rights and were forced to live on the peripheries.[13]

While this systematic exploitation of an entire section of society has been carried out for centuries, the terms commonly used to describe the people who are exploited—untouchables, depressed classes, *harijans*, Dalits and scheduled castes to name a few—are relatively new. 'Depressed class' was a British legal term that began to be used in the late 1870s. The first volume of the *Bombay Gazetteer* published in 1877, used the term 'Depressed castes', but in subsequent volumes caste was substituted by classes and this term was taken up by the reform movement, the local elite and European missionaries.[14] The term 'untouchable' was coined during the Census of 1901. Sir Herbert Risley was an Oxford-educated British ethnographer and colonial administrator who belonged to the Indian Civil Service. He was greatly fascinated by the caste system and when he became the Commissioner for the Census of 1901, he embarked on a grand experiment to classify and rank the castes. One of the five categories he identified for the enumeration was *Aprishya Shudra*, defined as 'castes whose touch is so impure as to pollute even Ganges water.' Two British Superintendents, R.C. Bramley and Captain A.D. Bannerman, carried out this enumeration for the state of Rajasthan. It was they who for the first time in print, called these castes untouchables.[15] It was subsequently taken up by Sayaji Rao Gaekwar III, the Maharaja of Baroda, who argued that all Indians, including the Brahmins, were depressed.

Till the 1930s, Mahatma Gandhi used the term *Antayaja* (last born) to refer to the Untouchables when he wrote in Gujarati. In English, he used the term 'suppressed classes'. It was after the Poona Pact that promised greater reservation of seats in legislatures for the depressed classes, that Gandhi began to increasingly use the term Harijan, literally, 'Children of God'. Historian Ramchandra Guha believes this is because he found the word to be, 'less pejorative than "Untouchable", less patronizing than the colonial coinage, "Depressed Classes", and more indigenous-sounding than his own earlier alternative, "suppressed classes".'[16] He borrowed the term from the 14th-century Gujarati poet Narsingh Mehta.

The term Depressed Classes was replaced with Scheduled Castes in the Government of India Act of 1935, designed to provide greater self-rule to the provinces. In 1936, a list of these castes was released through another Government of India Order.[17] After Independence, the Constituent Assembly continued to use the terms Scheduled Castes and Tribes and the 1936 Schedule was reproduced with some changes.

The term Dalit was coined by Jyotiba Phule and used intermittently by Ambedkar. However, it was with the Dalit Panthers Movement in Maharashtra in the 1970s that the term gained currency. A 'radical political movement that challenged the hegemony of Hindus and the power they wielded in the realm of culture and politics,'[18] the Panthers sought to expand the scope of the term 'Dalit' beyond untouchability and to imbue it with a new political identity. Their 1973 Manifesto sought to create a coalition and defined Dalits as, 'Members of scheduled castes and tribes, Neo-Buddhists, the working people, the landless and poor peasants, women and all those who are being exploited politically, economically and in the name of religion.'[19] Talking about Dalit literature, Baburao Bagul, an eminent Marathi writer, proclaimed, 'Dalit is the name for total revolution; it is revolution incarnate.'[20] Thus, what had emerged as a political self-designation for the Untouchables, was expanded to represent a coalition of those rendered powerless and exploited continually in the name of religion. This was important for consolidating the protesting voices and creating a comprehensive movement against caste-based discrimination.

Currently, every Indian state recognizes certain groups of people as Scheduled Castes (SC) and Scheduled Tribes (ST). These state lists are amended versions of the original 1936 list. As a result, some groups of people are deemed SC in one state, ST in another and none of the two in a third, generating confusion and artificial divides. There also exist systems of hierarchy and discrimination within the groups who are treated as Untouchables. Further, the inclusion of groups within these lists is no longer about affirmative action for equity, targetting those that have been exploited or discriminated against the most. Rather, as recent headlines have shown, it has become a political battleground for appeasement and identity politics. Thus, reframing the Dalit identity to express a collective injustice was a strong tool for amalgamation and consolidation.

The Dalit Foundation has taken this a step further. It has moved from a definition of Dalits as victims, to Dalits as active agents. Thus, to them the term Dalit signifies a moral position of equality. Any and every person who fights against discrimination, who stands for this equality is a Dalit.

Why then do I lay out these various definitions and trajectories the definitions have taken in this chapter? In common parlance, all these terms are used interchangeably. So too is the case with this Museum. To the extent possible, my attempt has been to stick to the vocabulary used by the people or the translators. Yet it is important to acknowledge that each of the terms identified above carries connotations and political positions. In this Museum, we acknowledge the baggage of history and politics that every term carries. We recognize that everyone has a different understanding of these terms. But here, the Dalit is any person who has been subjected to discrimination—social, economic and gender—as a result of the caste or community he or she was born into. He or she is equally any person who is fighting against this inequality and discrimination. In short, our definition of the Dalit is not confined to the constitutionally recognized Scheduled Castes.

Endnotes

1. R.R. Hunt, J.B. Worthen, *Mnemonics: Underlying Processes and Practical Applications* in Learning and Memory: A Comprehensive Reference, Vol. 2, 2008, Academic Press; pp. 145–56.
2. The Mandal Commission had been appointed by Prime Minister Morarji Desai in 1978 to examine the issue of reservations for socially and economically backward castes and to identify the caste groups that should benefit from these.
3. The only available work is a short book called, *Isn't This Plate Indian? Dalit Histories and Memories of Food*, published by Pune University. In 2013, under the initiative of late Professor Sharmila Rege at the Krantijyoti Savitribai Phule Women's Studies Centre in Pune University, a group of students explored the politics of food and created an anthology of Dalit food practices.
4. Ajit Kumar Jha, The Dalits: Still untouchable, *India Today*, 3 February 2016. Available at http://indiatoday.intoday.in/story/dalits-untouchable-rohith-vemula-caste-discrimination/1/587100.html
5. Parthasarathi Muthukkaruppan, Dalit: The making of a political subject. *Critical Quarterly*, Vol. 56, Issue 3, pp. 34–45. 2014. Available at https://doi.org/10.1111/criq.12136
6. A suggested and by no means exhaustive list of such articles is included at the end of this book.
7. Violence is not always physical. Mental and emotional violence and abuse were perpetrated on a daily basis against untouchable communities to ensure that they knew their place and never sought to rise out of the morass.
8. The purpose of this chapter is not to list, probe, discuss or debate the various theories on the origin of the caste system. That is beyond the scope of this book.
9. Susan Bayly, *Caste, Society and Politics in India from the Eighteenth Century to the Modern Age.* Cambridge University Press, 1999.

10. Smita Narula uses this term in her 1999 report, Broken People: Caste Violence against India's Untouchables. Available at https://www.hrw.org/report/1999/03/01/broken-people/caste-violence-against-indias-untouchables

11. B.R. Ambedkar, Castes in India: Their Mechanism, Genesis and Development. *Indian Antiquary* Vol. XLI (May 1917). Available at http://www.columbia.edu/itc/mealac/pritchett/00ambedkar/txt_ambedkar_castes.html

12. Dr. Babasaheb Ambedkar Source Material Publication Committee (2013). The Writings and Speeches of Dr. Babasaheb Ambedkar, Volume 7. Available at https://www.mea.gov.in/Images/attach/amb/Volume_07.pdf

13. Ambedkar also believed that originally there were just three varnas. The Shudras were a part of the Kshatriya varna. There was continuous feud between the Shudra kings and the Brahmins in which the latter were subjected to many indignities. As a result, they refused to perform the Upanayana, a traditional rite of passage that accepted a student's acceptance by a guru and his entry into a school of Hinduism, on the Shudras. This led to an erosion of the rank of the Shudras and they fell below the Vaishyas to form a fourth varna. According to Ambedkar, the Untouchables were not a product of racial discrimination, but rather of territorial segregation. The concept came into existence around 400 AD. When tribes began to settle down, they were always in danger of being attacked by other nomadic tribes. They employed Broken Men or people who were left without tribes as theirs had been eliminated in inter-tribal warfare, to protect them from other nomadic tribes in return for food and shelter. However, as these Broken Men were from alien tribes they could not be allowed to live amidst the settled tribes. Further, in order to guard against raids, it made sense for these men to live outside the villages. These Broken men became the Untouchables. For details on Ambedkar's theory on Shudras, read his book, *Who were the Shudras?*. And for his theory on the Untouchables read, *The Untouchables, Who are they?* Both are available at https://www.mea.gov.in/books-by-ambedkar.htm#inline-2

14. Simon Charsley, Untouchable: What is in a name?, *Journal of Royal Anthropological Institute*, 2:1 (1996), 1–22. Available at https://www.jstor.org/stable/3034630?seq=1#metadata_info_tab_contents

15. For a detailed account of the history of the term 'untouchable', read Charsley, 'Untouchable' 1996.

16. Ramachandra Guha, The rise and fall of the term Harijan, *The Telegraph*, 10 June 2017. Available at http://ramachandraguha.in/archives/the-rise-and-fall-of-the-term-harijan-the-telegraph.html

17. Please see http://socialjustice.nic.in/writereaddata/UploadFile/GOI-SC-ORDER-1936.pdf for a copy of the 1936 Order.

18. Parthasarathi Muthukkaruppan, Dalit: The making of a political subject. *Critical Quarterly*, Vol. 56, Issue 3, pp. 34–45. 2014. Available at https://doi.org/10.1111/criq.12136

19. The Manifesto can be viewed at http://ir.inflibnet.ac.in:8080/jspui/bitstream/10603/14528/15/15_appendicies.pdf

20. Quoted in Dabjani Ganguly, *Caste, Colonialism and Counter-Modernity: Notes on Postcolonial Hermeneutics of Caste*, Routledge, London and New York, 2005, p. 180.

The Gallery of Portraits

She wasn't doing a thing that I could see, except standing there leaning on the balcony railing, holding the universe together.

—J. D. Salinger, A Girl I Knew

In our world of big names, curiously, our true heroes tend to be anonymous. In this life of illusion and quasi-illusion, the person of solid virtues who can be admired for something more substantial than his well-knownness often proves to be the unsung hero.

—Daniel J. Boorstin

POSTCARD 1: YOUR GOD AND MINE!

Ambale village, Maharashtra

Sunita and her mother standing with their own Gods

Dear Reader,

Look around. Do you notice the muted yet magnificent colours that paint this warm and sunny gallery: each one a little different, and perhaps, just a little similar to the other? Proud, accessible, without the protection and insulation of a glass shell and yet somehow, still invisible to the outside world. Does it bother you, this lack of distance? This complete absence of the 'Do not Touch' signs exhorting you to simply observe from behind the glass partitions, to simply feel?

Truth be told, here, we do not want you at a distance. Touch, feel, live every postcard in this Museum. And then respond. This postcard, and every other in this Museum, narrates the story of a broken tea cup; a story that we have curated for you from different corners of this country.

This first postcard I write to you from the village of Ambale in the Ahmednagar district of Maharashtra. We—Pradip More,[1] the West zone co-ordinator for the Dalit Foundation who serves both as a guide and translator during my travels across Maharashtra, and I—are standing outside the only *Pardhi* house in this village, 74 km from Pune. The only Pardhi house inside the village, that is. The Pardhi are a nomadic tribe, what the locals call a *Ghumantu jaati* (travelling tribe), found primarily in the Ahmednagar, Satara, Solapur, Sangli and Usmanabad districts of Maharastra. Originally forest dwellers who lived off selling various forest products, they were left without shelter and livelihood when the new laws imposed by the British denied them access to these forests. In protest, some started thieving and attacking the colonialists. As a result, in 1871 the British government included them among the list of 150 criminal tribes, to be 'cured' through intense labour along with daily doses of flogging and caning. In one stroke, anyone born into a Pardhi household was automatically branded a criminal and targeted for life. Ironically, the British used the caste system to justify the heinous Criminal Tribes Act, 1871. While introducing the Act, T.V. Stephens, the Member-in-charge of Law and Order at the time explained: 'The special feature of India is the caste system. As it is, traders go by caste: a family of carpenters will be carpenters, a century or five centuries hence, if they last so long. It means a tribe whose ancestors were criminals from times immemorial, who are destined by the usages of caste to commit crime and whose descendents will be offenders against the law, until the whole tribe is exterminated or accounted for in the manner of the Thugs...reform is impossible for it is his trade, his caste, I may almost say his religion to commit crime.'[2]

Though the Pardhi were denotified in 1952 by a Government of India Act, the stigma continues till date. In the villages, no one wants a Pardhi neighbour. Earlier, the community moved around from place to place. Now they often live in a *paal* (temporary shelter made of plastic sheets and twigs), a couple of kilometres away from the village.

So the two-room house in whose raised courtyard I stand is remarkable, just like the woman who owns it—33-year-old Sunita Bhosle. Dressed in an orange and blue saree, her black hair tied back in a bun, Sunita launches into her story in broken Hindi.

Her father, I learn, was murdered when she was in Class 5. He was visiting Ranjangoan Mashidi, a village 18 km from their home where his sister had been married.

'No one knows what transpired. My father used to guard farms and run the household with the grains he was given,' recalls Sunita. Gradually, he managed to save ₹3000 and bought 3 acres of land. He stopped guarding farms much to the consternation of the landlords. One day he was found murdered in his own field.

'After that, life was hell. I have a younger brother and an elder sister. My sister was married at the age of 10 or 11 years. My mother, as you can see, is only able to use one hand. Six months before he died, my father had, in a fit of rage, hit her with a stone and rendered her disabled,' Sunita explains.

Sunita's father had married thrice. Her mother used to beat the other wives and finally managed to drive them away. This is what had piqued him on that fateful day. After her father's death, life took a turn for the worse. The little girl had to take the goats grazing, attend school and then, twice a day, go begging for food in the village. 'The local Congress MLA had been my father's friend. He put my brother into a school. There was no one else to earn, no money. The children made fun of me, my classmates called me names but what choice did I have? Often I stayed hungry or survived on *imli* (tamarind).'

As if this wasn't enough, they also had to face constant police harassment. 'Every time there was a theft in the village, the police would round up the Pardhi. We have never really left behind the tag of thievery. No one lets us live nearby or gives us a job. The ostracism continues.' The police often visited Sunita's *paal*—the house where I am standing, constructed under the Indira Awaas Yojana, came later—and this fuelled rumours. When she was barely 10, both Sunita and her brother were arrested on charges of theft but immediately released. One day her mother brought mats from her sister who lived in Shirur. New mats in the *paal* immediately raised the hackles of the villagers who informed the police. Sunita's mother was arrested and kept in lock-up for three days. 'It was automatically assumed that as a Pardhi the only way you can get new mats is by stealing them. The villagers were so wary of us. I just couldn't take it anymore; the constant scrutiny, suspicious glances, allegations and finger pointing. Within a year, I dropped out of school.'

A little later, Sunita heard of the Manavi Hakka Abhiyaan started by advocate Eknath Awad. They were holding a *morcha* (rally) at Parner to protest against the stripping of Vimal Kare, a Pardhi woman, accused of theft, by the police. 'The police said she was hiding 9 kg gold in her Nauwari saree and even in the absence of a female officer, they proceeded to strip-search her. When I heard of the morcha, I went there. I had first-hand experience of being targeted by the police. I remember that day so clearly. I was in my school uniform. Those were the only clothes I had.'

After the meeting Sunita decided to join the organization as a *karyakarta* (worker). 'It required no degree.' The organization began training the youth who had come in. Sunita, by then all of 14 years, went on a month-long *padyatra* (journey by foot) from Nagar to Nanded, in her school uniform. Gradually, she learnt of Savitri Bai Phule and Babasaheb Ambedkar, iconic leaders who had fought for the rights of Dalit communities. She became more vocal and started work on atrocities, education and land.

'I began to take out rallies and protest when the police arrested Pardhi men and boys on false cases. I was often targeted by the upper caste as I was trying to change the status quo. Attempts were made to kill me, most recently when I filed a complaint against the harassment of a 12-year-old Pardhi girl, but I am a hardy soul. I survived.'

In 2009, Sunita heard about the fellowship programme being run by the Dalit Foundation through Manushki, an NGO. She applied and her selection marked the beginning of a new phase in her life. Empowered by the fellowship and the subsequent interaction with other 'fighters' like her, she became more determined. 'And more organized,' she admits laughingly. 'Till I started training, I only knew how to shout slogans, hold placards and take out *morchas*. I had never thought of running an NGO. Here I learnt about leadership, about organized and sustained struggles, about taking people with you in your fight against oppression.' With the help of her fellowship and friends like Ranjeeta Pawar, Sunita started Kranti. 'Come to think of it, it was Pradip who came up with the name for my organization,' she says with a twinkle.

Today Sunita's life revolves around ensuring justice for the Pardhi. Every morning, she wakes up at 6 am to fill water, cook, bathe her mother, wash clothes and utensils, and carry out other household chores. Thereafter she boards a local tempo, bus or even a truck to visit Pardhi families in different areas. These visits often reveal cases of illegal detention, harassment and caste-based discrimination. The rest of the day, and those following it, are spent in running to government hospitals for medical certificates (in case of sexual harassment, rape or physical violence), filing FIRs, following up with police officials or gathering evidence to prove the innocence of illegally detained Pardhi boys. By now, all the local police officers know her and at times, this comes in handy. 'About two years ago, my mother was travelling with my niece on a bus. My niece does not know the Pardhi language and people immediately got suspicious. They reported a possible kidnapping to the police. When the bus stopped in Shirur, my mother was arrested.' Only when Sunita called the officer in-charge was her mother released.

'At times, this fight seems never ending. Often, I get home late at night. Sometimes, I end up staying in the villages, but I don't mind. I know my work is making a difference,' explains Sunita. It is perhaps this dedication that has drawn the attention of a Mumbai-based journalist who is now shadowing Sunita to write a book on her life and her struggles. So, if you want to learn more about this beautiful woman, all you need to do is brush up on your Marathi!

Before we leave, Sunita shows me around her house. The first room is the kitchen with a seating area. It opens into another room—the bedroom—with pink walls, almirahs stacked with clothes, utensils on shelves and strings of garlic drying on a rope near the ceiling. Sunita assures me that this is a familiar sight in her part of the country. Against one wall, there is a desk with framed photographs of Dr Ambedkar and Savitri Bai Phule. Right next to the desk, slightly lower is a small stand with a number of idols and pictures of Hindu Gods.

Pointing towards the desk, Sunita says, 'This is our temple.'

'Temple?' I ask confused.

'Yes, my mother worships the idols. And he,' she says looking at Babasaheb's photograph, 'is my God.'

Her mother, draped in a printed orange saree, grumbles a little in a local dialect that I am unable to understand.

Laughing Sunita tells me that when she framed and brought the two photographs inside the house, her mother locked her out for three whole days. 'You see, the Pardhi don't like to identify themselves as Dalit, and most don't recognize how much Babasaheb did for us.' This is because the Pardhi believe that Dalits are beef-eaters, whereas to them, the cow is sacred. Thus, while a Pardhi would even be willing to eat the leftovers from the plate of a Maratha, (s)he wouldn't accept fresh food from a Dalit household. They may be victims of discrimination and untouchability, but they too practise it—with other Dalit communities and with their own women.

'Once she is married, a Pardhi woman is treated as an untouchable, contaminated by intercourse. Not even her own parents or in-laws will eat anything cooked by her. Her clothes are not allowed inside her own house. Often, if the family can manage it, the stove where she cooks and the bathroom that she uses is separate. Her own daughter is not allowed to wash her clothes,' Sunita tells me. When guests come, it is the men or the unmarried girls of the household who cook and serve food. Married women are not allowed to touch the utensils, or even fetch a glass of water for themselves till the men have eaten.

Appalled, I ask, 'But this is unacceptable. How can we talk about the discrimination faced by the Pardhi, without also addressing the discrimination practised by them? Untouchability is wrong—wrong when it is against you, and equally wrong when it is by you.'

'I know. In my house, I eat food cooked by my mother and wash her clothes. We do not keep separate bathrooms or stoves. I also try and explain this to families when I visit them but these practices are so ingrained, that most are unwilling to even consider change. Eventually, it will happen, but it will take time. For that you will need many more Sunitas.'

Till then, this brave 33-year-old will keep waking up at the crack of dawn to raise her voice against injustice; keep teaching young boys and girls, by example, to become Sunita.

POSTCARD 2: AN ODE TO STUBBORNNESS

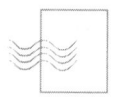

Umerga, Maharashtra

A Lambadi woman in her traditional attire at Sardarnagar *tanda*

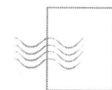

Umerga, Maharashtra

Babita, Prem and Ranjeeta (left to right) at their office near Umerga, Maharashtra

Dear Reader,

Have you ever been accused of the 'sin' of stubbornness? Of doing exactly what you want? Of living life on your own terms? Of just not listening? Ranjeeta has, time and again, throughout the 31 years of her life. And yet, she has no regrets. After all, her stubbornness has changed not just her life, but that of the 400 residents of her *tanda* (colony). Her stubbornness coupled with Prem's belief and Babita's determination. Misery and deprivation never faced more worthy opponents. This postcard is their story.

Ranjeeta, Babita and Prem are from a small Lambada *tanda*, located about 14 km from the city of Umerga in Osmanabad district of Maharashtra. At one point, it was simply known as Lambada *tanda* Number 1. Now it is called Sardarnagar. The Lambada or Banjara as they are frequently called, are a nomadic community. Over 5 million of them are spread out across the country, particularly in the states of Telangana, Andhra Pradesh, Karnataka and Maharashtra.[3] Traditionally this community travelled long distances transporting salt, food grains and even bamboo on oxen and bullocks. In fact, the term Lambani is believed to come from the Sanskrit *Lavana* meaning salt, which was their principal item of trade.[4] Some historians claim that the Banjara are the descendants of the Roma, who migrated to Rajasthan via Afghanistan, 2,300 years ago. A recent paper uses oral history (songs sung by the elders of the community) to trace the Banjara back to the 11th century. The songs talk of the Bhats of Rajasthan who sought to help Prithviraj Chauhan against Mohammad Ghori in the Battle of Tarain in 1192 AD. They were targeted by Ghori's army and dispersed into the forests to escape persecution. Hence the name Banjara, which comes from the Sanskrit *Vanachara*, literally forest wanderer. Some others trace the origin of the term Banjara to *Vanijyakaras*, meaning merchants.[5] Due to their horde of cattle, the Banjara served as commissariat traders for the Mughals, supplying the armies with arms and food grains. They followed the armies in their conquest of the Deccan and when the Southern campaign ended, the Banjara gave up the

The Gallery of Portraits

barren deserts for the Deccan plateau.[6] With the advent of modern means of transportation, the community lost their livelihood, and with the British branding them as a criminal tribe in 1871, their prestige.

Till a couple of decades back, the Lambada moved in caravans, under the leadership of a *Naik* (headman) and pitched their tents on '*banjar*' or fallow fields outside villages. These temporary Banjara colonies (now increasingly permanent) are called *tandas*.

Sardarnagar is one such *tanda*. Here too the opinion on their lineage is divided. Some people claim that their ancestors were from Gulbarga in Karnataka, while others trace their lineage to Rajasthan. According to Ganesh Shankar Pawar, Ranjeeta's father, the *tanda* was started in 1972. Ranjeeta recounts the story. About half a century ago, Venkatrao Patil was the local *zamindar* (landlord). When a caravan of Banjara, headed by Ranjeeta's grandfather, reached the area, he employed them on his fields. After a few years, he offered them land in exchange for cattle dung. Thus, for the next five to six years, the *tanda*, which at that time was made up of four families, supplied him with dung every year. Finally, about two decades ago, the land was divided and formal deeds handed over to all families. That is when the temporary shelters were converted to permanent houses. Today there are 72 families that live here.

Ranjeeta

Though Ranjeeta's grandfather was the Naik of this *tanda*, she was born in Assam. After their wedding, like most people in their *tanda*, Ranjeeta's parents worked as construction labour in Mumbai. Those were tough days. 'People would harass me. Often when the women were sleeping on the footpath at night, men would come and try to slip in next to them, taking liberties. Within two months of childbirth, I would be back at the construction site, lifting bricks, with a child on my hip, or in the shade next to the work site,' recalls her mother.

It was in these conditions that Ranjeeta's elder brother and two sisters were born. Then, in 1981, her father joined the army and the family began to travel with him. Around this time Ranjeeta was born. Soon after her birth, Ranjeeta's mother came back to Sardarnagar with her children.

In those days, in Sardarnagar, like in most Lambada *tandas*, every household used to brew liquor. Women and girls would get up at four in the morning and start preparations. By the time the day was fully awake, the drink would be ready. The children would taste the drink to ensure that the flavour was just right. Thus, they got addicted early on in life. Some customers would come to the *tanda* and buy the brew from the young girls. But as police raids became more frequent, children started conducting business behind the bushes that lined the road to Kader, the village closest to the *tanda*. During Ranjeeta's childhood, the drink sold at ₹10 per bottle.

Ranjeeta's house was no different from the others in her village, though her mother claims that she only started brewing because her husband would spend a large amount of money on drinking whenever he was home. Like the other kids in the *tanda*, her sisters brewed alcohol, but Ranjeeta was defiant. 'I would do all the work reserved for boys. Cycle to the village for flour and provisions, fetch water from the well; anything but the brewing. I used to see how the men who came to take the drinks looked at the girls. I despised it,' she recalls. Her mother agrees. 'She was such a stubborn child. If we forced her, she would make herself ill and faint. So we let her be.'

Ranjeeta's four sisters were married when they were barely 13 or 14 years old. This was the norm in her *tanda* but once again Ranjeeta rebelled. She refused to marry. 'Initially there used to be six girls in our class. Five left school after class seven. My father wanted to marry me off, but I wouldn't listen,' she tells me.

The Gallery of Portraits

Meanwhile, an incident took place which shook the young girl's world and made her even more determined to not live like the others in her *tanda*. 'I was in class six. By then, our family had stopped brewing alcohol. But others in the locality did and police raids were common. During the annual *jatra* (festival), my father came home and as usual he brought liquor. He drank and took off. Suddenly the police came. My mother tried to hide the bottle, but the policeman found it and arrested all the adults in the house—my mother, two *chachas* (father's younger brothers) and *phuphi* (father's sister). I ran after their car for a long time, crying but to no avail. It was three days before my mother came home. The policemen made lewd remarks about her but because of my *chachas* they didn't do much else,' Ranjeeta recalls with a shudder. Her mother tells me that the incident scared her so badly that whenever there was a police raid in the locality thereafter—and there was one almost every week—she would pretend to go to the toilet and run away.

Ranjeeta passed Class 10 with 66 per cent marks. At that time, this was unheard of in her *tanda*. She wanted to study further but her father and elder brother refused. They believed that girls didn't need to study further. Her elder brother even beat her up when she argued. After much cajoling, her father agreed to let her sit for the Class 11 entrance examination to the Shri Krishna Mahavidyalaya, located 7 km away in Gunjoti. She wanted to study Science, but he insisted on Arts and finally she took admission into the Commerce stream. 'But for one year he didn't let me attend classes. Then finally, in Class 12, my mother and I managed to convince him. Babita, who was my senior, had already set an example.' Now of course, her father claims credit for her success. He says he always believed that girls should be educated. His wife and Ranjeeta simply share an amused look.

Ranjeeta secured 67 per cent marks in Class 12 and this time, the villagers convinced her father that she had a bright future. He asked her to sit for the Police Service Examination but she got rejected in the orals. Finally, she persuaded him to let her try for D.Ed (Diploma in Education). Her elder brother had already taken this exam but he never supported her. So even though she cleared the entrance examination and secured a seat at a college in Latur district, for a long time she wasn't allowed to go. Egged on by relatives and his own conservative views, her father refused to send a girl out of town for two long years.

'At that time, there was an NGO that was encouraging Self Help Group (SHG) formation. They came to our village and I formed an SHG for them. Meanwhile, Prem had also finished his Art of Living course. Babita, he and I had already managed to get alcohol brewing banned in our *tanda*.'

'Wow! That couldn't have been easy. After all, you did say that it was the main occupation of the Lambada here,' I exclaimed.

'It was, but two things had happened that made our job slightly easier. When I had been in Class 10, my cousin's husband who had come to our village, died of liver cirrhosis. His relatives blamed us and even threatened us. Meanwhile, another boy died from liver complications. All this had already made the villagers angry with the Lambadas. So, Prem, Babita and I went from house to house, explaining to the people that alcohol was only ruining us. Little kids were getting addicted and dying young, the villagers were ready to chase us away and the police kept harassing us. Finally, in 2003 the *Jaat* panchayat (caste panchayat) banned the practice and announced that anyone who brewed alcohol would be punished. That was the turning point for the *tanda*.' In the Lambada *tanda*, the verdict of the *Jaat* panchayat, headed by a Naik and comprising seven members, is sacrosanct.

By this time, Ranjeeta had once again shown her stubborn streak and her parents let her join the college in Ahmednagar, Latur.

'My perspective and therefore my life, changed. I saw so many girls studying, planning careers and I decided that when I go back, I too would teach children.' It was while she was attending college in Ahmednagar town of Latur that Ranjeeta came across the Nav Maharashtra Community Foundation that worked on ensuring education for Lambada children. Three days every week she received training with them. Thereafter, she worked with them on overcoming the language barrier for Lambada kids—the schools taught in Marathi while the children spoke Lambadi, a mix of Rajasthani, Gujarati, Sanskrit and Marathi. She trained 55 teachers from seven different institutions.

'Around this time, I also became cognizant of the atrocities committed against Dalits and began attending protests. Consequently, I fell short of attendance and was not allowed to sit for the college exams till I explained to my Principal what I had been doing. Then she encouraged me.'

By 2007, Ranjeeta had finished her course and come back to Sardarnagar to join her friends, Prem and Babita. Here once again, she told her parents of her ambitions. By now, even her father had given up. He simply told her that as she was too stubborn to listen to anyone she could do as she pleased. Thus began the two-hour bridge classes called *Shakaushalas* for the Lambadi kids. In 2008, the trio formed Samarthya (Capability). They took training from Pratham, a large NGO that works to provide quality education for underpriviledged children and started conducting tests for children living in five *tandas* near Umerga.

Ranjeeta was now 24 and by Lambada standards, firmly on the shelf. 'People said no one will marry such a stubborn girl. She fights even with government officials. Then I met Rajendra at a conference. He was a *Kaikadi* and inter-caste marriages were strictly taboo amongst us. It took us almost two years to convince both our parents but finally we got married. I am lucky, my husband understands me and my work. Within 15 days of my wedding, I was in the field. My husband and four-year-old son, Raman, live in Shirur with my mother-in-law while I shuttle between there and here,' she finishes with a smile.

Babita

Babita's story is slightly different. Over a delicious home-cooked meal comprising *paalak pooris (spinach bread), halwa*, mango and peanut chutney and a vegetable curry made of drumsticks, she tells me about her life. 'I was born on 14 May 1984 in Mumbai where my parents worked as construction labourers. I spent the first few years of my life in the city, but then my *chacha*, who is paralysed, called me back to the village, saying that Mumbai is no place for a girl to grow up in.' Adjusting to the *tanda* after living in the city was not easy. Till Class 4, Babita studied at the school in the *tanda*. But there was no government middle school in the vicinity. So, for Classes 5 through 10 the children had to go to a private school in the village—the Lokmanya Tilak Vidyalaya. By now Babita was old enough to join alcohol brewing. Every morning the nine-year-old would get up at three in the morning to brew the liquor. Then she would rush to school and after returning at 4 pm, she would start selling the alcohol.

At my request, Babita and Ranjeeta describe the process used by the Lambada in her *tanda* to brew liquor. 'We mix 2.5–5 kg of jaggery with water and put it in an earthen pot for 3–4 days. Then one day before the brewing we add *Nausagar, the material that provides the high*,' they explain. On the day of brewing, the jaggery and water mixture treated with Nausagar is put into a groundnut oil can and covered with a plate of German (aluminium). A trough of cold water is placed atop the plate. When a fire is lit below the groundnut oil container, the mixture evaporates. A pipe inside the groundnut oil container collects the vapour, which gets converted to alcohol when it passes through the trough of cold water.

Babita's was a tough life. In addition to attending school and brewing and selling alcohol, the lean little girl also had to cook, clean the house and accompany her uncle to the police station and courts whenever there was a raid. But she survived, often on sheer will power. 'It wasn't just the work, there was also the discrimination. The village children would call us names, tease us about our dress, the ornaments we wore in our hair. I used to run all the way from school to escape their taunts. I loved singing and dancing but was never given the chance to participate in any event in school. The teacher would ask us to sit at the back of the class. All this disturbed me. I was in Class 7, when Ranjeeta got admitted to Class 5 in my school. We decided we would no longer sit at the back.' Together, and without any help from teachers or students, these two young girls wrote and performed a play called *Patni Fashionwali* (Fashionable wife) at the school function, wherein Ranjeeta played Babita's husband. They won many accolades and the first prize. The very next year, they performed a Banjara dance and once again won the first prize.

Earlier in the day when I had visited the *tanda*, I had seen Ranjeeta and Babita join the other women in the community as they step danced to the beat of the *Halgi*—a round, flat-faced drum similar to the *Dappu* of Andhra Pradesh. Seeing the women move to the rhythmic music in their colourful costumes, it was easy to understand why the two young girls had won the first prize. With the success of the play and their dance, their talent was recognized and they participated in all the school events. 'Now the school even has our names written with pride. But when I joined Class 11 at the new school in Gunjoti, once again the discrimination and struggle started. When I wasn't allowed to join the annual event, I participated in the fashion show and won the second prize for my dress.'

She was wearing a banjara dress, one of the most intricate and complex dresses I have seen thus far. The women wear a voluminous, ankle-length colourful cotton skirt called the *Phetia*. The blouse is called *Kaacheri* and is composed of many pieces. Two scraps of cloth with intricate mirror work cover the fabric over both breasts. This is called the *Katli*. A big piece of mirror, called *peti*, rests on the stomach.

The Banjaras use a *Cheent* or a wide, long stole to cover their heads. One section of this falls on their forehead and outlines their face. This is the *Ghoongto*. It is made up of large mirrors (almost 8–10 cm in diameter) and has coins called *Chavali* hanging from it. Often the ghoongto can take up to three days to make and comprises really old coins. The Ghoongto I saw in the village had coins which dated back at least 50 years. Traditionally, these coins were the ones that a woman received as gifts during her wedding ceremony—perhaps they signified the blessings of her relatives. She took them off when her husband died. In fact, a widow took off all the mirror work and coins from her dress. Some say that the Banjara women wore mirrors to ward off animals—the beasts of prey were scared when they saw their own reflection—as they were often left alone in their caravans when the men went trading.

In addition to these garments, traditionally the women wore lots of silver (and if they couldn't afford it, metal) ornaments: *Kasotia* (armlets), *Phula* (bracelet), *Kase* (anklet), *Bichuwa* (toe rings), *Bhuria* (a big silver nose ring), *Rapiya* (a big necklace made of money or rupaiya as it is called in Hindi), *Patri* (a neckpiece of small beads) and *Hasli* (a huge silver neckpiece).

The most distinguishing feature of a Banjara woman's appearance, however, is the *Chotla* and the *Ghugri*. The Chotla refers to the huge silver or metallic ornaments that resemble chunky long earrings and are woven into their hair. The women learn to live with this heavy jewellery and open it once a week to wash their hair. The Ghugri is worn by married woman and is a huge round piece of metal or silver just above the Chotla. These days, the new generation has given up on the Chotla and the Ghugri. The rest, they still wear at festivals.

'I decided to showcase my culture, which people made fun of, to win appreciation and I did,' Babita explains. At that time, this young girl also dreamt of becoming a Chartered Accountant but life had other plans for her. While visiting Ranjeeta's house, Babita would often bump into Balaji, a Lambada boy from another *tanda* who was friends with Ranjeeta's elder brother. Cupid struck and in Class 11, Babita got engaged. Ranjeeta teases her good naturedly as she recalls how she and Babita had to threaten Balaji into the engagement. 'We felt he was stalling. In those days boys often took advantage of girls. So we told him, either you marry Babita or quit coming here,' she giggles. Faced by two such strong women, Balaji quickly proposed and at 17, just after she finished her Class 12, Babita got married. For some time after the wedding, both she and Balaji stayed at home, living off their father-in-law's income. Meanwhile, Babita too had come under Prem's influence. She began teaching school dropouts under the Mahatma Phule Education Guarantee Scheme.

'It wasn't easy. Most girls didn't want to study. The alcohol brewing hadn't completely stopped by then. Whenever I went to their house, people would close the windows to keep me out. For two years, I did that,' says Babita. Then one day, she, Ranjeeta and Prem decided that they needed to change things in their *tanda*. And Samarthya was created.

Prem

Born on 10 June 1979 to a pair of construction workers in Mumbai, Premling Manu Rathod, the soft-spoken man who guided and inspired these two young girls, had what he calls a very unremarkable childhood. At the age of six, he was sent to live with his *Dadi* (grandmother) in the *tanda*. When his *Dadi* took him to school for admission, the teacher recorded his name as Premling instead of Prem Singh. The new name stuck. With three brothers and two sisters, Prem lived the life of most Lambada children in the *tanda*, drinking, selling alcohol, consuming addictive substances like *khaini* (chewing tobacco). He participated in *tanda* festivals and pursued his studies because by then one batch of children had already graduated from the newly opened Ashram School. 'They went on to become engineers, get jobs,' he says. Then in 2000, when he was in his third year in college, Prem attended an Art of Living workshop. 'It was on a lark. Many students were doing it. So I did too.' That changed his life. With his openness to new ideas, he saw all that was amiss with his community and his own life. He completed the entire course and then decided that he would follow the path shown by his newfound beliefs. For two years, he worked in the tribal areas of Yavatmal. 'I learnt about organization, about struggle, about bringing change. Yet I also realized that no one was doing this for our community. So, I went back to the *tanda*, reconnected with Babita and Ranjeeta and we started working with Self Help Groups and children.'

The Prem of today does not even drink tea, leave alone alcohol. 'He is a saint. Ask Avita, his wife. He has given up everything, even meat,' the girls tease. After some cheerful banter, Prem tells me why he stopped eating meat. 'That was 17 years ago. I went with my friends to fish at the lake. For the first time, I noticed something beyond the gaiety and excitement of the people when a fish was caught. I saw the fish; I saw her struggling. When we sat down to eat and that fish was served, I only saw her struggles at the lakeside. I couldn't eat. After that day, I gave up all non-vegetarian food.'

I smile at the bonhomie in the room and the easy camaraderie born out of shared convictions and a lifetime of shared struggles.

This trio of brave and vivacious youngsters got their first break in the form of a Dalit Foundation Fellowship in 2009. With the exposure and training the fellowship provided they gained new perspectives and began to focus on atrocities and education. 'We realized that in our community, there were five things that kept the children from studying: the distance from schools, seasonal migration by parents, child marriage, discrimination in school and the language barrier. So one by one we started addressing them. We campaigned for facilities in our localities. We enabled women to start shops so that they could stay back and the children could attend school,' Ranjeeta explains.

To address the language barrier, they conduct two-hour classes, between 5 pm and 7 pm, every day in 10 *tandas*. 'We have also trained 15 local youth from the community. We call them *Prerak* or animators and they work for the upliftment of their *tanda*. Unlike in Sardarnagar, in other *tandas* alcohol brewing continues; children still get addicted and drop out of school,' Babita adds.

The efforts of the three friends have clearly borne fruit. In 2012, for the first time, Sardarnagar got electricity. The residents now have ration cards; toilets have been constructed. Samarthya's area of operation has also expanded to 20 *tandas* in the area. Very soon, they hope to see the progress of Sardarnagar reflected in these *tandas* as well.

Today Ranjeeta, Babita and Prem have many more dreams that they chase with just as much stubbornness and determination. Prem wants to ensure provision of amenities in all the 52 Lambadi *tandas* around Umerga. Ranjeeta wants to resume her studies. 'I want to engage intellectually. Do a BA (Bachelor of Arts) and then an LLB (Bachelor of Law) perhaps. Meanwhile, I continue to write stories and poems,' she confesses.

As I watch these three friends interact with the young children in their *tanda*, I realize that sometimes all you need is stubbornness. Because your stubbornness gives you the strength to weather all storms, to forge your own path and walk it, even if it means doing so alone. Stubbornness is often nothing but a reflection of your innate strength. And sometimes, your stubbornness is what keeps your world afloat. Sometimes your stubbornness is CHANGE!

POSTCARD 3: YES, YES, YES, I AM A BHANGI

Kanpur, Uttar Pradesh

Deo Kumar (second from the right) with his team at the Apna Theatre office in Haddigodam, Kanpur

Dear Reader,

As a child, I always thought the term Bhangi was an adjective used to refer to anyone who was filthy, dishevelled, even intoxicated. It was many years before I realized that Bhangi is not an adjective but a noun. That it refers not to qualities of an individual but to a group of people, people who have traditionally kept our surroundings and our houses clean. Ironically, the very same people, who cleaned the filth from our lives were abused, abhorred and ostracized to an extent that their very name became synonymous with filthy.

'Even among the Dalits, the Bhangi was the lowest of the low. Other Dalit communities like Dhobi (washermen), Chamar (leather workers) and Khateek (butchers) did not mix with us. They still don't,' explains 43-year-old Deo Kumar.

Stout, with a broad face, olive complexion and curly black hair, Deo works as a Supervisor with the Municipal Corporation of

Kanpur. 'That is my job, what keeps the house running. It is not my identity,' he asserts. And indeed, it is not. So today, I introduce you not to Deo Kumar, an employee of the Municipal Corporation of Kanpur but to Deo Kumar—writer, director, theatre artist, lyricist, sculptor and above all, a man who has worked ceaselessly for the rights of Dalits for the last 24 years.

The third child of Prabhu Dayal and Ganga Devi, Deo was born on 6 February 1972 in the Haddigodam *mohalla* of Kanpur. 'There were some 150–200 Mehtar or Bhangi houses in our area. In fact, since it was predominantly a Bhangi neighbourhood, people from other communities who lived in the area were worried that they would be thought of as Bhangi. They never wrote Haddigodam as their address. Instead, they started calling the area Dalel Purva. If you see someone saying he is from Haddigodam, assume he is a Bhangi. If he says he is from Dalel Purva, know that he is not, though he lives in the same locality.'

Today, this discrimination and segregation makes his blood boil, but as a child Deo was oblivious to it. He did not question when he was told not to visit certain houses or go near some temple or road. 'During Eid, our Muslim neighbours would put food into our utensils. Yet they never invited us in or let us eat in their plates. This was the way of things. We never questioned it.'

Deo's parents were firm believers in the power of education. His mother had not received much formal schooling, yet her command over Sanskrit and Hindi was perfect. 'She was an *ayah* (helper) at the municipal school. She cleaned premises, fetched children and dropped them back. But she valued education and kept learning on her own. Later she would teach other children.' So Ganga Devi and Prabhu Dayal ensured that all their four children—two sons and two daughters—received an education. Till Class 8, Deo studied at the Rishi Sudarshan Vidya Mandir in his *basti*. Everyone in the school, be it his classmates or teachers, was a Bhangi. There were no abuses, no name calling at school. 'That only started when I went outside for my inter [mediate studies]. People would taunt me about my scholarship, fees and other things. But at that time, I just let it slide. It was a part of life.'

Instead of getting rattled by the injustice around him, Deo used his time to indulge his creativity. While he never learnt how to play any instrument, he would often draw and sculpt. He developed a taste for the theatre early in life and would perform *Ram Lilas* with other children of his neighbourhood. Of course, he always chose to portray Ram.

When he was in Class 8, Deo heard the story of Angulimal. The story inspired the 12-year-old to write and direct his first play. Deo's love for the theatre kept growing. His *nataks* (plays) often centred around religious epics like the *Ramayana* and the *Mahabharata*. Then in 1990, he read Premchand's *Nashe Mein Dooba* and performed it at the 15th August programme in his *basti*. While his portrayal of the drunkard Lallu won accolades from all, his father was not happy. Prabhu Dayal had lived a tough life. He had managed to study by living with his *Bua* (father's sister) in Kanpur, but soon after had returned to his village in Hamirpur district to play the *naqqara* and the *dhol* like other members of his community. He fitted skins on the musical instruments and performed at weddings and functions. 'Later my father moved to the city and found a job as a sweeper at the municipal slaughterhouse. Because he was educated, he eventually got promoted to the post of a sanitary supervisor. Having seen such hardship, it was natural that he wanted his children to be secure. Theatre did not provide that. It did not get regular jobs,' Deo explains without rancour.

Deo's maternal uncle, Ram Gopal Gautam, was a follower of Buddha and Ambedkar. Around this time, he presented a book on Dr Bhimrao Ambedkar to Deo. 'That book changed my life. Till then I had been a practising Hindu. I kept fasts, observed rituals. I accepted all the discrimination and injustice I was subjected to without question. But reading Babasaheb's works created an *aakrosh* (anger) within me. I began to question; the more I read, the more determined I became to change things. Suddenly, I had a new purpose in life.'

Yet suddenly, life became tougher. In 1991, Prabhu Dayal passed away. Deo was pursuing his BSc at the time. He was forced to drop out of college and concentrate on making a living. Government policies guaranteed him a job in lieu of his father but it was two years before he got the post. In the interim, he sold vegetables, worked as a security guard and even joined a factory that packaged oil.

Meanwhile, his mental churning continued. Since childhood Deo had believed in the might of the pen. Now he employed it to fight against injustice and to spread social messages. In 1993, his first book, *More Bazaar*, was published. It told the story of people who worked in others' houses and ate their *jhootan* (leftovers.)

Theatre had always been Deo's first love but now it was no longer a mere art form. It became a tool of enlightenment, a potent weapon to fight against discrimination. 'I realized that our people were mostly uneducated. They had never read the *Ramayana* or any of the religious epics. Yet they knew the stories by heart as they had seen them in *nataks* (plays) and *nautankis* (street plays), in *Ram Lilas* (re-enactment of the Ramayana), year after year. So I decided that the theatre would be my instrument of change.' Deo began writing *nataks* that spoke against the social ills that were prevalent in his community. 'I realized that the change has to come from within. A tough life and discrimination had led to a high incidence of intoxication among people from the Mehtar and Bhangi communities. Alcohol and drugs were common. Our *nataks* started targeting them. We spoke of the importance of education and the need to break away from caste-based occupations.' In 1992, Deo formed the Apna Theatre Group with eight youths from his own community. Over the next few years, the team size went up to 25. They would go to different Dalit *bastis* and perform.

Deo had never formally learnt how to write plays or act in them. Once he approached renowned play director Santosh Gupta to learn from him. Santosh told him, 'I don't teach. If you can learn, do so.' He connected him to Harish Chand Naqqara who ran the Nautanki Prashikshan Kendra. Every day Deo would hang around at the rehearsals and pick up pointers about sets, acting, directing and most importantly, about the *nautanki* as a mode of theatre. 'I particularly liked the *naqqara*. In *bastis* and *mohallas*, the sound of the *naqqara* could be heard from afar and people would know a *natak* is happening. These instruments are great crowd pullers. I also began incorporating the tunes from *nautanki* into my *nataks*. It increased receptivity.'

In fact, Deo's most popular play, *Dastaan*, incorporated the tones and techniques of *nautanki*. The original play, written when Deo was merely 21, was one hour and 15 minutes long. Over the years it became a five-to six-hour long marathon. 'We also have a six-minute version of the play. When the Bahujan Samaj Party came to power in Uttar Pradesh in 1997, a Chatrapati Shahu *mela* (fair) was organised in Kanpur. Seasoned artists from all over the country attended it. I was given a chance to perform *Dastaan*, albeit in six minutes. I played Ambedkar. That day, Kanshiramji was present at the performance and he had tears in his eyes when he saw the *natak*. After the play, he called me and shook hands (with me), conveying his appreciation,' Deo recalls.

And yet, even as he basked in the appreciation that his plays garnered, Deo felt the need for more active engagement with his community. In 1998, he formed the Swayam Sudhar Samiti with 12 members. The Samiti would organize day-long camps, starting at 6 am. 'I had begun penning songs on social issues. We would start the camp with these songs. Thereafter, we would tell people about Babasaheb's ideals. We would organize talks by activists on culture, history and various other topics. But we had no funding and gradually the team began to fall apart.'

But Deo did not give up. In 2001, he began to bring out the *Jai Bhim Bulletin*—a paper that talked about Dalit rights and sought to create awareness. His colleague, Vinay would go from house to house on a bicycle, carrying the newspaper, and with it Babasaheb's world view. Times were tough and resources were scarce. Then at a meeting in Lucknow, Deo met Pushpa Valmiki and told her about his work. Pushpa connected him to the Dalit Foundation. 'I applied for the fellowship and won it. That turned the tide. We got money for Apna Theatre but more importantly, the exposure helped our thought process to evolve. Earlier, my endeavours began with me—they were about the self. Interacting with different people through the fellowship taught me to think about society. The three years of support that we received infused fresh life and enthusiasm into the organization.'

Today, Deo and his colleagues use their own resources and donations to bring out *Jai Bhim Jai Samaj*, a weekly paper. They focus on books, meetings and *vichaargoshtis* (brainstorming sessions). That Deo has been able to mobilize the youth is evident. His small shop-sized office in Gwal Toli is filled with his young team—students who heard Deo speak in their *basti* and decided to become his fellow travellers. 21-year-old Manish is a BSc first year student. 'In 2012, Deo *bhai* had organised a *baalmela* (a fair for children). I was standing and watching, when he noticed me. He asked me my name. Later I went back and read his books. I knew I had to join him.' The other young men gathered in his office, Rohit, Vinay and Kunwarjeet, all had similar tales to tell.

Even as he spreads the message of education, Deo is trying to finish his own graduation. As I turn to leave his office, I cast a look at the many books Deo has written. One in particular catches my eye. It is called, 'Haan haan haan, Main Bhangi hoon'. (Yes, Yes, Yes, I am a Bhangi). Noticing my interest, Deo explains, 'A Bhangi is someone who gives, who suffers for others, who cleans up society's mess. A Bhangi is therefore noble. Yet, all our life we try to run away from the name. We look at it as an abuse and as soon as we land a job or "make it" in life, we wish to disown this identity. Why?'

There is little research or evidence on the origin of the term Bhangi. Etymologically, most scholars trace it to *bhang* or hemp. Others reiterate its meaning as an occupational sub-group referring to people who cleaned the night soil and worked as sweepers. Tales on why a particular group of people were forced to do this abound. And yet, Deo does not lend credence to them.

'I plan to do my PhD on the origin and meaning of this term. I believe it has been reviled and distorted over the years. The term needs to be resurrected and re-understood, for the community to reclaim its dignity. My dream is to see an India where the Bhangi is treated at par with every other person, where people are proud to be called Bhangis,' says Deo with an almost embarrassed laugh. 'It's very big, this dream. Almost impossible, I know.' But isn't that how dreams are supposed to be? Big enough to seem impossible and yet potent enough to change the world!

POSTCARD 4

> Do you hear the People Sing?
> Singing a song of Angry Men?
> It is the music of a people
> Who will not be slaves again!
> When the beating of your heart
> Echoes the beating of the drums
> There is a life about to start
> When tomorrow comes!
> **—Les Miserables**
>
> It will not stop, it will not stop,
> it will not stop
> This war of hunger will not stop
> It will not stop
> Until the rule of the looters ends
> This armed struggle will not stop
> It will not stop
> The plough that dug the furrows
> Says these furrows are mine
> The hands that planted the saplings
> Say these saplings are ours
> The sickle that cuts the crop
> Says this harvest is ours
> It will not stop
> The blacksmith's fire is flaring up
> The potter's kiln is blazing
> The *maadiga*'s tambourine goes
> *dhanadhanadhana* announcing the
> message in drumbeats
> It will not stop
> **—Sung by Gaddar**[7]
>
> I sing of revolution

Chwidikada Village, Coastal Andhra Pradesh

Dear Reader,

Ramamurthy G is a tall man of average built, with greying hair and a thick moustache, more salt than pepper. Dressed in a full sleeved shirt with indigo and white stripes, he sits gingerly in a chair inside a small, one-room office in Chwidikada village, 36 km from the town of Anakapalli in Vishakapatnam district of Andhra Pradesh. Despite running a temperature and being unwell—he walks with a limp and has a handkerchief tied around one hand—he has

The Museum of Broken Tea Cups

come all the way from K R Petta in the neighbouring district of Vizianagram for a meeting called by the Dalit Foundation. They are looking for people to support through their group fellowship programme and 54-year-old Ramamurthy is representing the Dalit Bahujan Kala Mandali, a *dappu* group he started in 1985.

The *dappu* is a traditional percussion instrument that is associated with Dalit communities—particularly the Madiga—in Andhra Pradesh and Telangana. It consists of a wooden frame, 6–8 inches in radius, with a buffalo skin tightly stretched across it. It is played with two wooden sticks—a nine-inch-long round stick called the *sirre* and a thinner and longer stick called the *pulla*. For centuries, the *dappu* has been used in festivals and rituals and as a public announcement system. Then rights groups like Ramamurthy's appropriated what had become a symbol of injustice and caste discrimination to spread the message of equality and human dignity.

Ramamurthy's parents were agricultural labourers. After finishing Class 12 he pursued a course in blacksmithery from the Industrial Training Institute (ITI). Yet, as with most Dalit youth in his area, he did not get a job. So, he too took up work as an agricultural labourer.

'At that time, every village in coastal Andhra (Pradesh) had an Ambedkar Yuvajan Sangham. These were groups of Dalits that monitored cases of atrocities and caste-based violence in the villages. They were the brainchild of Arjuna Rao, who was the Collector of Vishakapatnam district in the mid-1970s. A native of Nellore and a Dalit himself, he started the *sangham* to unite all Dalits and to lobby with the government for their rights. Nine educated Dalit youth from every village were selected to form the core committee. All Dalit families were members,' he explains. Ramamurthy tells me how the movement grew across the countryside and how Dalits were encouraged to set aside their differences and fight collectively for their rights. He first attended a Sangham meeting immediately after he passed Class 12 and was much inspired by what he heard. Thereafter, an 18-year-old

Ramamurthy would accompany a local state government employee from village to village to encourage the formation of these Sanghams. 'Often, we had to work clandestinely. This was a time when lots of caste-based atrocities were taking place. If the upper caste got wind of our intentions, we would be in trouble. So we moved secretly, convincing villagers to organize themselves.'

On 17 July 1985, six Dalits were brutally murdered and another 20 grievously injured in an attack by upper caste men in the tobacco-growing village of Karamchedu in the Prakasham district of Andhra Pradesh. This time, Dalits across the state rose in protest. Katti Padma Rao, founder of the Dalit Mahasabha, launched a Chalo Karamchedu Movement. 'The Ambedkar Yuvajan Sanghams organized groups of 10 Dalits from every village. These groups travelled to a huge rally in the Prakasham district. We had been experiencing caste-based violence all of our lives. The rally marked a turning point for us. We united to say, enough is enough. We won't tolerate any more atrocities and discrimination. I convinced my parents to go there.'

Listening to the speakers in Prakasham added fuel to the fire burning inside Ramamurthy. He heard the famous Vittal Rao Gaddar singing of emancipation and Dalit Rights and suddenly he had found his way forward.

Wikipedia describes Gummadi Vittal Rao as a revolutionary Telugu balladeer and a local Naxal activist from the state of Telangana, who earned the title of 'Gaddar' after his first book of songs. Gaddar formed the Jana Natya Mandali in 1972 and started singing of revolution in the villages. 'I heard Gaddar and realized that he is singing about our issues. So I joined forces with him.' Ramamurthy tells me that he was lucky enough to work with Gaddar on many occasions.

In 1985 Ramamurthy started the Bahujan Kala Mandali with 10 members. The Mandali would go from village to village, singing of Ambedkar, land rights, Dalit problems and government schemes to the beat of the *dappu*. 'Our aim was to create awareness at the *Mandal*, that is, the block level. We did this through songs and stories, communicating with the villagers in a language that they understood.' In Andhra Pradesh, a *Mandal* consists of 20–35 villages and covers a population of upto 70,000.

For years the Bahujan Kala Mandali persisted, taking the Ambedkarite thought far and wide. Life was tough. Ramamurthy still had to work in the fields—in his own one-acre plot as well as those of others—to sustain his family. In 1986, he married Laksmi. His wife, an Anganwadi worker, asked him to give up the Mandali. It did not bring any money and the lifestyle was unpredictable. But Ramamurthy was determined. Today, one of his daughters is married and another is pursuing her graduation. His son is pursuing a Master's in Social Work. Ironically it was his daughter's wedding that finally led Ramamurthy to quit the Mandali he had created and nurtured.

'I had to take a loan for the wedding. To repay it, I took up a job as a supervisor in a construction company. The Mandali continued without me. Now I have almost paid off my debts. In a few months, I will be able to rejoin the Mandali,' he says, his brown eyes full of hope; a hope that resonates in his powerful voice as he sings one of his motivational songs for us.

POSTCARD 5: A WEAVE LESS ORDINARY

Banbaspali Village, Western Orissa

Kuntavati

Dear Reader,

It's 8 pm, yet the dark night offers little respite from the sweltering Oriya heat. Above me, the sky is aglitter with countless sparkling gems, its freshly donned obsidian cloak drawing attention to every speck of stardust scattered by fairies frolicking around with abandoned gaiety. Yet, as I spend a little more time admiring the brilliance of their almost callous handiwork, carefully stitched patterns begin to emerge—the Big Dipper, Orion and many more whose names I do not know. The hazy shroud donned by the Big Smoke Factory that is our national capital has never given us a chance to get better acquainted.

Now, as I stand outside my car in a village in Western Orissa, less than 20 km from the Chhattisgarh border, I try to remedy this unintentional slight. Meanwhile, the darkness around me reverberates with the triumphant exultation of mosquitoes that have managed to evade my defensive swats to savour the red wine flowing through my veins. We are in the village of Banbaspali, just off State Highway 13 in the Bargarh district of Orissa. This part of Western Orissa is renowned for its handloom weaves, particularly the Sambalpuri *Ikat*. In fact, it is reported that Bargarh, which had a population of nearly 1.5 million according to the 2011 census, has more than 12,000 looms, the most in any district in the state. Its weavers have received 58 National Awards, 30 State Awards, seven Sant Kabir Awards and two Padma Shri honours. Yet less than a score of these winners are women. The few who are there have generally won it jointly with a male weaver.

In these parts, it is the men who operate the looms—ancient decrepit pit looms with the fly shuttle, often housed in a small enclosure called the *Bunashala*, next to their homes. The women and children carry out the pre-loom procedures like dyeing, warping, bobbin winding and sizing. In simple terms, they separate and rewind the yarn bundles obtained from the traders, dye or colour it using chemicals, and wind or warp it using wooden pegs. It is hard work. Writing in the early 20th century, P. T. Mansfield of the Indian Civil Services estimated that warping of yarn for one warp alone involves eight to ten miles of walking. Yet in general, women do not weave. I had noticed this in village after village as I had sought out weavers. Then as I was visiting Sarandapali, the adjoining village, I heard whispers about a woman weaver. In places like Kaithun, where the Kota Dorian is woven, this may be commonplace. But here, in western Orissa, it is a big deal.

And thus, I find myself waiting in the pitch dark on a narrow village road as Balakishore, my guide, who himself comes from a family of weavers in Sarandapali, goes from house to house to find out if what we had heard in his village is indeed true. Suddenly the almost rhythmic monotone of the buzzing bloodsuckers is broken by a sound of voices. In the small stretches of visibility created by two or three mobile phone torches, I see a dozen people coming towards me. Among them is Kuntavati Sika, the 30-something woman weaver I have come looking for.

In another postcard I will, dear reader, tell you more about the Sambalpuri *Ikat* and the weavers who have been keeping the art alive, but this postcard is about Kuntavati—one of Bargarh's few woman weavers. 'Perhaps the only one who actually weaves for a livelihood. Others learn or know how to, but they simply aid their husbands, fathers and brothers, take over for small intervals when times are tough or create pieces to win awards,' Balakishore whispers.

At first glance Kuntavati looks no different from any other married, young woman inhabiting the villages of Western Orissa. Brown eyes set wide apart in a round face, black hair oiled and pulled back into a callous bun, a short thick neck, an exquisite albeit worn-out red and white Sambalpuri sari draped around her short frame, red and white bangles her only ornament. Yet two minutes into the conversation her confidence and ready smile set her apart.

'You came to meet me. Why?' she asks with genuine surprise.

'Because you weave.'

'So do many others. It's common enough here. That is how we earn our livelihood,' she says with a shrug.

'But not many women weave.'

Another shrug. Suddenly her face breaks into a big smile.

With twinkling eyes, she tells me, 'My father is also a weaver. I used to watch him at work. I liked what he did. I didn't want to simply do the warping and the winding of thread. I wanted to learn how the simple yarn was transformed into saris that people around me were wearing.' Indeed Orissa is one of the only states in the country, where the countryside has not been invaded by Surat—the hub of cheap, mill-made, synthetic sarees. Throughout my trip, I had seen women of all ages walking and working in cotton sarees.

'So I would observe my father. Whenever the loom was idle, I would sit and learn. By the time I was 14, I knew how to weave.'

For the next two years Kuntavati continued to weave from her father's home. Then at the age of 16, she was married within her village. But she did not give up her work.

'My husband works as a *coolie* in Tamil Nadu. Every four to five months, he visits us for a little while. But my family has been supportive. My father-in-law has his own loom, but he helps me as well.'

'How do you juggle housework and weaving?'

'When the children were small, it was much more difficult. I could spend less time on the loom. Now the children take care of most of the housework. My daughters also help with the winding and the warping of yarn.'

Kuntavati has four daughters and one son. With the children grown up—her eldest daughter is 16—she now has the luxury of getting up at seven and directly sitting at her loom. Apart from a short break to bathe and eat some lunch, she works non-stop till 5 pm. After that she takes care of dinner and helps her girls with housework.

'I have my own loom,' she tells me with great pride. On this she weaves two saris a week. 'But the earning is not much. The *Seth (merchant)* gives me ₹600 for the two saris.'

Like most Dalit weavers in these villages, Kuntavati does job work, that is, she weaves as per the design and instruction of the traders. The raw materials, that is, the *bandha* or the dyed yarn, is also provided by the traders, saving weavers the hassle of procuring raw materials and marketing finished goods. Of course, this also means that they get paid very little. The sari for which Kuntavati gets ₹300 is sold for at least three to four times the price.

I ask Kuntavati if she has faced the censure of society for taking up the loom. She looks at the ever-growing crowd of villagers around her and simply shrugs. 'I like my work. It brings in money. My family supports me,' she says. I can almost sense the unspoken, 'Does anything else matter?' at the end.

I ask about her siblings and if they also weave.

'I have a brother and a sister. My brother also weaves, but I am better,' she says, the sparkle back in her eyes. Her two oldest daughters, who are standing next to her, laugh.

'Are you teaching them to weave?'

'Yes, but they are studying. They are enrolled at the Dumberpali High School.' She has herself studied till Class 5, Kuntavati tells me.

Padmavati, her daughter, is 16 years old. She tells me that like her mother she too likes to weave but she won't take it up as a profession.

'I have passed Class 10 with E grade. I want to study further and become a Science teacher.'

Her sister, who is dressed in a pink *salwar suit*, also dreams of teaching.

Yet when I ask about their schools, the girls become uneasy. With hesitation they tell me about the untouchability that they experience.

'It's not as bad as earlier. We are allowed to sit with the other children for the mid-day meals, but no one touches us. In the village, we still have a separate well or boring. If we oppose or try to go near their well, we are abused,' they confess.

For Kuntavati however, this is a part of life. Just like she does not let the opinion of others dim her smile, she doesn't let this bother her either. She is surprised when I ask her if I can write about her.

'I do what I know to do, what I like to do and what I have to do,' she says simply.

My last glimpse of her as I get into the car is of a smile as radiant as any of the twinkling jewels above me.

Endnotes

1. Pradip is now the Deputy Director of the Dalit Foundation.
2. K. M. Kapadia, The criminal tribes of India. *Sociological Bulletin*, Vol. 1, Issue 2, pp. 99–125. First Published 1 September 1952.
3. History - Home of Lambadi gormati, n.d. http://lambadi.weebly.com/history.html. Last accessed 10 August 2019
4. B.G. Halbar, 1986, *Lamani Economy and Society in Change*, Mittal Publications, cited in http://shodhganga.inflibnet.ac.in/bitstream/10603/136659/12/12_chapter%206.pdf
5. B. Suresh Lal, 2016, A Historical Study of the Origin and Migration of Banjara Tribe in Telangana State, *International Journal of Current Research*, 8, (10), 40261–67. Available at https://www.researchgate.net/publication/311562515_A_HISTORICAL_STUDY_OF_ORIGIN_AND_MIGRATION_OF_BANJARA_TRIBE_IN_TELANGANA_STATE; last accessed 1 December 2018.
6. To learn more about the Banjara, read The Art and Literature of Banjara Lambanis by D. B. Naik and The Banjara by S. G. Deogaonkar and S. S. Deogaonkar
7. Gaddar, n.d., It will not stop, *The Little Magazine*, Vol VII: issue 3 & 4. Translated by Parsa Venkateshwar Rao Jr and Antara Dev Sen. Available at http://www.littlemag.com/security/gaddar.html

Theatre of the Invisible

Baraj says with hands clasped, 'Master our days are gone.
New men have come now, new styles and customs in the world.
The court we kept is deserted—only the two of us are left.
Don't ask anyone to listen to me now, I beg you at your feet, my Lord.
The singer alone does not make a song, there has to be someone who hears:
One man opens his throat to sing, the other sings in his mind.
Only when waves fall on the shore do they make a harmonious sound;
Only when the leaves shake the woods do we hear a rustling in the leaves.
Only from a marriage of two forces does music arise in this world.
Where there is no love, where listeners are dumb, there never can be song.'

—**Rabindranath Tagore**, *Broken Song*

Dear Reader,

This vibrant amphitheatre that you see reverberating with the sounds, sights and smells of life, this is where it all began. When we set out to curate this Museum, we were looking for the contribution made by Dalit communities, the cultural capital that they had created over the centuries, despite all odds. All discourse about Dalits is generally centred around the theme of discrimination. They are looked upon as victims, as groups of people who have suffered greatly—which they undoubtedly have—and who need to be empowered. Yet, no one talks about how much these groups, who have been denied everything by society, have contributed to it. No one talks of their rich legacy and immense knowledge because to do so would be to value them, respect them. For a society that has only deigned to acknowledge them when some heartrending story of torture has jarred its conscience, this is perhaps too utopian a dream.

And yet, we have only to look around us to see why the Dalits are the most significant cultural philanthropists that we can possibly encounter. We all value hygiene and cleanliness, take great pride in keeping our homes immaculate. Yet, who ensured that our homes and surroundings did not stink? Who cleaned our waste? The Dalits. Till date most sweepers and cleaners in municipal corporations belong to Dalit communities. The irony is that the people who remove the filth from our lives are abused as filthy.

Let's move on. Postmortem, that great scientific study of the human body to find out what ended the life that flowed within. Who do you think does it? Doctors? Cutting open a dead body, often one that has been rotting, is no small feat. It takes great fortitude and courage. It is often a Dalit who cuts open the bodies for postmortem and who then deftly sews it together again.

Now for the more pleasant things in life. The clothes we wear, for instance. Many *Bunkar* (weaver) communities were Dalit. Other castes, though they may eat animals, would not deign to touch their bones outside their plates. Some say that this is why weaving which involved the use of pieces of bone in the traditional loom was the domain of the Dalit. And those lovely shoes that you and I would never be caught without outside? The Chamars or leather-working castes made them. Today the production may be mechanized and the designs may be created by big names who charge a bomb for their creativity, but for centuries the creators and designers of chappals, sandals and shoes in India were these Dalit communities. Yet, they were never allowed to wear their creations, at least not in front of the other castes that benefited from their talent and acumen.

But the creative genius of Dalit communities is not limited to our closets. Let's move to the kitchen and the dining table—the two places where they were never allowed. Be it the earthen pots of the Kumbhar (potter) or the stone plates, grinders and mortar-pestles made by the Vadar, we cook and eat in vessels created by Dalit hands. Yet once these utensils enter our household, we say their touch pollutes them.

Enough talk of grimness though. Cultural connoisseurs that we are, let the beats of a *dappu* or a *naqqara* drown the cacophony of our thoughts. But who has been playing these instruments all these years? Beating the drum to announce and to entertain? Singing ballads to educate and to enthral? It has been the Dalit. Almost all the musical instruments that we see today are a legacy of these communities. They may or may not have been invented by them but they have been preserved, nurtured and developed by the Madiga, the Mahar, the Mehtar, the Valmiki, the Bhangi, and the Turi Barot. This is particularly true of the drums, most of which use animal hide.

And finally dance, that godly art which, as Indian mythology tells us, can enchant the most pious of men. Classical forms like Bharatanatyam and Odissi are important accomplishments that we wish to include in the repertoire of our kids. Where did they originate? Bharatanatyam can be traced to the Sadir dance of the Thevadiyal of Tamil Nadu; Odissi to the sensuous Mahris of Orissa; Mohiniattam to the Tevidicchi of Kerala—all devadasis. Yet, even as their art form was sanitized and co-opted, they, the creators, were ostracized and reviled. They were not given the reverence due to a *Guru* (teacher). And that is the tragedy of our times. The teacher was simply used and abused, never acknowledged. The same is true of folk dance forms like the Lavani. When the Kolhati women, the original progenitors of this dance form perform, they are looked upon as 'loose'. But when women from other communities learn this dance, they acquire acclaim on stage and in theatre.

The list of the cultural accomplishments of communities that are traditionally seen as 'uncouth' is endless. There are Godna artists that will put to shame any modern tattoo maker, not to mention the Chitrakathi and Kalamkari painters. All these great accoutrements for cultural connoisseurs have Dalit roots, roots which are seldom acknowledged.

This Museum is an attempt to trace these roots, document them. The human capital that you see in the other galleries is something we encountered along the way. And it was so invaluable, so inspiring, that we could not leave it untended, unseen, unappreciated.

But this gallery is about the legacy of ostracized communities. This is about seeking, learning, respecting. It is about seeing the people who have remained invisible even as their creations have won accolades. The task is humongous. It cannot be completed by one person or one group. We invite you to join in our quest to better understand our cultural heritage and to recognize the faces that have dedicated their lives to create and preserve it.

Meanwhile, immerse yourself in the Theatre of the Invisible!

POSTCARD 1: THE BEATS OF HUMILIATION

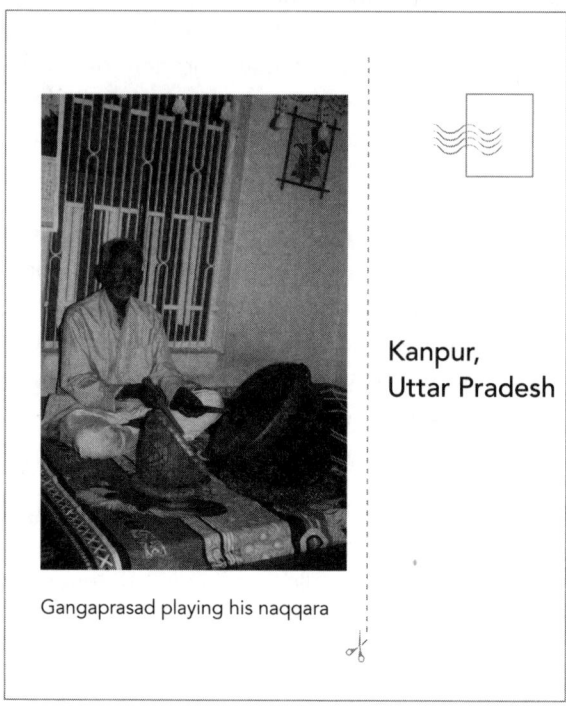

Kanpur, Uttar Pradesh

Gangaprasad playing his naqqara

Dear Reader,

Today I write to you from the largest city in Uttar Pradesh, Kanpur, once renowned as the Manchester of India. It is a hot and sultry May afternoon with outside temperatures ranging between 39 and 41 degrees celsius. I am traversing the city, on a two-wheeler, in an attempt to find the musicians and *nautanki* players who were once an integral part of its cultural fabric.

Here, in the bylanes of Kanpur, the Swachh Bharat Abhiyaan (Clean India Mission) seems non-existent. The city is filthy. My quest takes me to a small double-storey home in Purani Chowki *mohalla*, the house of 85-year-old Gangaprasad Naqqarawadak.

I enter a tiny courtyard. Beyond it is a small receiving room—no more than 6×8 square feet in size. A single bed and a sofa sit along the freshly painted green walls. On the bed, dressed in a crisp biscuit-coloured *kurta*, with an orange *gamcha* (towel) and a white pyjama, rests the *naqqarchi* I have come to visit. Thin, but not frail, a white moustache and a small white beard break the monotony of his rich espresso skin and imbue him with an air of distinction. His eyes are sunken, brown pupils ringed with a light grey. They light up when he recalls his days as a *naqqarchi*, as *naqqara* players were called.

'I started playing at the age of 10. My father worked as agricultural labour but playing was his hobby. It is from him that I first learnt how to play the *naqqara*,' Gangaprasad tells me.

Naqqara is a kettledrum instrument that derives its name from the Arabic verb *naqr*, meaning 'to strike, beat'. Its origin and presence in India remain shrouded in mystery. Some believe that it was brought to India from Persia. Others quote ancient texts and cite excavations to prove the prevalence of kettledrum instruments in India as early as 3000 BC. Irrespective of its origin, the fact remains that the *naqqara* was popular in Rajasthan, where it was called the *Nagada*, and gained much acclaim in Mughal courts. It is said that Emperor Akbar was not only extremely partial towards this instrument which finds mention in the 16th-century *Ain-i-Akbari*, he was also an exceptional player himself. Since its advent, the *naqqara* has served multiple purposes—as a public announcement system, as an adrenaline booster during wars, and as a source of entertainment, especially when combined with the *sarangi* (wooden stringed instrument) at weddings and the harmonium at *nautankis*.

'*Naqqara* consists of two drums—the *nar* (male) and the *mada* (female). In both, a buffalo skin is stretched across a round bowl-shaped body. Ropes interlock to keep the leather in place. For the smaller drum, called the *jheelnagaria*, the body is made of mud. It is heated before playing. The bigger drum, made of metal, is called the *Nagada* and is cooled before playing,' explains Gangaprasad.

As we wait for the *nagaria* to warm up, Gangaprasad reminisces about his life and his days in the *nautanki*. 'I studied till Class 3 at the Harijan school. So, I was quite well educated for someone from my caste and profession.' Gangaprasad belongs to the Mehtar community. Traditionally, people from this community worked as manual scavengers, sweepers and drum beaters. They were ostracized and discriminated against in a rigid caste-based society.

'By the time I was a teenager, I had learnt to play most instruments, including the *sitar*, the *bansuri* and the *dholak*. Music was my interest, my passion. From the age of 10, I started visiting people's houses and playing. Soon what my father taught me was no longer enough. So I trained under Pyaare Ustaad. Then Rashid Khan Saheb from Aligarh came to Kanpur with the Gulabibai Natak Mandali. He became my *guru*. By the time I was 20, I had started performing in *nautankis*.'

Nautanki is a form of folk theatre that engages the audience through a musical retelling of ballads and verses. It is believed to have evolved from the *Swang* and the *Bhagat* traditions of North India. *Swang* literally means impersonation and is an open-air theatre form. The *Bhagat* tradition of Agra is over 400 years old and began as dramatized devotional singing by the devotees of the Vaishnava cult. Tales of valour, romance and legendary kings were added later.[1]

Nautanki, which is often regarded as entertainment for the masses, uses a mix of Braj, Persian, Hindi, Urdu and Awadhi languages. It involves a recitation of epics, singing, miming, clowning, emotional dramatization and some dancing. It became extremely popular during the early 20th century when troupes of artists called *mandalis* (groups) or *akhadas* moved from place to place, entertaining audiences. Some say that *nautanki* troupes were called *akhadas*, literally wrestling arenas, as the form of singing they indulged in required extensive stamina.

'There are two distinct schools in *nautanki*—the Hathrasi school from Hathras and Mathura and Kanpur schools,' Gangaprasad informs me. The Hathrasi school is older, operatic in form and emphasizes the singing. The Kanpuri School developed during colonial times. It meshed the prose dialogue delivery from Parsi Theatre with Hathrasi singing to come up with a new, fast-paced style of performance.[2] Besides these two, there are three other distinct *akhadas* of *nautanki*: Muzzafarnagar, Kannauj and Saharanpur, each named after the town where it emerged.

'During my youth, *nautankis* were very popular. Shri Krishna Pehelwan Nautanki and Mohan Ustaad from Kannauj were the two big *nautanki* companies that travelled all over the country. I joined the Shri Krishna company and travelled as far as Delhi and Mumbai. In those days, our company stayed near the Rail Bazaar station. There were some 20–25 actors. People would come from afar to seek us out. For the *melas* (fairs) we got a fixed fee. For the *nautankis*, the *naqqara* players got ₹3 per day and the *dholak* players ₹2.' The company would move from village to village in bullock carts, the *saajinde* (instrumentalists) in one cart and the artists in another. At the *melas*, they would sleep in tents or simply in the bullock carts. Food and props were provided by the community. 'The *saajinde* were from the Mehtar and Valmiki communities; the actors from the higher castes. So we had to stay and eat separately. We were not allowed to eat at the *bhandara (community feast)* and later, when we travelled by lorries and trucks, we had to sit where the actors took their shoes off. But at that time, we didn't protest. We had a role to play and were allowed no other. It was how things were. Besides, we were too busy going from one place to another, earning a livelihood and enjoying our art. It was quite a life. We would travel for weeks or months,' Gangaprasad recalls.

He proceeds to describe a typical *nautanki* night. 'Normally we performed in a huge *maidan* (field) in the village or just outside it. A small stage or elevated platform was set up and people would gather around it. At the *melas*, this happened inside a tent. Initially there were no sound systems, so the beginning of the evening was announced by the beating of the *naqqaras*. While other instruments like the harmonium, *dholak* and *sarangi* were also used in performances, the *naqqara* remained the most important *saaz* (instrument). In fact, the *nautanki* is named after the *naqqara*,' he explains with a twinkle in his eye. The animation in his voice and across his features are a testimony to both his love for his art and his pride in it.

'The nautanki is named after the *naqqara*?' I ask dumbfounded.

He nods enthusiastically and I do not have the heart to remind him of the ballad of Princess Nautanki. The story goes that Nautanki, the Princess of Multan, is a renowned ethereal beauty who rejects all suitors on some pretext or the other. In the neighbouring kingdom, live two brothers—Bhup Chand and Phool Chand. One day, Phool, the younger brother, comes home after hunting and demands food immediately. His sister-in-law taunts him saying that he is behaving as if he is married to the great Nautanki herself. Insulted, Phool vows to return only after he has married Nautanki and sets out for Multan. Once in the city, he convinces the flower woman of the palace to carry to Nautanki a beautiful garland woven by him. When Nautanki quizzes the florist, she claims that the garland has been prepared by her daughter-in-law who is visiting. Nautanki expresses a desire to meet the lady and Phool Chand, disguised as a woman, enters her bedchamber. Nautanki falls instantly in love with the woman. She claims that had Phool been a man, she would have married him. The clever Phool advises her to close her eyes and pray to the Almighty to turn him into a man. As the princess prays, he removes his disguise and the lovebirds unite. When the King hears of this, he orders Phool's execution. An angry Nautanki rides to his rescue with a sword and a cup of poison. Seeing her love, the king relents and the Princess marries Phool.

Most people believe that *nautanki* theatre is named after this popular play, which first appeared in published form as Khushi Ram's *Sangit Rani Nautanki Ka* (The musical drama of Queen Nautanki) in 1882. Some attribute it to the Sanskrit '*natak*' meaning play, others to '*nau takas*', literally nine rupees, the price for hosting a *nautanki* company. A few believe the word refers to a distinctive music and drumming style—*nay tankar*, or 'new sound', lending credence to Gangaprasad's theory. Whatever, the origin of the word, the fact remains that the *naqqara* was the distinctive feature of *nautanki*. It was used to announce the entry and exit of every character, to denote the change of scenes and to add much needed pace and emphasis to certain parts of the musical dialogue.

'Every *nautanki* would begin with the *saaz*. Once the audience began to gather, we would play the *nagma* or instrumental music. For an hour, there were no words, no song. Just the tones of the harmonium, *naqqara* and *dholak* enticing the public.' This was followed by *Mangalacharana* or devotional songs offered by the actors as prayers. Finally, the *Ranga* or the Director would step up, sing a dramatic event from the story and usher in the characters.

Initially, the *nautanki* had an all male cast. Men dressed up as women. Then in the 1930s, a young Bedia woman, Gulab Bai, breached this all male bastion. Thereafter, more and more women, mostly from the Dalit communities, began to perform in the *nautanki*. 'In my time, there were two main narrators—*Nat* and *Nati*—one male, one female. The *nautanki* progressed as a musical exchange between them, interspersed with dance and emotions. We used to perform all night, often without any breaks. And people used to sit and listen. No one went home. Those nights were special,' he says with a fond smile and a faraway look in his eyes.

For 20 years, the veteran *naqqarchi* travelled across the country, enthralling audiences with the varied beats of his *naqqara*. Then, in 1970, he was offered a job by an insurance company. He accepted.

'I haven't performed publicly since,' he says with a sigh. Then his grandson brings in his *naqqaras* and once again his face lights up, his spine grows straight. He arranges the two instruments on the bed carefully and then picks up two small narrow wooden sticks. 'These are called the *Chobh*,' he explains. For the next half hour, I sit spellbound as his hands use the *Chobh* to create one lively tune after another. His posture is straight, his face almost impassive, but his hands! I am mesmerized by the rhythm, the sheer artistry with which he moves them. And the speed! There is no time for the brain to tell the hands what to do, for the hands to process the information and comply. Instead they seem to have a mind of their own. Or perhaps they simply know, they remember. They beat swiftly, elegantly, with nary a pause. If hearing the *naqqara* is a feast for the ears, then watching Gangaprasad play is a treat for the eyes.

'Why did you give it up?' I ask, unable to hold the question any longer.

He grows quiet, a look of acute sadness and loss on his face. His younger son, Surajdin, who had learnt to play the *naqqara* and *dholak* from his father explains. 'It sounds romantic and I guess, for my father it was, this life dedicated to his music. But it was very hard on the family. He was away for months and the earnings were paltry. There was no fixed income, no guarantee,' he explains. So, when finally a job came by, Ganagaprasad's wife and children convinced him to take it up. 'It provided security,' his wife says simply.

And security was important. Ask Gangaprasad's elder son, the man who had to pull rickshaws to keep his family from starvation while his father was away, entertaining villagers. 'My father pulled rickshaws, took up whatever job was available to help his siblings study. He himself studied under the streetlight,' explains Rohit, Gangaprasad's 24-year-old grandson.

Rohit was 11 when he joined Apna Theatre, an organization that uses *nukkad nataks* (street plays) to fight untouchability and other social ills. Today he is pursuing his Master's in Social Work and hopes to work with an NGO. 'But my father wants me to give the Staff Selection Commission exam and get a government job. He has seen so much struggle and insecurity in his life that he wants to ensure a secure future for us,' shrugs Rohit.

'Do you play the *naqqara*?' I ask.

He shakes his head. As do the other children sitting around him.

'Today's generation plays the *bhangra dhol*. They say that times have changed and that this would at least get them a job in band parties. I taught my younger son the *naqqara* and then even took a few *shagirds* (students). Alas, I have outlived my students and there is no one really to carry my *kala* (art) forward,' laments Gangaprasad.

Surajdin intervenes. 'You see for my father, playing the *naqqara* was a *kala*. For me, it was a source of livelihood. I did a few *nautankis* but quit the minute I got a job. Today, *nautankis* are dying. They no longer enjoy the status they did. Earlier it was patronized by the masses—it was their only form of entertainment, and in some cases, information. Now they have TV, films and the internet. No one cares for old ballads and mythical tales. No one really looks for a *naqqara* player. The young have no reason to learn the instrument.'

No reason and no inclination. To them it is not an art form, but a profession that reeks of caste-based hierarchies and discrimination. Rohit sums it up. 'What has the instrument given us? A missing father? A missing husband? Insecurity and uncertainty? My grandfather says he did not pay heed to the discrimination but admits it was there. His talent was the life of every wedding and yet no priest would perform his wedding because he was a Mehtar. He couldn't enter people's homes; sit with them; eat with them. He could not take up another profession or even become a narrator in the *nautanki* company. It was as if people in our community could only play drums or sweep. This instrument became a tool of discrimination, of perpetuating stereotypes. Why should I learn to play? What legacy do you want me to carry forward? And for whom?'

POSTCARD 2

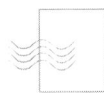

Jamkhed, Maharashtra

Kaajal with her ghunghroos

Jamkhed, Maharashtra

Lavani dancer (photocredit: Kunal Vijayakar)

Dear Reader,

Dressed in a red chiffon saree with a shiny red bindi, she sits quietly on the floor, oblivious to the mayhem around her. Fair skinned, with big kohl-rimmed eyes and chest-length straight black hair partially held back by a tie, she is beautiful. And young, no more than 18 years is my guess. With acute concentration she wraps a shoddy maroon length of cloth around her feet. Then she starts circling it with a long string of large *ghungroos*.[3]

'Those must be heavy,' I venture. She continues to focus on her *ghungroos*, the slight smile hovering on her lips and the twitch of a facial muscle the only indication that she has heard me.

There is something about the stoic air with which she carries out her task that draws my attention, despite the flurry of activity that is going on around me. I remember myself at 18—bubbling with excitement, full of dreams for the future. Perhaps this is why the restraint, which seems to cloak every movement of hers, unsettles me. 'Doesn't it tire you?' I try again.

This time she looks up and tilts her head almost imperceptibly towards the middle-aged *tabla* player in a full-sleeve shirt with white and blue checks, sitting on the floor next to her. Without so much as a sound, the message is sent. 'Wait for the music to stop.' And why not? As a Lavani dancer Kaajal has learnt to communicate with her expressions—to tell stories with the tilt of her head, the lift of an eyebrow, the slightest turn of her lips.

It is 9 pm and I am inside a small room at the Sanskritik Kala Kendra in Jamkhed. This is where 70 people—about 50 female dancers, all of them from the Kolhati community, and 20 musicians and cooks spend their days and nights. It is here that they live, entertain and earn.

All around me the beats of the *tabla* mesh with the tantalizing notes of the harmonium and the incessant tinkling of *ghungroos*. I sit on a small platform that runs along one wall. It is covered with a rundown mattress. The room is small—barely 7 × 7 square feet in size—and is currently occupied by six Lavani dancers between the ages of 18 and 45, two instrumentalists—both middle-aged men—and three visitors—my colleagues and me. It serves as a private *baithak*. Here small groups get to enjoy the lithe movements and gyrations of the dancers for a pre-negotiated fee, much like the *kothas* (brothels) immortalized by Bollywood. Only the pomp and show, the rich furnishings, trademark hookahs and liquor bottles are missing. Those, I learn, are simply accoutrements added by Bollywood stylists to enhance the sensuousness of the experience.

YaRav ji, BassaBhav ji… the slightly off-key notes reverberate across the room. A middle-aged dancer, her body draped loosely in another red chiffon sari much like Kaajal's, sensuously throws the *pallu* (edge of her saree) over her head. Then she bows, quirks an eyebrow, taps her chin with her finger and with studied grace bites into her lower lip, even as her feet move to the popular Marathi number. Behind her, Kaajal slowly gets up and begins to keep rhythm with her now *ghungroo*-clad feet. Gradually her body begins to move to the music but her face remains blank, her hands by her side. It is clear that Alka Tai, as the tall, fair skinned and generously built woman dancing before me is called, is the leader of Alka Sangeeta—the name splayed in bold red paint across the harmonium. For the next 20 minutes she continues to enchant us with her *ada* (coquetry) and her dance. Every time she gets out of breath and takes a break, one of the other dancers steps in and the show goes on.

After every song, there is a brief consultation about the next number. The women are perplexed when we ask for the traditional ballads. 'These days people generally ask for popular Bollywood or Marathi film numbers,' explains Alka Tai. 'Does it bother you?' I ask. She shrugs nonchalantly.

In the last few years Lavani has come back into the limelight. While popular raunchy numbers like *Chikni Chameli* and *Mala*

Jau Se have ingrained it in the psyche of the middle class, studies and performances by a few artists have also led to improved media coverage. In 2017, the Mumbai editions of most newspapers have featured stories about the origin and comeback of the Lavani. The credit for this sudden visibility goes to *Natarang*—a film starring Atul Kulkarni that traces the life of a *Tamasha* artist—and to *Sangeet Bari*, originally a play and now a book in Marathi by Bhushan Korgaonkar.

It is said that Lavani as a dance form is more than 400 years old but it gained popularity during the rule of the Peshwas who used it as a tool to legitimize the institution of slavery of lower caste women. Lavani had two forms: spiritual and *shringarik* (or erotic). It was the latter that found patronage in the Peshwa times. According to the late Sharmila Rege, renowned sociologist and Head of Women's Studies Department at the University of Pune, any lower caste woman accused of adultery could be sold by the Peshwa state to fill their coffers or forced into employment at their various factories or dancing houses. Thus, they encouraged Lavani—a dance form wherein nubile dancers from the Kolhati community showcased the eroticism and desire of the female, as seen through male eyes (the song writers were mostly male) for an entirely male audience. The idea, according to Rege, was to construct the lower caste women as amoral and sexually insatiable. During the reign of Bajirao Peshwa II, Lavani moved from private *natakshalas* (theatres) to public performances or *tamasha* for a male audience. With the end of Peshwa rule, the Lavani dancers were left struggling without patrons. Both the British and the new middle class that emerged began to view the Lavani and the *Tamasha* or folk theatre in which it was performed as 'amoral' and 'licentious'. The early 1900s saw the emergence of spontaneous theatre called *Vag* in Maharashtra, where all the roles were performed by male artists. The Kolhati women responded by forming groups called *sangeet barees (homes of music)*. They would go from village to village and perform. In these *barees*, the all male audience would bid for the Lavani to be performed on a song of their choice. Soon a contract system emerged, where the *sangeet baree* women would stay and perform in theatres that began to be known as *Kala Kendras* (Centres of Art). Today, there are seven *Kala Kendras* in Jamkhed itself.

The Lavani dancers belong to the Kolhati, Dombari and Kawlateen communities. The rule in these communities is that once a woman dons *ghungroos*—the hallmark of a Lavani dancer—she will never get married. Thus, if she craves love, companionship, economic security or children, a series of wealthy patrons is her only recourse.

At the end of the Lavani performance, I follow Kaajal out of the room. She moves across an open courtyard, brimming with women (the artists) and men (the customers) and enters a small room. 'This is where I stay with my group. 'Ab batao tumko kya poochna hai,' (Now tell me what you want to know) she says as she sits on a mat and begins to unravel the string of *ghunghroos* she had so painstakingly adorned. The room is small, without any beds or furniture. Just a plastic chair which Kaajal pulls up for me. Along the walls are a few trunks and almirahs that contain the belongings of the group members.

'How much do those weigh?' I ask pointing at the *ghunghroos*.

'I have never really weighed them. Must be around 5 Kg. Here, you can feel their weight,' she says thrusting them at me.

'These are heavy. Don't you get tired?' I reiterate my earlier question.

A patient look followed by a shake of the head. 'We are used to them now. If we dance without them, we feel tired.'

'How long have you been dancing?'

'Five years.'

'You started dancing at the age of 13?' I ask startled.

'No. I am 21 now. I first came here when I was 16.'

I prod some more. 'That's still very young. Life here must be very different from what you were used to?'

She simply shrugs.

'Weren't you worried?'

'Alka Tai, who runs this *Kala Kendra*, is my *Atiya* (father's sister). What was there to worry? Yes, I miss my family, but my elder sister Reshma is also here.'

Sensing her discomfort—or perhaps, it is my own reluctance to pry into her personal life—I ask Kaajal about her *kala* and life at the *Kala Kendra*. Another intense stare comes my way.

'Make no mistake. This is our livelihood. No one looks at it as an art form. You won't see people applauding or awarding us. Those are for other women. When a Kolhati girl dons the *ghunghroos*, there is no respect, no love for the dance, just a material need.'

Her candour leaves me speechless. There is no complaint in her tone. No rage. No inflection of any emotion. It is simply a statement of fact.

This is in sharp contrast to an earlier conversation I had had with Arun Hirabai Jadhav. The son and brother of a Lavani dancer, Arun, along with his wife Uma, started Gramin Vikas Kendra, an NGO that works for the rights of marginalized communities, in 1995.

Sitting in his small office in Jamkhed, under the watchful eyes of social reformers like Dr Ambedkar, Shahu Maharaj, Jyotiba Phule and Maulana Azad, Arun had angrily outlined the caste-based discrimination that underlies the life of Lavani dancers. 'You say it is an art form, a cultural heritage. Yet what has it brought us? Our women are harassed when they go out. They are looked down upon. Children don't know their fathers or their names.' I had pointed out that with Lavani capturing the public imagination, things could change. 'The Kolhati women could perform on the stage and in theatre. They no longer have to stay in these *Kala Kendras*. Perhaps, they could even teach women who want to learn the dance.'

'Oh yes and who would learn from them? It is true that public interest in Lavani is reviving. But don't get fooled. The women you see in theatres and in cultural festivals are not from the Kolhati community. They are women from the upper castes. We nurtured the dance form and yet, when it gets respect, it is not us who are recognized,' he had said bitterly.

I remember his impassioned words as a few more artists walk into Kaajal's room.

Shingroo, a middle-aged woman, clad in a nightie, jumps into our conversation. 'This is like any other profession. We perform and we earn.'

'So why choose it if not for the love of dance? Why not do something else?'

'What else can we do? People look at women from our community differently. We can study but we still don't get jobs in sales or in offices. If somehow we do land a job, we are inundated with indecent propositions. At least in the *Kala Kendra* we choose who we are with. Outside, it is a free for all,' Shingroo says.

In a soft voice, Kaajal adds, 'I love dance. Always have. When I was a kid I used to watch Alka Tai and copy her actions. I even performed in my school programmes. But I never intended to don these *ghunghroos*.'

'Why?'

'Because once you wear them, people look at you in a different way. They believe you are available. So what if I only dance?

So what if after the performance I return directly to this room? People don't care. They don't want to know this. I am still available.'

The air in the room grows heavy, as if unable to stand the weight of Kaajal's hurt and her accusation. I want to ask her more; to understand better but at that point the unshed tears shimmering in her beautiful eyes win over my urge to know.

Instead, I learn about life at the *Kala Kendra* from the motley group surrounding me.

Each *Kala Kendra* is made up of a few groups with 10–12 people each. These include not just dancers but even musicians and a cook to take care of the food and the cleaning. Performances typically start at about 6:30 pm and go on till midnight or a little after. Customers pay for a group, not individual dancers. Rates are normally by the hour and depend on the size of the room selected. Half of it goes to the *Kala Kendra* owner—in this case, to Alka Tai. Then some money is put aside for food and other group expenses. The rest is divided among the dancers and the musicians, every 4–5 days. In addition to this, customers often shower money on dancers if they are happy with the performance. This money is kept by the artist and does not have to be shared.

'Some people make ₹6000–8000 in a month. I make around 20,000.' Kaajal tells me.

A few of the women surrounding me have children. Reshma, Kaajal's older sister is one of them. Her son is two years old and stays with her mother in Jamkhed. She sees him every 15 days.

'I miss him but look at the *mahaul* (ambience). You can't raise children here. They stay with us till they are about one. Then we send them to live with our parents,' Reshma explains.

'And the father?'

'I am lucky. He visits the child, even supports us financially. Many others don't.' I learn that the children of Lavani dancers are known by their mothers' names. Their fathers seldom acknowledge them.

None of the dancers want their children to grow up in a *Kala Kendra* or to join it later.

'Each of us is here because we had no option. I had dreams of getting married, of having a career. My *Mausi* (maternal aunt) is a doctor in Mumbai. She used to go to college and I, to school. Afterwards she would take me with her to work in the fields. This is how I studied till Class 8. Then my father passed away. My older sister joined this *Kala Kendra* to make ends meet. But we are five sisters and one brother,' Kaajal tells me. Two years after her father's death, 16-year-old Kaajal followed in her sister's footsteps. She worked at Alka Tai's *Kala Kendra* for a year and then moved on to the Arya Bhushan and the Shiprapur *Kala Kendras* in Pune. Her *Mausi*, she tells me in a voice choked with emotion, hasn't spoken to her since.

'In Pune, the money was better. People were also better behaved. Here they pass all kinds of raucous comments and we have to continue dancing as if nothing is amiss. There it was different. We performed on the stage more often. In Jamkhed, it is mostly private *baithaks*.' While on stage, the Lavani dancers wear the *Nauwari* (nine feet) Paithani sari. In *baithaks*, they simply wear regular sarees, loosely draped to allow for leg movement.

'At least on the stage we feel more like artists. There are no cat-calls,' Kaajal says with a shrug.

'Then why did you come back?'

Another shrug greets me. 'Alka Tai called me back.'

Perhaps it was the call of the known or the fact that her family is now in Jamkhed. By being in this *Kala Kendra* she can meet them more often. Whatever the reason, two years ago, Kaajal moved back to the Sanskritik Kala Kendra. But it wasn't an easy decision. Most *Kala Kendra* owners lend money to the dancers when they come in. Moving from one *Kendra* to another necessitates the settling of this debt, which is often done by taking money from the next *Kala Kendra*. Thus, the cycle continues.

Kaajal shares with me the educational achievements of her siblings with great pride. Her love for her siblings is evident when she speaks of them. 'Two of them are in college, one in Class 12 and another in Class 8. They keep telling me that I should quit. That they will find some work. But how can I? I have to get my sisters married. I have to see that they finish their education. My father had borrowed a lot of money. Those debts have to be repaid,' she explains. Yet, she is confident that one day her siblings will rescue her from this life.

'What will you do after this?'

'I will rest. I am so tired.'

'Would you like to study further?'

Sadly, she shakes her head. 'Our world is different. Even if I quit dancing, people's attitude towards me will not change. They laugh at me now and they will laugh at me then. Studies are not an option. Neither is another job. I will most likely open a beauty parlour,' she confides.

'And will you marry? Fulfil your dream?'

'How can I? These *ghungroos*, they are like chains. If I am lucky I will find someone who will take care of me. Perhaps he will set me up with a house. Pay the theatre owner and take me away from this world. Give me a child. That's the best I can hope for.'

The dejected stoop of her shoulders and the hopelessness in her tone unravels something within me. I have an overwhelming urge to give her some hope, to make her believe that she can have a life beyond the *Kala Kendra*. I tell her of devadasis and Bedia dancers who have found love. I give her examples of people who married despite society's diktats. If marriage is what you wish for, it is possible, I insist.

'These men and women that you are talking about, did their community accept them?' she asks calmly.

'But why do you care about a community that only ostracizes and mocks you? You can build a life of your own.'

'Perhaps you are right. But, what of my mother? Of my sisters and brother? Of my nephew? What will happen to them? Either they will have to cut all ties with me or face the ire of the community. Who will marry them? I love them. I am here for them. How will I stay away from them? And how will I live with myself if my actions destroy their lives? No, this is why one should never don these *ghungroos*. Now this is my lot in life.'

Kaajal's words continue to ring in my ears as I leave the *Kala Kendra*.

POSTCARD 3: ROOTS OF REBELLION

Vithalbai with his Bungal in Patan, Gujarat

Patan, Gujarat

A Chaupra

Patan, Gujarat

Dear Reader,

Do you remember *Amar Chitra Katha*? Those great Indian educational comic books that our parents were only too happy to sit us down with on hot summer afternoons? In 1975, they published the story of Jasma of the Odes (*[sic]*: Oad or Odh), a folklore from Gujarat from the Oad community.

According to legend, Jasma was a beautiful *Apsara* (celestial nymph) sent by Indra to disrupt the meditation of the great sage Nala. Enraged, the sage cursed her to life as a mortal, married to an ugly, crippled man. But Jasma was no simpering miss. She called out the sage on his hypocrisy and cursed him to life as the very cripple who would become her husband. Thus, the divinely beautiful Jasma was born to Dhalo Dhond, the *Nayak* (leader) of the Oad tribe.

The Oad are a nomadic tribe spread across Sindh and Punjab in Pakistan and various states in North and Western India. They are known as great diggers and navvies: historically they have built roads, *vaavs* (stepwells), lakes, wells, etc. When Jasma came of age, her stepmother, who like all stepmothers in lore was evil, tricked her doting father into marrying Jasma off to Rooda, a cripple. Initially repelled, Jasma soon saw the beauty that lay within her husband's heart and accepted her marriage. At that time, Siddhraj Jaisingh Solanki (reign 1094–1143), often regarded as one of the greatest kings of Gujarat, was in power. One day, Jivaji Barot, his court poet, saw the beautiful Jasma and wrote paeans to her beauty. When he recited them to the king, the latter immediately expressed a desire to see this celestial being. This was the time when Gujarat was facing an acute drought and Solanki's wife had, in her dreams, received divine orders to build a huge lake. The King sought to kill two birds with a single stone. He ordered that a huge Sahastraling Sarovar be built (so named as it had small temples with a 1000 Shivlings around it) in Patan. For this he summoned the Oad. At the building site, the king saw the beautiful Jasma and fell in love with her. Her asked her to marry him but Jasma brushed aside his proposal. She told the king that she was already married. An incensed Siddhraj ordered the death of her husband and her tribe who rose in protest. Left with no choice

Jasma committed Sati,[4] but not before she had cursed the king. She ordained that no water would flow into the great Sarovar being built by the king and that he would never experience the joys of having an heir.

The *Amar Chitra Katha* version of the story glosses over the caste dimension and proceeds to a happy ending by suggesting that the Gods revive Jasma, her husband and her tribe, but not so the local lore that I hear standing at the Sahastraling Sarovar, in Patan, 130 km from Ahmedabad. It is mid-afternoon and the Sarovar is deserted. The few tourists who have braved the brutal April sun have stopped at the neighbouring Rani ki Vaav (Queen's stepwell), a UNESCO world heritage site. 'This place is of great significance to Dalits but few tourists venture here,' Manoj, a short man in a pink full-sleeve shirt who is acting as my translator, tells me.

'Why, because Jasma was a Dalit?' I ask.

'There is that. In fact, there is a temple dedicated to Jasma that has been built here. But the importance of this place lies in another story. Do you remember the tale of Veer Meghmaya that the Turi Barot narrated this morning? This is where he sacrificed his life.'

I turn back towards the dry ruins that seem to be radiating heat under the stark afternoon sun. The Sarovar makes for an interesting study in architecture—the 5-km-long stone tank was built to receive the waters of the River Saraswati. But it is much more than a complex web of reservoirs and channels. It is perhaps one of the biggest symbols of protest against caste and gender-based exploitation. It is a place where a woman—and a Dalit woman at that—asserted her right to reject a man, even if he was a king. It is also the place where Mayo, a young Dedh 'untouchable' sacrificed his life to win freedom from untouchability for his people.

I had first heard the story of Mayo from Martin Macwan, the 56-year-old Director of the Dalit Foundation. We were travelling in the Surendarnagar district of Gujarat to visit some schools and Martin was telling me about the history of untouchability in the region. 'Earlier Dalits had to tie a spittoon around their neck, so that the earth was not contaminated by their saliva. And their shirts had three sleeves,' he told me.

'Why?'

'The third was for the broom which was tied behind them to wipe out their very footprints. They could not wear shoes and cross the house of any "upper caste" person. In some places they were made to wear bells to warn others that they were coming. A Dalit bridegroom could not sit on a horse. The list is endless. There is an old Gujarati film called *Bhavni Bhavai* made by Ketan Mehta. It is based on the story of Veer Meghmaya who is a hero among the Dalits here. Watch it and you'll understand,' he had explained.

Then earlier this morning, I had heard the complete local version of the tale of Mayo. I was sitting inside a house, just a few kilometres from the Sarovar where I stand currently. Most people come to Patan for the renowned Rani ki Vaav, the Jain temples, the Sun temple at Modhera and the exquisite Patola sarees. Yet it was neither my love for history nor handlooms that had drawn me to this ancient city. I had travelled here in search of the *Bhavai*, a Gujarati folk theatre that is fading away, and the men—yes, it is only men—who have traditionally been performing it.

Much like the *Nautanki* of Uttar Pradesh, the *Yashagana* of Andhra Pradesh and the *Tamasha* of Maharashtra, *Bhavai* is a form of folk dance-drama that has entertained the rural masses in Gujarat for over 600 years now. Traditionally, it is performed by the Targala or the Nayak, i.e., men from the Turi Barot community.

'There may have been some form of religious folk theatre dedicated to the Goddess Amba that prevailed earlier, but *Bhavai* as we know it can be traced to a Brahmin priest Asait Thakore who lived in Siddhapur village in the 14th century.' The speaker is a tall, lean man in a full-sleeve green kurta with a Nehru collar. Clean-shaven, with a broad forehead made even more prominent by a receding hairline and a shining pate, tufts of salt and pepper hair moving well beyond his shoulders, Vithalbhai Kunjiram Nayak is a renowned Bhavai player. We are seated on handmade *chattais* (reed mats) inside an 8×8 room in his house in Patan.

It is believed that a Muslim *subedar* (an army officer) once abducted Ganga, the daughter of Hemala Patel from Unza village of Gujarat. When Asait heard this, he went to the *subedar* and demanded the release of Ganga, claiming her as his own daughter. The shrewd *subedar* was aware of the caste sensibilities of the local folk. He demanded that Asait share a meal with Ganga from the same plate to prove his parentage. Asait ate with Ganga and managed to rescue her but he was ex-communicated by his own community for eating with a 'lower caste' person. It is said that an angry Asait who was also a renowned poet composed 360 *veshas* or playlets (standalone drama scenes) and travelled from place to place, performing them. His first *vesha* was *Ramdeva* and he is believed to have enlisted musicians from the neighbouring town of Vadanagara to perform it.

'Sixty of the original 360 have survived. These compositions of Asait, over a period of time, came to be known as Bhavai. The performers who worked with him and their descendants came to be known as Bhavayyas or Nayaks,' Vithalbhai says as he opens a tattered old album. Inside, there are a few certificates from different government agencies where Vithal and his troupe, the Hathi Group, have performed over the years. There are also a number of pictures of various Bhavai performances. The costumes are elaborate as are the props. There are men dressed as elephants and horses. One picture in particular catches my eye. It is of a woman wearing a *chania choli* (a flared skirt with a short blouse), with lots of jewellery and three metal pots on her head.

'Who is this?'

Vithal gives me a shy smile. 'Me.'

The Bhavai, I learn, has only male performers. 'Bhavai troupes travel from village to village. Our womenfolk don't mingle with strange men. So men don the traditional *chania cholis*, wear hair-dos and make up and essay their parts,' he elaborates. Thus, while all three of Vithal's sons are Bhavai performers, his two daughters know nothing of the profession.

Bhavai troupes typically comprise 15–20 members. These include instrumentalists, cooks, actors and a *sutradhar* or *nayak* who is the narrator and group leader. The musicians play *pakhawaj* (flat faced drums), *jhanjha* (cymbals), *sarangi* (stringed instrument) and the harmonium, but the distinguishing *saaz* is the *bhungal*. Vithalbhai and his son Jagdishbhai take out three big copper pipes. 'These are joined together to form the *bhungal*,' Jagdish explains. 'The upper part is called the *phuga*, the middle the *vaan*, and the lower portion the *chamchi*. Once it is assembled, the instrument is four feet long. For ease of storage and transport, we dismantle it.'

The *bhungal* is a long, thin trumpet-like horn, tongued for tonality and pitch. The breath is modulated to create various pitches. It is played in pairs—a high pitched one for the female characters and a low pitched one for the male ones. Much like the *naqqara*, its strident sounds are used to announce a change of scene, the entry and exit of characters and to provide rhythm for dances.

'Every Bhavai troupe has marked areas. For instance, we have 42 villages. While we go to others when performances are requested, these are our traditional circuits. Before we leave for a performance, we go and blow the *bhungal* in front of the Chamunda Devi and the Phulba Ma temples. They are our ancestral deities and we invoke their blessings.'

The troupe then goes to the Vankar (weaver) and Rohit (Chamar or the leather workers) *mohallas* of a village. 'While we play for the upper castes when they ask us to, our traditional patrons have been the Vankar and the Rohit. We stay in their *mohallas*. In the evenings, we call on the community elders and seek their permission to perform the Bhavai. Unless there has been a recent death in the community, they never refuse. After all, it is on their request that our caste was created,' Vithalbhai explains.

I am confused. How were two Dalit communities responsible for the creation of another? 'I am sorry, I don't understand. Didn't you say that your community is a descendent of Asait Thakore?'

'That we are. But the story goes back further. Don't you know of Mayo?'

Though I had heard bits and pieces of the story, I shake my head, unable to make the connection. And then I hear the famous tale.

After Jasma Odhan cursed Siddhraj Solanki, the Sahastraling Sarovar remained dry. Everywhere people and cattle were dying from the drought. The king called and consulted many astrologers to find a way to break the curse. Finally, they hit upon a solution. 'Sacrifice a man with 32 *gunas* (virtues) at the Sarovar and it will fill up,' they decreed. A search was launched and finally the priests identified two men who fit the bill—the king himself and an untouchable Dedh youth called Mayo, who lived in a village near Patan. While the king did want to save his people, he had no intention of sacrificing himself. Hence, Mayo was summoned. Knowing that he did not have a choice, Mayo agreed to sacrifice his life on one condition. He pointed out that his community was poor and suffered greatly from the curse of untouchability. He requested the king to remove this. To give the community the right to have houses within the city, wear new clothes, worship the Goddess Amba, keep *pipal* and *tulsi* plants and have access to the Barot who compose genealogies. The king agreed and Mayo was beheaded at the Sarovar. It is said that the Sarovar instantly filled with water. Thus, not only did the brave man win the right to a life of dignity for his community, he also saved thousands from death.

Some versions of the tale, including the one in the famous *Bhavni Bhavai* suggested by Martin, claim that Mayo was actually the son of the king himself. A jealous queen had conspired with the court astrologer to convince the king that he would die if he saw his son's face. In an act of self-preservation, the king had ordered that his son be killed. The soldiers entrusted with the task put him in a cradle and tossed him into the river. The baby travelled downstream to a Dalit *basti* and was rescued by a childless Dalit couple who raised him as their own. This I discovered later when I watched the movie and researched the story.

'So you see, Mayo asked for Barot, literally meaning poets and genealogists, for the Vankar and the Rohit. Now it is said that there were two brothers who belonged to the Nayak community. They would compose genealogies and perform *nataks* at the palace to entertain the rich and the upper castes. Instead of allowing the untouchables access to the palace, the king decreed that one of the brothers be given to the Dalit communities for entertainment and for maintaining their records. The elder brother gave the younger brother to the community. The younger brother used to play the *tutari*, a bugle-like instrument resembling a trumpet that is frequently used in Maharashtra. Earlier it was employed during wars to boost the morale of soldiers. The *tutari* player became a Turi, and his descendants, the Turi Barot. So you see the community asked for us and can't turn us away,' Vithalbhai concludes his tale with a flourish.

It is some time before I am able to journey forward 1000 years and return to the present; the present where Vithal's sons are recounting a Bhavai tour for me.

After seeking the blessings of the elders, the *bhungal* is played to inform the villagers that a Bhavai troupe has arrived. A Bhavai is not just a source of entertainment but a community event. Everyone chips in. A small gathering is held in the evening and people pledge different forms of support to the troupe. 'Some people say we will give so many bags of rice, others offer sugar, tea leaves, etc. Someone will offer us a *charpai* or room in their house for the duration of the Bhavai,' explains Rajeshbhai Vithalbhai Nayak, Vithal's eldest son. Dressed in a purple t-shirt and jeans with a big black moustache and jet black hair that falls well below his shoulders, he exudes an air of confidence. After all, he is the *Nayak* or leader of the Hathi group. As I learn about the lifestyle of the Turi Barot, I also catch a glimpse of how caste still plays a role in the lives of the villagers. There may have been a Mayo and King Siddhraj may have abolished untouchability at his insistence, but many of the discriminatory practices and attitudes have filtered down through the centuries.

'We stay and perform in the Vankar and Rohit *mohallas* of the village for two days. The upper caste people may come to see our performances and if they like it the *mukhiya* (village headman) may invite us to perform in the main village square. In that case we extend our stay to five days. Often the upper castes will come and enjoy our performances but they won't eat with us or invite us into their homes.' Unfortunately, while this community of *kalakaars* (artists) faces discrimination, they also discriminate against other castes themselves. They only accept food or stay in the houses of the Vankar or Rohit. They do not visit the Valmiki *mohalla* or accept anything from them.

The morning after their arrival, the Bhavai troupe goes from house to house collecting the materials promised by the villagers. The actors rest and get ready, while the cooks prepare breakfast and lunch. After lunch, they decide which *veshas* will be performed and who will do what part. The props are prepared with support from the local communities. 'We only carry our instruments and dresses with us. In Bhavai, there is no fixed script. We know the *veshas* and allot parts. Thereafter the actors improvize and perform. We don't memorize any dialogues and in case someone gets stuck, we have prompters,' explains Rajesh.

And this is what makes Bhavai so vibrant. No two performances are the same. As actors grow, so do their performances and their plays. They incorporate local contexts and ensure that the plays are not just rib-tickling but also relevant. You can watch the same Bhavai, performed by the same troupe a year later and it may turn out to be a completely novel experience.

'Every performance begins with the *Nayak* invoking the Goddess Amba and seeking her blessings. Thereafter the actors and musicians come in. Dance is an integral component of Bhavai; most scenes begin and end with it. But the hallmark of Bhavai is humour, often supplied by an actor called the *Ranglo*,' Rajesh tells me just as he gets up to leave for a meeting.

In the past, Bhavai was used to poke fun at the customs, figures and practices that discriminated against the Dalit communities. Most *veshas* involve kings and noblemen and these characters were often depicted as ignorant bumblers. More importantly, the professional working classes who were branded as untouchables, and whose existence was always invisibilized, find a place in these *nataks*. The stories, lives and often, heroics, of the Oad, the Banjara (nomad), the Kumbhar (potter), the Fakir (mendicant), the Maniar (bangle maker) and the Chamar are depicted in great detail.

'Bhavai performances typically start around 9 pm and carry on till 4 am. Earlier we performed with the *mashaals* (wooden torches), then came the lanterns and now there are tubelights to light up the arena as we sing, dance and act. For two days few people in the village sleep. We work on an empty stomach. We eat dinner only when the Bhavai is over,' Vithalbhai tells me.

'That's not a very healthy lifestyle,' I venture. 'Doesn't it lead to problems?'

'Of course, it does. Blowing the *bhungal* requires a lot of energy. It's also not good for the lungs. Besides, when we play, air fills our stomach and our food intake goes down. Many also suffer from hearing problems due to the raucous sounds of the *bhungal*. Constant travel, crazy schedules with little sleep and erratic eating habits—this is our legacy but what option do we have? This is our livelihood and this is how it is done.'

'What about the women?'

'What about them? They stay at home, take care of the house and the children.'

'You are always travelling. What kind of family life is that? Why not take them with you?'

'We don't know where we will be staying and for how long. We don't know the kind of quarters or food we will receive. Where will they sleep, bathe? Besides the children have to go to school. Earlier, we received substantial fees. It wasn't just in the form of money. People would pledge 150–200 *mann* of wheat or rice.'

'Mann?'

'One *mann* is equivalent to 20 kg. We would divide this amongst the troupe.'

'Equally?'

'Oh no. Every person's share is determined by the role he played. Naturally, the *nayak* gets the biggest portion, followed by the main actors and the *bhungal* players.'

'So you are out all year, while your families stay here?'

'No. We mostly travel during winters. The Bhavai season starts after Dussehra and carries on for three to four months. Normally we go after the harvest, so that we receive ample foodgrains from the villages.'

'And the rest of the time?'

'We perform at weddings, often playing musical instruments. I get ₹2500–3000 for playing the *shehnai* at a wedding. We work as labour and also maintain the *chaupra*.'

'Chaupra?'

'Genealogical records of different Vankar and Rohit families. That is what Meghamaya had asked for—Barots who would record the *vanshavali* (family history) of his community.'

This, I learn, is the other occupation of the Turi Barot—they are mythographers and genealogists par excellence. Every birth, death and wedding is meticulously recorded in their records. That is not all. The *chaupras* also contain details of the bride's family, ancestral gods and goddesses and property records.

'If you ever want to settle a property dispute or know how a land changed hands, you have only to consult the *chaupra* of a Vai Vancha, as the Turi Barot who maintains genealogical records is called. These records go back centuries. There is a *chaupra* with Mayo's story as well.'

'Wow. So you are also a Vai Vancha?'

'No, not me. I started going with Bhavai troupes since I was 18. First, I would observe and learn—after all, there is no formal training—and then I started performing. But you are lucky. A Vai Vancha from another village is visiting us today,' says Vithal.

This is how I meet Gaudabhai of Godana village from Sahmi Tehsil of Patan.

Dressed in a peach kurta with a khadi green-and-white striped jacket, and a white cotton stole, Gaudabhai must be in his 60s.

'The villages are divided amongst the different Vai Vanchas and each person's area is called a *garaag*. I have 35–40 villages in Morbi in my *garaag*. When there is a birth in the family of a Vankar in our *garaag*, we are informed. We record the event in huge registers called the *chaupra*. People inherit lands and properties. We inherit the *chaupra*. It is our source of livelihood,' Gaudabhai explains.

'So every time there is a birth or a death or a wedding, you go to their house and record the event?' I ask.

'No. Making an entry into the *chaupra* is a big event. It is called a *prasang*. Normally, unless someone is very well-to-do, they don't independently host a *prasang*. A few families get together and call us. It could be a week after the birth or even a few years.'

The Vai Vancha is usually accompanied by his sons, his nephews or his successors, all of whom are male. This, Gaudabhai explains, is to ensure a seamless transition between generations—the new generation learns the craft and also becomes acquainted with the families in their *garaag*. Like the Bhavai performers, this group of 4–5 people stay at the home of one of their Vankar hosts. At the *prasang*, not just villagers, but relatives and friends from different villages are invited. 'We recite the genealogy of the family and make new notations in the *chaupra*. In the evening, when everyone gathers, we narrate the *kathas* (stories). I was 17 when I started reciting them.'

At the end of the *prasang*, the Vai Vancha get *bakshis* (tips) from the villagers and from their hosts. 'There is no fixed fee. But the *bakshis* is usually substantial. I have received gold rings, necklaces, a bed, utensils of brass and copper, silver items and cash.'

'Do people still do this?'

'Oh yes. Vankar families from our villages keep their *chaupra* updated. Wherever they migrate, they call us. I have gone to Mumbai, Ahmedabad, Kutch. Normally, we visit a village once every couple of years. Our records are so meticulously kept that you could use them in a court of law for property disputes,' he says, eyes shining with pride. Some *chaupra*s, I learn, are 500–600 years old. They are huge registers that have a page for every family in the *garaag* of the Vai Vancha.

'But how do you include all this information in just one or two pages?'

Gaudabhai simply smiles and I am intrigued.

'May I see your *chaupra*?' I request.

He shakes his head regretfully. 'Had I known you were coming, I would have brought it with me. I was simply visiting a family member and we don't carry our *chaupras* with us. Besides you won't be able to read them.'

'Don't worry, I can read a bit of Gujarati. I just wish you had it here,' I say.

Both Gaudabhai and Vithalbhai start laughing. 'That's the thing. We do not write in Gujarati or Devanagari. Earlier we did not have the right to study. Some people who had managed to learn despite the caste restrictions evolved a special *lipi* (script). That is the language that we write in, the language that we teach our children. Only the Vai Vancha know it,' Gaudabhai explains.

His explanation further piques my curiosity and I begin to enquire about other Vai Vanchas who may be staying nearby. 'My father is a Vai Vancha. He stays in Chanasma town. It's about 17 km from here,' Manoj, a Dalit rights activist and my guide, offers shyly.

I find myself travelling to a small single-storey house in Chanasma. Manoj's father is a thin, elderly man. There is little vision left in his cataract-afflicted eyes and his hearing is poor. Dressed in a white *dhoti* and *kurta* he sits on the floor and insists that we take the only chairs in the house. When he hears my request, his wrinkled face lights up. He very carefully brings a bundle wrapped in a vermillion red cloth from a steel almirah that sits in the tiny space that serves as the family's receiving room. With great respect he touches the bundle to his forehead, chants a few words—a prayer, perhaps—and then opens it. There are two registers with tattered covers and white cotton threads wrapped abound them. Both are in landscape format. The bigger of the two must be 6 inches in height and 10–12 inches in breadth. Inside, the yellowed pages are filled neatly with row after row of black script. Occasionally there are markings in red. As Gaudabhai had predicted, neither Manoj nor I can read the *chaupra*.

Manoj's uncle, also a Vai Vancha, offers to read a few entries for us. Carefully, he opens a page and begins 'Dinesh Lavjina...'. As he squints to read the entries, another voice continues the recitation. Startled, I look up and see Manoj's father calmly narrating the genealogy. Manoj smiles even as his uncle follows the script with a finger, nodding all the while.

'I am not able to read them now, but I wrote these *Vanshavalis* (family histories). For many years, I recited them. I know them by heart,' his father explains. And that I learn is the mark of a true Vai Vancha. He records the history meticulously for the next generations, but for his own part, he knows them verbatim.

'How old is this *chaupra*?'

'This one isn't that old. Must be 150 years or so. Open the first page. Do you see a note with the stamp on it? That is my father's will bequeathing me the *chaupra*,' he says.

'So technically you will be getting these *chaupras*, right? Yet you haven't learnt the script,' I ask Manoj.

'I chose a different path,' he says simply. Yet, implicit in his answer is the questioning of an age-old system where professions were hereditary. Why should the son of a Vai Vancha be only a Vai Vancha? For that matter, why shouldn't the child—male or female—from another community, be it the Thakore, the Mehtar or the Vankar perform the Bhavai? Why not treat the Vai Vancha or the Bhavayya as a guru and learn his art from him? This would perhaps infuse a new life and dignity into this fading art form.

'With the onslaught of the electronic media, the demand for Bhavai is fading. More importantly, the youngsters today do not wish to learn it. They detest the casteism implicit in the performances,' laments Vithalbhai.

'Casteism in the performances?'

'You see we have to bow to our patrons, offer them *salaam*s, dance for them and ask for money at the end. The *veshas* are adopted to sing their praises, even as other communities are ridiculed. Then we have to dress up as women and people make fun of us. The young men today don't like this. They look for other alternatives.'

'All the more reason to involve the other communities as performers.'

'No, we do not want other communities to take up the Bhavai. Some Thakores have started performing a few Ram Kathas. They haven't learnt it from us and even if they did, they would never acknowledge it.'

'But what if they did? Wouldn't you want that respect?'

'No, this is our heritage and our source of livelihood. It is one of the few definite assets that we have. If others take this from us, where will we go? The Bhavai performers you see on the dance shows and on theatre platforms are not Turi Barots. When other communities learn this art form, they take away all the programmes and the limelight because they have better access and because casteism still operates,' Jagdishbhai, Vithal's son, answers.

'Won't acknowledging you as a guru bring you money as well as respect? Won't it disrupt the hierarchy that fuels the caste system?'

Both Jagdish and Vithalbhai shake their head.

'So will you teach your son to perform the Bhavai?' I ask Jagdish.

'Of course. He is only five now. He may decide to do something else when he grows up but I will make sure he learns the Bhavai. It is our *virasat* (heritage), our identity and our security. If he doesn't find another job, he could always perform and earn. After all, music is in our veins. It is said that even when our children fight, there is a rhythm in their arguments.'

POSTCARD 4: A WARPED WEAVE

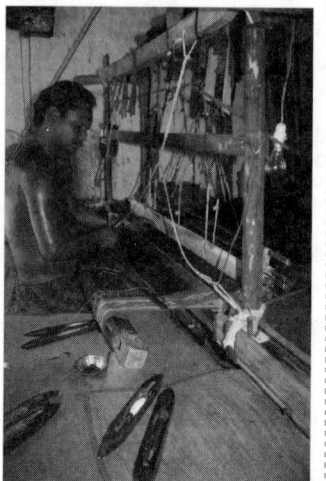

A Kureel weaver on his loom in Bargarh district, Orissa

Bargarh and Balangir, Orissa

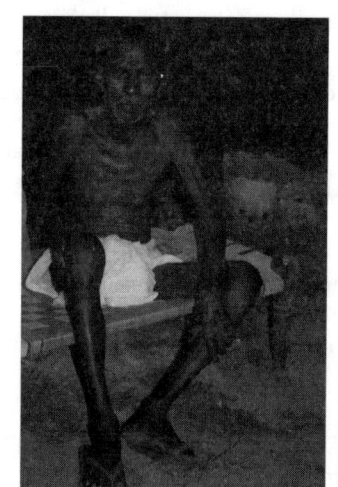
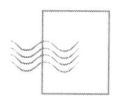

95-year-old Shatrughan Chhatriya outside his house in Balangir

Bargarh and Balangir, Orissa

The Museum of Broken Tea Cups

Dear Reader,

I have a confession to make. For over a decade now I have been carrying on a not-so-clandestine love affair with the handwoven fabrics of India. What started out purely as a work relationship has blossomed into a passion, or as my family insists, an obsession. Perhaps now you will indulge my excitement over a visit to Western Orissa—the place where the famous Sambalpuri Ikat is created.

My association with Orissa is almost as old as my just confessed love affair. It is a favourite destination—the state does boast some of the finest handloom products in the country! Yet I had never made it to the western part of the state. So, on a hot, sultry May day I find myself on a train from Bhubhaneshwar to Balangir, the infamous B of KBK (Koraput Balangir Kalahandi), a region synonymous with poverty, deprivation and malnutrition.

Nine hours later—trains never run on time on this route—I am at the district headquarters, the jaundice-afflicted town of Balangir. Droughts and epidemics are common in this erstwhile kingdom of Rajendra Narayan Singhdeo, the man who went on to become the Chief Minister of Orissa in 1967. Almost 40 per cent of the district's population belongs to the Scheduled Castes or the Scheduled Tribes.

By the time I reach Chesta Chhatriya's brick home, 25 km from the town, dusk is gathering. A glow of lanterns and a group of three men standing next to the National Highway, 5 km after the block headquarters of Loisinga, tell me that I have reached my destination.

It is a simple house located in the middle of a field. The bricks that make the walls are clearly visible as is the cement holding them together. The corrugated metal sheet roofing is covered with large swaths of plastic. There is no electricity as it is a couple of kilometres from the nearest village. Here, Chesta, along with his 29-year-old wife Kanchan Kalsia, plans to start a hostel for children in Classes 1–8. This, he says, is the only way children from his community will get educated in a district with one of the highest out-migration rates in the country.

It is estimated that almost 1.5 lakh people migrate out of Balangir every winter. This led the district administration to announce 135 seasonal hostels in 2014 to prevent children from dropping out of schools. But in a country where caste still continues to hold sway, even this does not guarantee access to education for children belonging to Dalit communities. This is where people like Chesta come in.

Tall, with a square face, shining olive skin, a thick black moustache and equally black, albeit thinning hair, Chesta is dressed in a simple half sleeve white shirt and black trousers. He is a Gana or a Ganda. This community accounts for over 66 per cent of the Scheduled Caste population in Balangir and is also found in large numbers in the neighbouring districts of Sambalpur, Sundargarh and Bargah. Traditionally, they were weavers who also served as village watchmen, musicians and messengers. Though they claim to be a warrior caste that served in the militia of former princely states, they were regarded as untouchables and till date, the Gandapara (Ganda hamlets) are found outside villages and towns.

What brings me to Chesta's house is not his plans for the hostel—I heard of them only when I visited him—but his ancestral profession. A frail man with just a white loincloth tied around his waist sits on a white *charpai* outside Chesta's house. Every bone and rib on his dark body is clearly visible, even in the dim light of the lantern. He is 95-year-old Shatrughan Chhatriya, Chesta's grandfather. 'I started weaving *kapta* when I was 12 years old. My father taught me,' he says.

'Kapta?'

'It is a shorter sari worn traditionally by the women in Orissa. About 1.5 m wide and 5.5 m long, it is thicker than the usual saris—uses a 20-count thread—and has *pallus* on both sides. This ensures the opacity of the fabric and women can wear it without petticoats and blouses.' An ingenious idea not only because it reduces the need for tailors, but also because it keeps the wearer cool during the blistering Oriya summers. The sari is tied in such a manner that it hangs a little below the knees, leaving the calves bare—again a practical measure for women working in the paddy fields. A *pallu* thrown over the left shoulder and secured by wrapping it under the right one, ensures that the bosom is gracefully covered and that the cloth does not flutter or get tangled in bushes. This style is passé now. Increasingly women in Orissa are draping themselves in six yards of finely spun fabric over petticoats and stylized blouses.

'Only the elderly women and some in rural areas forgo the blouse these days. For some reason the very practical style of our forefathers is suddenly regarded as immodest,' laments the nonagenarian. He adds that this trend of adopting the blouse and wearing finer saris started over 60–70 years back. It was when a weavers' society from Sambalpur visited his village of Tangrupadar in the neighbouring Bargarh district, that a young Shatrughan learnt how to weave the Sambalpuri Ikat.

'While it took a little longer to make this sari—two pieces of *kapta* are woven in three days whereas it takes four to weave two simple Sambalpuris—it fetched a much better price. So whenever possible we made the switch.'

It is believed that Sambalpuri Ikat came to Western Orissa with the Bhulia community in 1192 AD. This group migrated here when the Chauhan empire was defeated by the Ghouris. Unlike Bandhani, in Ikat the thread is dyed with the design before the cloth is woven. In some cases, only one thread—that is either the warp or the weft—is dyed. While this variety is produced in Sambalpur and the neighbouring districts, this region is most noted for its double Ikat. This is an extremely fine art—it requires the design to be made on both the warp and the weft threads and then their placement is done in a very calculated manner to ensure that it is reflected accurately in the woven cloth. It also takes much longer to weave—in some cases up to 10 days for a single sari. But the Ganda don't make these finer saris.

'Making the switch wasn't easy. In our society caste boundaries were very strong. The Sambalpuri Ikat was the craft of the Bhulia. We were regarded as untouchables. Who would teach us? We could switch from the *kapta* to making saris, but the Ikat was a very different thing. Till date it is the Bhulia who make the finest Sambalpuri Ikats. Only they know how to make the *bandha*.' The dyed thread on which the design has already been created is known as *bandha*. It is the foundation of the Sambalpuri Ikat and the art is zealously guarded by the Bhulia community.

'I know different scavenger communities and people who work with leather were stigmatized by the Varna system, but why the Ganda?'

'Who knows? They said we were impure because we ate beef and removed caracasses. People were happy to listen to us play but because our drums and instruments used cow flesh, we were ostracized.'

'But not your music or the cloth you wove?'

'No. Our art was accepted. What they discriminated against was our person. We could not enter the houses of other communities or visit temples. They kept separate utensils for us and if we touched anything of theirs, they would throw it away. If we were eating and some food fell on the ground, we were made to use cow dung to purify the area.'

'Did you have your own temples like some Dalit communities?'

'No, instead we worshipped the Pidar. It is believed to be the spirit of our ancestors. When there is a death in the family, we go into mourning for 10 days and eat no non-vegetarian food, oil or spice. On the 11th day, the bereaved family organizes *a bhoj* (food) for all the *baradinia* (blood relatives) and the *jaati bhai* (other villagers). Non-vegetarian food is prepared by the villagers and the Birtia performs rituals.' Since Brahmins do not enter the homes or come near the Ganda, the Birtia perform all the rituals for them. They too are regarded as untouchables. The night before the *bhoj*, the family of the bereaved goes with the Birtia to fetch the soul of the dead. This they establish in a small place in the house called the Pidar.

'Our people may have started worshipping idols; they may pay obeisance to Gods like Rama and Krishna now but till date every Gana house will have a Pidar,' Shatrugan tells me. And till date the discrimination continues, albeit more discreetly, his daughter-in-law Kanchan says.

'We were the first batch of students for whom the mid-day meal scheme was introduced. At that time, we were made to sit separately. We couldn't eat with the other children. That is no longer the case. But even today rice and ghee from Gana households is not accepted for Ganesh and Saraswati puja functions in schools. We can only contribute the *agarbatti*,' she explains. In the flickering light of the lantern I can barely make out Kanchan's features. Stout with a round face, she is dressed in a purple and pink cotton nightgown.

'My son is in nursery. We send him to a private school. In our village school, there is a teacher who creates a ruckus if a Gana child even touches her table,' she explains. This is why she and her husband are planning to open a hostel. 'We have registered an NGO and currently have 12 children. These are children whose parents have migrated for work. We provide them with food and shelter. But the need is much greater.' Kanchan insists that they will even accept Ghasia children into their home and hostel.

The Ghasia community are considered among the lowest of the low in Orissa's caste order. They do the scavenging and the cleaning. They also rear pigs and make musical instruments. Unfortunately, the discrimination faced by the Gana has not sensitized them to the violence faced by other communities. So Shatrughan tells me matter-of-factly that he will never eat in a Ghasia household.

'They do dirty work,' he explains.

Kanchan and Chesta simply shake their heads and change the topic. Chesta tells me that not only did he learn weaving but he will also teach his children the profession. 'What if they can't find a job? At least if they know how to weave, they will be able to earn and get by,' he says. Narayanan Mahanand, Chesta's friend who is visiting from Haldi village in the neighbouring district of Sonepur echoes his sentiments. He has even taught his 17-year-old daughter Tanmayi to weave—a remarkable thing given that in this part of Orissa, it is the men who weave.

'I make ₹10,000 a month. The *thekedaar* (middleman or commissioning agent) provides the raw materials and I weave about 12 saris or suit pieces in a month,' he says.

Shatrughan laughs. 'How times have changed. When I stopped weaving 35 years ago, I used to get ₹30–50 if I sold the *kapta* in the market and ₹5 for making *gamchas*,' he reminisces. Today the weavers from the Gana and Kuli Meher communities do mostly job work for traders. This saves them the hassle of procuring raw materials and marketing their own goods. However, it also ensures that their earnings are much lower than the actual selling price of the sari. Depending on his (because almost all the weavers are male) skill, an average weaver earns between ₹5000–10,000 a month, if his entire family chips in. In a district where most people migrate for work, this is good money.

So, unlike in Varanasi, Pochampally and Kaithun where the children of weavers are taking to pulling rickshaws and doing all sorts of manual labour, here in Western Orissa they are still learning to weave. Every weaving household I visited in the districts of Balangir and Bargarh had a similar story to tell. The task is arduous, it doesn't fetch as much as they would like but at least it ensures employment and income. It is a legacy that this generation of weavers is still anxious to pass on, a legacy which the current generation is still willing to embrace, albeit mostly as a Plan B.

POSTCARD 5: ORCHESTRA OF THE OSTRACIZED

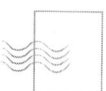

Mapada and Patrapalli villages, Orissa

The Mohuri, the queen of instruments in the orchestras of Western Orissa

Mapada and Patrapalli villages, Orissa

Tula playing the Mohuri

Dear Reader,

'With peacock feathers artfully arranged around our arms, *ghungroos* called *chaap* tied around our waist and feet, long hair made up in style, earrings, piercings, face-powder and cosmetics, we were a sight to behold. Girls queued up to see us.' As he sits on a brown plastic chair inside a tiny room, eyes dancing with mirth and fond memories, Bishwanath Baghel looks decades younger than his 97 years. Few lines have the temerity to mar his shimmering coppery skin. His wavy black hair with their salt and pepper roots are slicked back neatly in a Johnny Depp-esque bob. Moisture glistens on his late afternoon stubble, as the temperature rockets to an unforgiving 40 degrees Celsius. There is no electricity or fan inside the room. But the nonagenarian sitting before me in a short grey t-shirt and a printed brown loincloth folded above his knees, is oblivious to the heat inside the small brick house. I am in Mapada, a village of 120 Dalit households in the Balangir district of Orissa.

'Our whole body was our costume! Oh, the colours we wore! I took over an hour to get ready. You should have seen me. I would perform cartwheels and acrobatics. My father was a *bajania* (a community of acrobats and performers from Gujarat). I could lift a needle or a blade with my eyelids,' he reminisces. Baghel was part of a music troupe called Singh Bajaa.

In the Bora Sambhar region of Western Orissa, bordering Chhattisgarh, these music troupes were once an integral part of social life. Called the Ganda Bajaa, they were instrumental musical orchestras, composed solely of men belonging to the Ganda or Pano communities. The word Ganda literally translates into foul-smelling and is a reference to the activity of tanning leather for the drums and musical instruments. The Ganda people were considered 'polluted' as they played instruments made of cowhide and touched their own saliva while playing aerophones like *mohuri*. Ironically, as we have seen before, while the people who made the music and the instruments were considered impure, their music was not. It marked all important events in the life of the community, be they weddings, funerals or religious rituals. The rhythmic beats of the Ganda orchestra were used to invoke the goddess and call her to earth, yet the Ganda were not allowed into her sanctum.

Social anthropologist Lidia Julianna Guzy is Director of the Marginalised and Endangered Worldviews Study Centre (MEWSC) at the National University of Ireland. She spent 30 months in the rural regions of Western Orissa with Surendra Kumar Sahu, a local folk musician and music director, to create what is perhaps the only anthropological documentation of the Ganda Bajaa, their music and its ritual significance. In her book, *Marginalised Music: Music, Religion and Politics from Western Orissa*, she notes, 'Music in the Bora Sambhar region has both: a polluting, marginalizing as well as a purifying, sacred character…. The instruments mediate and manifest the other world of the goddesses, while the subaltern social status of the musician, as we have seen, paradoxically qualifies them for communication with the divine world. But although it is the musician alone, who has the capacity to control the goddess, he remains socially marginalized even while interacting with her.'[5]

Tula Bivhar is in his 60s. A resident of Mapada, he is an active member of the Murri Bajaa orchestra. 'People call us to play at weddings and festivals. Often, we stay for a couple of days during the *jatra* and Diwali and three days during wedding ceremonies. The people who call orchestras have to arrange for food and stay. But we are considered untouchables. Earlier, we were either asked to go and stay with Dalit families in the village or were given some space in a shed next to the house. We had to eat separately and throw the leaves on which we ate. Now people are less cruel, but we are still considered untouchables,' he says as he squats on the floor under the clothesline in Baghel's home.

Baghel denies facing any discrimination. 'We were in demand. So, we named conditions when people came to invite us. Being healthy and talented, we were worried that people would practise witchcraft on us. We never accepted cooked food. Instead we asked for dry rations and cooked our own food,' he said. He admitted that they were never allowed inside the house and had to stay in the shed next door. Someone drew water from the well and gave it to them. They were never offered any plates used in the household; just leaves and old aluminium utensils. Yet he never considered these forms of discrimination. They were the norm.

'Those were heady days. We were a group of six. We didn't really care. February–March, June–July were peak season. In those days, our group got up to ₹1000. That was a lot of money. Most of the invitations were from Tatanagar which has a huge migrant population and what is now Chhattisgarh. We travelled by foot and bullock carts,' Baghel recounted.

'And the rest of the time?'

'We collected forest produce.'

Baghel started playing at the age of 15, one year after he got married. His entire family—father, uncles, grandfather—had been in the orchestra. For him, joining one was the obvious choice. He started with the *dhol* and moved on to the *nissan* and the *mohuri*. 'I had studied till class seven and got a job as the peon in a government school. They paid just ₹2 per day. I could earn much more with the orchestra. I even got selected for a police job, but my mother refused to let me join.'

But life in the orchestra was not easy for the family. While Baghel travelled from place to place, his wife worked as an agricultural labourer trying to make ends meet. Soon she ran off and Baghel married a second time. 'But we were unable to have children, so I married again and begot four sons.' His third wife passed away some time back. Today, Baghel stays with his one surviving wife, four sons, daughters-in-law and grandchildren. Their house comprises a few small, one-room brick structures with *khaprail* (clay tiles) rooftops, arranged around a courtyard. For all his joy in playing with the orchestra, Baghel did not pass on his music to his children.

'For me, it was a source of livelihood. But my children went to school. The eldest is engaged in agriculture. Another is a teacher, while the youngest two are still studying. My eldest grand-daughter is pursuing nursing training in Bhubhaneshwar. Why should they play?' he asks. Baghel himself stopped playing in 1985.

Mukesh Suna disagrees. He is a strapping young man in his 20s, clad in a purple t-shirt and a loincloth. A white, handwoven cotton scarf sits carelessly around his neck. Some years ago, he started the Mulniwasi Adhikar Sangharsh Manch (Forum for the Struggle of Indigenous People) to ensure the protection and promotion of the traditional instruments and practices of the Ganda community. 'Earlier, the Ganda used to make beautiful carved wooden combs but that art is now lost. Soon, we'll lose our music too,' he says. This could destroy the fabric of the Ganda community because as Guzy points out, often 'Local meaning is generated and transmitted through techniques of acoustic and visual, oral or literal representation.... Music thus operates as an embodied and communicating system which resonates a local history and a culturally specific emotional memory.'[6]

A Ganda orchestra comprises five to seven players who primarily use five instruments: *dhol, tassa, nissan, mohuri* and *kastal/jhang*. The former three are membranophones that produce sound by a stretched membrane made of animal skin. I ask to see the instruments and Tula goes to fetch them. As we await Tula in a shaded area behind the houses, Mukesh tells me more about them.

The *dhol*, which is the leading instrument of the village orchestra is a large drum (90–150 cm in length) made from the trunk of a tree. 'Strips of cow hide run along the length of the drum and are attached to it by rings. The right side of the hollow drum is slightly smaller than the left and covered with calf or goat skin. It is called the *taali* and played with the hand. The left side called the *dhaaya* or *pita* is strung with cowhide and played with wooden or rubber sticks called *khana*,' he explains. It is believed that the voice of the goddess appears first in the deep sounds of the *dhol* drum and directs the rhythm of the entire orchestra.[7]

The *tassa* or *timkri* is a small drum made of clay and strung with goat skin on top. It is played by striking two wooden sticks on the skin clad head of the drum, and produces a high, thin sound. Both the *tassa* and the *dhol* are slung from the neck of the musician.

'And this,' says Tula as he returns with a big drum tied around his waist, 'is the *nissan*.'

Believed to be the oldest instrument of the village orchestra, the *nissan* has a tapered form, and resembles a melon cut in half. It is made of wooden and iron sheets, strung with buffalo or cow skin at the top. The playing surface is often decorated with colourful paintings. The *nissan* is played with two sticks called *chimta*, made of wood or, as was the case here, with old tyres. According to Guzy, 'The *nissan* is always played with maximum strength, thus producing a deep and penetrating sound which is compared to the sound of the thunderstorm and identified with the horrifying strength of Goddess Nissani.'[8]

Tula explains that at times, the orchestra also uses a variety of tambourine called *dafli*. It consists of a broad circular wooden frame, about 10 inches in diameter, with a double row of bells. *Kastal* or *jhang* are iron cymbals and the *jhumka* is a rattle. Their sounds are associated with the Goddess Gantheswari, the goddess of the bells.

Most Ganda musicians know how to play multiple instruments in an orchestra though each generally has one that he prefers. For Tula, the *mohuri* trumps all. An oboe-like wind instrument, a *mohuri* is considered the most difficult instrument in the orchestra. Less than 24 inches in length, it consists of a hollow bamboo pipe with holes and a metallic front to amplify the sound. The mouthpiece made of *taalpatta* (palm leaf) is crafted by the player himself. It is said that only the Ganda know how to play this instrument whose sound is crucial to changing the character of the music and the rhythm. 'In the orchestra, I play the *mohuri*. My father was a labourer, but my elder brother played. I needed to earn, so when I turned 15, I asked a *bajaawala* (an orchestra member) to teach me. I learnt to play the *nissan, tasa and dhol*, but my heart lies with the *mohuri*,' he says as the air vibrates with the rich, almost sensuous notes of his beloved instrument.

By now we are surrounded by a group of young boys. 'Are you learning how to play?' I ask. The kids look away. 'Children nowadays are ashamed of playing. They go to school,' says Tula sadly. He has four daughters and two sons. The girls are not taught to play and boys are just not interested. 'Only my youngest son is learning, thanks to the movement to preserve our heritage. But the truth is that the orchestras are dying. We only get 5–12 assignments in a year. For each, our group of five earns between ₹3000–5000. For the rest, we have to take up labour work.'

'What if you have an alternative?' I ask

Tula shakes his head. 'I learnt how to play so that I could feed my family and myself. All these years, the music has kept me going. Now I won't give it up even if I find another job. I will play till the day I can,' he says with a gentle smile.

Few however share Tula's gratitude. For most, joining the orchestra was not a choice, but the only available option. They see it 'not as a medium for the emotional transmission of ideas,'[9] or even as an art form, but a source of livelihood. For their children, they aspire for 'something better'.

38-year-old Vijay Chhuria lives in Patrapalli, a village that consists of three or four large orchestras. Here the groups have 17–18 members and conduct as many as 70–80 programmes between the months of January and July every year. The instruments are more ornate, decorated with red cloth, balloons, balls and gold lace. 'We earn roughly ₹1000 per head per programme,' says Vijay whose two-storey brick house is lined with instruments that hang alongside clothes on the wall. He has an eight-year-old son and a daughter. 'I play the *dhol*. My children want to learn to play it too, but I won't teach them. I started playing at the age of 12. This is not what I want for my kids,' he says firmly.

This sentiment is echoed by most families in Patrapalli. Vijay's 63-year-old uncle, Aunthu Churria is also a *Dholya* (dhol player) with the Maa Someshwari Dhulduli Bajaa. He is dressed in a checked cotton loincloth, tied below his generous belly. The upper half of his torso is bare, except for a necklace of rudraksh beads. A long, thick black moustache and a bright red *tika* (a mark on the forehead made with vermillion, a symbol of valour, protection and goodluck among Hindus) sit prominently on his face. Aunthu shows us the different instruments and how they are played. 'My entire family is in this profession. I had no option. But my 18-year-old son is training in Nagpur—learning about Babasaheb Ambedkar and Buddhism. He wants to sit for the JNU and IISS entrance exams to fight against discrimination,' Aunthu says with obvious pride. Most of the young boys in the village are either already enrolled in or want to earn a Bachelor of Social Work degree.

'What would you like to do after that?' I ask the motley group of young men that had been walking with me around the village, as I went from home to home in search of orchestra players.

There are a few nudges, uncomfortable smiles. A lanky young man finally speaks up. 'Tell us what we can do. We only know that we want a better life. It is true that the orchestras now face less discrimination than before. They often refuse to go and play if someone is being openly disrespectful. But we still don't eat together. There are separate rows. We want more than grudging concessions. We want a different life,' he says.

POSTCARD 6: SOFTLY WAILS THE NIGHTINGALE

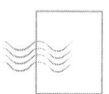

Kukusda, Chhattisgarh

Mandar, the instrument played by the Dewar musicians

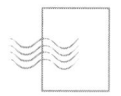

Kukusda, Chhattisgarh

Rekha Dewar outside her house in Kukusda, Chhattisgarh

Dear Reader,

In January 2015, the third edition of the Sirpur Music and Dance Festival was held on the banks of the river Mahanadi, in the erstwhile capital of the Somvanshi kings of South Kosala, some 80 km from the city of Raipur, the capital of Chhattisgarh state. The performers included some of the biggest names from the world of dance and music—Kathak exponent Pandit Birju Maharaj, Grammy award winning percussionist Peter Lockett, Sitar virtuoso Ustaad Shujaat Khan, Japanese Taiko player Leonard Eto and Bollywood singer Anuradha Paudwal. The opening act, in the precincts of the 7th-century Laxmana Temple, was the traditional Dewar Geet from the plains of Chhattisgarh, performed by Rekha Dewar and her troupe.

The Dewar are a group of travelling mendicants and musicians believed to have descended from the Gond and the Kawar tribes. According to lore, they trace their origin to a Binjhia tribal named Gopal Rai. A great wrestler, Rai accompanied Raja Kalyan Sai of Ratanpur to Akbar's court. There he not only seized and held a crazed elephant belonging to the emperor, he even defeated the champion wrestler. Raja Kalyan Sai asked him to compose a triumphal song in honour of the occasion. Rai dedicated his song to Devi Maha Mai or the Great Mother and since then writing and singing such songs has been the profession of his descendants, the Dewar.

A nomadic tribe, till recently the Dewar moved around in groups of five or six and lived in small makeshift huts outside villages. The men would sell metal ornaments or train animals, while the women would entertain villagers by singing, dancing and etching tattoos. They acted as village bards, narrating tales of yore. They also worked as magicians and tantric healers. In lieu of their performance and services, they received foodgrains and cloth from the villagers, particularly the Gonds and the Baiga. The women were also exploited sexually. As vagabond singers, they were forced to curry sexual favours in return for food and board. If they were young and good looking, they would often find a protector who would lay claim to them and look after their material needs for a few years at least. Then they were once again left to fend for themselves. I had heard about the skill of the Dewar singers and the power of Rekha Dewar's voice from Madhukar Gorakh, a well-known theatre artist and social activist from Bilaspur, who at one time headed the Indian People's Theatre Association.

On a hot summer afternoon, I set off for Kukusda village, some 50 km from the city of Bilaspur. The distance isn't great, but in the absence of roads, signages and Google Maps—yes, Kukusda is not on Google Maps yet—it is a few hours before we reach Rekha's two-storey house, situated outside the village of Kukusda in Patharia block.

The cement is still wet. The upper storey has just been constructed. Outside, work is on. Young boys are filling troughs with freshly mixed cement even as a goat and a calf loiter around. Next to the house there is a bicycle and a motorcycle. I have grown accustomed to the heat by now. As our surroundings turn dusky, we decide to sit outside. Rekha brings out a few cots for us.

She is a middle-aged woman, in her forties. Slim, of average height with twinkling hazel eyes. Her raven hair lies flat, oiled, parted and tightly plaited. A prominent line of red sits in the neat parting of her hair proclaiming her marital status. On her forehead is a big red *bindi*. Gold *jhumkis* dangle from her ears, while a gold nosering glitters against her warm sepia skin. She is dressed in an elbow-length bottle-green blouse and a shiny sky-blue sari. Her wrists are adorned with numerous red and green glass bangles, fringed with gold ones. Her moves are graceful, her smile welcoming and her mannerism confident yet shy.

'I was born here in Kukusda. My Nanhua (Nana) used to play the *Mandar*,' she tells me in Chhattisgarhi. Madhukar Gorakh, the elderly thespian acts as translator.

'*Mandar?*'

'It is a cylindrical drum made of mud. Here, let me show you one.' With that she goes inside the house to fetch a drum covered with red and yellow plastic stripes. One side is broader than the other. About 24 inches in length, it has a long strap that is used to sling it around the neck, while playing.

'I was 8 years old when I started accompanying my Nanhua and dancing to his beats. We are a nomadic tribe. Every season, when the threshing and winnowing of rice was done, we would go and perform for the farmers. Then we would ask them for rice. This has always been the traditional way of life for the Dewar. There were no schools, no permanent homes. I don't even know my birth date or year,' she explains.

There are two types of Dewar: the *gavaiya* (singers) and the *nachkaar* or the dancers. Both would go from village to village, singing, dancing and begging for alms. The Dewar *sarangi* (a long string instrument played with a bow) and the *mandar* were their instruments of choice. Whenever a boy was born in the village or a wedding took place, the Dewar singers and dancers were called to perform.

Every night, when the rest of the world went to bed, young Rekha would learn songs and ballads from her mother Thanvarin. 'Unlike others in my community I did not learn how to make tattoos or work with *jaribooti* (herbs). I focused on music and dance. It was all around me. My father, Dasrat Dewar, also played the *sarangi* and sang. Only my brother chose not to learn to play. Instead he started rearing pigs.'

By the time she was 15, Rekha had joined a group called Nava Anjuri and started performing professionally. 'I sang, danced and even acted in programmes. We were 15 people in the group. For each performance we received about ₹2000, which was divided amongst us. We travelled as far as Delhi. In fact, in 1984, in a single year, we did 160 programmes. Those days we were in demand,' she reminisces.

The harmonium player in the group was a Thakur youth called Vijay Singh. 'He was a connoisseur and wanted to learn Chhattisgarhi folk music. He would learn all forms of music—Bhartari, Dhola Maaru, Dasmat Kaina, Chanda Gwalin, Karma, Danda, Bhojli, Sua, Danda, Dewar—and then teach me. He became my Guruji.' As was the practice in those times, he also set up the 15-year-old beauty in a house.

Rekha tells me that Vijay Singh did a Gandharva Vivaah with her. A Gandharva Vivaah is one where two people consensually enter into a relationship, without any rituals, witnesses or family participation.

Vijay has his own family and does not live with Rekha or her children. Yet, she sees no reason to complain. 'I was lucky. Not only did he teach me much of what I know, Guruji looks after the children and me. The other Dewar girls have no one to protect them. They move from place to place and get exploited. This is our lot in life.' Vijay's name and the prominently displayed *sindoor*, *bindi* and bangles—all signs of a married woman—have kept her safe, Rekha insists.

As a tired and dusty sun retreats behind the green horizon, Rekha begins to sing. She sings of gods and goddesses, of the saga of King Bhartari, of lost love and of separation. I don't understand the words, but the power of her voice holds me in thrall. With perfect ease she moves from one form of music to another, from one pitch to another, prefacing each piece with—'This is a Karma geet', 'This is the Bhartari', 'This is the Dewar Vandana'.

The last piece is a Bhartari and she explains the saga to me. 'The Bhartari is in the form of a dialogue—a question and answer. Originally it was sung with the *ektaal tamura*, the *dafli* and the *kartaal*. It is the story of Raja Bhartari who goes hunting. He sees a hundred doe but just one black buck. The doe request him to kill any of them but leave the buck as he is the only male in their herd. But Bhartari insists that being a Kshatriya he can't kill a female and hunts the buck. The doe curse him saying that just as we are bereft and crying today, so will your wife be. She will never experience the pleasure of having a husband.'

After some time Bhartari is married to Shyama Dai. After her marriage Shyama realizes that Bhartari was her son in her previous life and their marriage bed breaks. When Bhartari demands his conjugal rights, she tells her husband there is a reason why the marriage cannot be consummated. The Bhartari tells this story through the conversation that takes place, first between the king and Shyama Dai and later, between the king and Shyama's sister.

'This is a long saga that recounts the queen's longing and unrequited wishes, the king's penance and his abdication,' Rekha says with a smile. By now, the youngsters have finished their work and they all sit around her in devout silence. Among them is her son Purshottam who is studying in Class 11.

'Are you teaching the kids?' I ask.

She shakes her head sadly. 'I want to teach but no one is interested in learning. There is no livelihood, no future in this line, only shame. For us begging was a way of life. But today, the children want a different life for themselves. My daughter is 21. I taught her all my songs. I had dreamt that she too would become a singer, but she got married and gave up singing.' Neither of her two sons—Purshottam or his elder brother who is in college—wants to touch the *mandar* or the *sarangi* that hangs next to the countless pictures of gods and goddesses inside Rekha's house. Instead they are learning the *tabla*.

I ask Rekha what is driving the youngsters away—the begging or the art itself, which has become not just the symbol of a caste-based occupation, but a tool for exploitation, especially of young girls. After all, despite the singing of religious hymns and the magical powers that they are believed to possess, the Dewar are treated as untouchables.

'It is true that we were regarded as untouchables, but I have never faced any discrimination myself. No, what is driving the children away is the lack of income and prestige. At one time, I was inundated with requests to perform. Today, I get invited to one government programme every couple of years. We have no land of our own.' I learn that Kukusda was a jungle when the Dewar families came here. Rekha tells me that it was the Dewar who cleared the land and built their houses. The village came much later. Yet, till date the Dewar families do not have land deeds.

'For all practical purposes, this is *kabja* (encroached) land and we can be thrown out any time. Why will the children learn?' she says her eyes full of sorrow.

'Music has enriched my life. The songs I sing are not just words and tunes; they carry hundreds of years of history, of pain, anguish, triumph and happiness. I wish there was a way to carry them forward without the stigma and the economic hardship. I wish our tradition would be recognized as an art form, a *kala*,' she whispers into the dark night.

Endnotes

1. Brisbane, K., Chaturvedi, R., Majumdar, R., Soo Pong, C. & Tanokura, M. (eds) (1998). *The World Encyclopedia of Contemporary Theatre, Vol. 5: Asia/Pacific.* Routledge, p. 165.
2. A Brief History of the Nautanki Performance Tradition, n.d. http://www.devnautanki.com/about_history.html. Last Accessed: 11 August 2019
3. A *ghungroo* is a musical anklet made of tiny, closely spaced bells. It is often worn by dancers in India.

4. An old Hindu practice in which the widow ended her life by sitting on the funeral pyre of her deceased husband. At the instance of reformers like Raja Ram Mohan Roy the practice was first banned by the British in Bengal and subsequently, all over India under the Sati (Prevention) Act 1987.
5. Lidia Julianna Guzy. (2013). *Marginalised Music: Music, Religion and Politics from Western Odisha/India*. Wien: LIT Verlag, pp. 18 and 74.
6. Ibid., p. 10
7. Descriptions of the musical instruments are based on observation, conversations with musicians, and Guzy's detailed work on the subject.
8. Guzy, *Marginalised Music*, p. 50.
9. Ibid., p. 13.

Budding Artists

'I am those who are free and never fear
I am the secrets that will never die
I am the voice of those who do not give in
I am meaning amid the chaos....
I am those who are free and never fear
I am the secrets that will never die
I am the voice of those who do not give in
I am the secret of the red rose
Whose colour the years loved
Whose scent the rivers buried
And who sprouted as fire
Calling those who are free
I am a star shining in the darkness
I am a thorn in the throat of the oppressor
I am a wind touched by fire
I am the soul of those who are not forgotten
I am the voice of those who have not died
Let's make clay out of steel
And build with it a new love
That becomes birds
That becomes a home
That becomes wind and rain.'

—**Emel Mathhouthi,** *Kelmti Horra*

'Beware; for I am fearless, and therefore powerful.'

—**Mary Shelley,** *Frankenstein*

POSTCARD 1: A TALE OF TWO SCHOOLS AND 251 STUDENTS

Satara, Western Maharashtra

Clockwise from the top left Pragati Ranjeet More, Vaishnavi Venkat Pawar, Aishwarya Suresh Nikam, Aishwarya Umesh Dharase and Ganesh Arun Jadhav at the Bhartiya Bhalke Vimukta Vikas Va Sanshodhan Sanstha, Maharashtra

Dear Reader,

In the bustling centre of Satara, a town in Western Maharashtra, lies the Pratap Singh High School. Red lettering on a blue board, outside a double-storey cream and brown brick building, proudly proclaims the school, albeit in Marathi. This was once a sprawling royal palace. Then Maharaja Pratap Singh Bhonsle, the erstwhile king of Satara handed it over to the British to start a school. Bedrooms, galleries and hallways were converted into classrooms and in circa 1851, Satara High School, where the

Budding Artists

sons of princes, landlords and officials from all across the country would come to study, was started.

In the year 1900, yet another student joined their ranks: nine-year-old Bhiva Ramji Ambavadekar, the son of Ramji Sakpal, a retired subedar-major of the British army. It was in this school that young Bhiva, who was later to adopt the name of his Brahmin teacher and become Bhim Rao Ambedkar, had his first brush with untouchability. He was not allowed to sit with other students, drink water from the school pot with his own hands or study Sanskrit. This was because Bhima was a Mahar and his community had long been treated as untouchable. Though he had managed to breach the citadel and get admission, his path continued to be littered with obstacles.

In the tattered yellow pages of the school's register, the evidence of Bhima's presence is neatly recorded. Next to his admission record is his name, written in his own hand, in Mori script. Dalits from all across the country come to see this school and the register whose pages have now been painstakingly laminated by the Dalit Foundation. Pages laden with history; pages that now lie open before me.

My visit to Satara is essentially the tale of two schools: one that is historical and another where history is currently being made. The Government High School (renamed Pratap Singh High School in 1951) where India's constitution maker studied from classes 1 to 4, and the residential school being run by the Bhartiya Bhatke Vimukta Vikas Va Sanshodhan Sanstha. More importantly, it is the tale of 251 students. One, whose story we all know—the man who conquered all obstacles to become India's foremost lawmaker, who led the crusade against untouchability and caste-based discrimination, who many revere as 'God'—Dr Bhim Rao Ambedkar. And 250 others, whose stories are still being written. I'll give you a head start on them.

Ten kilometres from the Pratap Singh High School, on the road to the famous Kaas Plateau, Maharashtra's very own Valley of Flowers, is the picturesque campus of the Bhartiya Bhatke Vimukta Vikas Va Sanshodhan Sanstha (Indian Institute of Research and Development of Nomadic and De-notified Tribes). Inside, there is a School of Social Work, a junior college, hostels and an Ashram school with 250 students from classes 1 to 10.

At 2 pm on a weekday, the place is abuzz with activity. Students and teachers have just returned from an invigorating lunch break, ready to resume their quest for knowledge. I head to the first floor of the double-storeyed institute building that embraces a circular courtyard. Here in a small corner room, a group of 50 students await me—the youngest is 12 years old, the oldest 16. Some play the *tabla*, the *dholki* and the Congo drums. Others create music on the synthesizer and the harmonium. Together they form the school's orchestra—one that has won name and fame in the district. They are often invited to sing for All India Radio and at local programmes. As the strong voices of the girls and the boys in the group decry casteism and call for equality through their songs, a new energy pervades the room, and with it, a new hope.

It is these students whose stories I wish to tell. But where do I begin? Do I tell you about 14-year-old Kaajal Manu Rathod, a petite girl in a pink salwar suit who came here from Kagneri Tanda in Karnataka when she was barely six years old. She dreams of becoming an engineer and ensuring the progress of her village. Or perhaps I should introduce you to Parshuram Bhimrao from Bacheri village of Sholapur district, who wants to bat like M.S. Dhoni and also become a doctor. 15-year-old Shekhar Vilas Jave wants to become the Prime Minister so that he can provide homes for the homeless, jobs for the jobless and end caste-based discrimination. His parents and elder brother sell *Vada Paav* (a local dish made of buns) to feed the family and he has had first-hand experience with discrimination.

Mayuri Bharat Pawar draws inspiration from Mahatma Phule and wants to become a district collector. Her first task, she says, would be to ensure that everyone gets access to clean drinking water. Mayuri has no father but she wants to make her mother, who works as a domestic help, proud.

Puja Ashok Chawan is in Class 9. When she joined the Ashram school in Class 1, she was a scared and traumatized kid. Her father had set her mother ablaze. Her mother survived. She moved out of her marital home and sent her two children to this school while she worked to make ends meet. She is Puja's hero.

Adarsh Shinde, a Dalit Marathi singer who pens revolutionary songs is 13-year-old Prasad Manohar Jadhav's role model. In a powerful voice, which he uses to enthral one and all, Manohar shares his dream of becoming a singer. 'I have been singing since I was in Class 1. I used to sing in the *kirtan mandalis* (devotional music groups) in our village,' he tells me.

The first thing that strikes you about 15-year-old Sarika Anand Mote is her unwavering smile and sunny disposition. Her face lights up as she recounts her dream of becoming a police officer to punish those who harass girls. Savitribai Phule is her inspiration.

I could carry on, tell you so many stories, because each of them is remarkable. Each child present in the room with me in this Ashram school has faced great hardship and violence. They have seen more pain in their short lives than most people do in an entire lifetime. Yet they shoulder on. They study, they play, they sing and they dream of making this world a better place. They are people who are determined to make history today; people whom history will acknowledge tomorrow. I wish I could introduce you to them all but how much can I include in a postcard? So, I'll tell you five stories here. Five stories that you can read each time you feel life has dealt you a rotten hand. Five stories that will give you the courage to carry on whenever you are about to give up.

Aishwarya

Aishwarya Umesh Dharase is 13 years old. Slim, with a deep sepia skin tone, she wears a bright, sleeveless red and gold salwar suit. Her jet black hair is oiled and tightly pulled back into a pony. 'I want to become a lawyer and fight for the truth,' this Class 7 student tells me. She also wants to learn to play the harmonium and the *tabla*. After all, she spent the first few years of her life around these musical instruments. Aishwarya's parents lived in the Bijapur district of Karnataka. Her father played the *dholki*, *tabla* and *pakhawaj* in an orchestra, while her mother was a singer. She also sewed garments to feed her family. Then one day, when she was barely six years old, Aishwarya's mother died in an accident. Shortly after, her father abandoned her. 'I was very small then. I didn't understand what was happening. Suddenly I had no family, no one to call my own,' she tells me matter-of-factly. Life as Aishwarya knew it was over. Initially her paternal grandparents looked after her. Soon however, her *mausi* (maternal aunt) took over. Aishwarya does not know if she is related to her *mausi* by blood. She doesn't know her maternal grandparents either. '*Mausi* says my mother was her sister and she treats me like her own daughter. That's all that matters. I have seen her work in the fields to raise me. It is her name—Bharti—that I write when I am asked for my mother's name.'

Bharti first got Aishwarya admitted into a Kannada-medium school but she wasn't happy with the quality of education. She decided to send her to the Ashram school where her own daughter Vaishnavi was studying. It was in Class 6 that Aishwarya came to Satara. 'I have been here for a little over a year now. Each day I learn new things. When I feel low, I think of my *mausi*. She is my inspiration. One day I will make her proud,' she tells me, the quiver in her voice only emphasizing the determined look on her face.

Pragati

Next to her sits a slim bespectacled girl in a white, printed salwar suit. 13-year-old Pragati Ranjeet More is a student of Class 8. Eyes brimming with tears, she narrates her story. 'When I was born, my mother abandoned me in the hospital and went to live with her parents. She didn't take me home. Didn't hold or hug me.' Pragati's father collected her from the hospital and took her to Pune. There he left the tiny infant with his sister. 'My *bua* raised me. She put me in a school in the city. Then one day my *dadi* turned up. She said that I shouldn't stay in Pune. She fought with my *bua* and brought me to Phaltan in Satara district. Since that day my *bua* stopped talking to us.'

Young Pragati was once again uprooted. She lost the only life and family she had known. But she was a survivor. She began to adjust to her new life. Just as she was learning to cope, another tragedy befell the family. Their house in Phaltan collapsed. They had to move to Satara. Pragati's father used to be a construction worker. But he drank heavily and gradually stopped working. In fact, it was his drinking that had driven Pragati's mother away. In Satara, her grandfather took up work in a hotel to feed the family. Pragati enrolled in a nearby school. One day, when she was in Class 3, her grandmother and father fought bitterly.

'My *dadi* burnt herself. She died,' Pragati recounts in a stony voice. Her mother used this opportunity to divorce her father. That was when she discovered that she had a younger brother. 'My mother never came to see me. I didn't know that my father used to visit her. After they divorced, I found out that I had a younger brother, Omkar. He is now in Class 4.'

Despite all the tragedies that life had heaped on her, Pragati did not give up. She had learnt how to cook when she was barely five years old. While her grandfather helped her with the housework, he also had to go out and earn. So young Pragati went to school, did housework, cooked and looked after her brother. One day, in the newspapers, she read about the Ashram school in Satara. She quietly went to her father and said she wanted to join the school. He agreed. Thus began a new journey.

'I don't know what more life has in store for us. My brother and I have no one to look after us. I used to call my mother occasionally, but now I can no longer get through to her number. My father wants to remarry but my grandfather has been opposing his decision. He is worried that my father's alcoholism will drive away any woman he marries. I don't really know what the future holds for us. Right now, I take one day at a time and I study hard,' she tells me. I can still see the unshed tears shimmering in her eyes, yet not one has trickled down her young, oval face. Sensing my concern, she gives me a wobbly smile. 'Don't worry, we'll be fine,' she reassures me, or perhaps she is reassuring herself. This reassurance, this hope, I can see is important for her. It is what keeps her moving. I give her a quick hug. 'Of course, you will be fine. You are such a bright girl. And what will you do when you grow up?'

'My father wants me to join the police.'

'And you?'

'I want to be a doctor. You see our village had no doctor in it. I want to go there and help the people,' she says shyly and I wish her luck with my entire being.

Aishwarya

My next hero is 12-year-old Aishwarya Suresh Nikam. This Class 7 student, dressed in a beautiful sea green anarkali suit, is one of the lead singers in the orchestra. One side of her beautiful face is scarred, from her forehead to the chin. Even her hands, covered by the net sleeves of her dress, bear severe burn marks. She is from Upsinghe village. 'In our village, every family has a member in the military,' she tells me.

'So your father is in the army?'

'No. My parents are agricultural labourers but my *Bade papa* is in the army.'

'Your father's elder brother? Do you also want to join the army when you grow up?'

'No and no. I want to be a doctor and my *bade papa* is not related to us by blood. But he is more than any relative can ever be,' she says with a smile.

'You must be wondering about my scars.'

'No. I am wondering about you and why you would like to be a doctor,' I confess. 'You don't need to talk about your burn marks unless you want to.'

She shrugs. 'When I was a month old, my father went to Sholapur for some work. My mother took me to visit my *nana* and *nani*.' At that time there was no electricity in her grandparents' home. Her mother lit an earthen lamp in the room. Aishwarya was sleeping on a bedsheet on the floor. Suddenly a cat came and knocked the lamp over. The oil from the lamp reached the bedsheet and burnt Aishwarya. Her family rushed her to the doctor but her burns were severe. 'The doctor was certain I wouldn't survive but my mother begged him to save me. We were very poor. The doctor had a friend in the military called Ganesh Deshmukh. He told him about my case. Ganesh Deshmukh immediately offered to pay for my treatment. "Just save the girl," he said. He is my *Bade papa*,' she says with a slight smile. Aishwarya survived but was too young to get any surgery done. Meanwhile, her home was also destroyed. Once again her *bade papa* came to the rescue. She moved into his house.

'He treats me like his own daughter. When I was three, he got my surgery done. And when I was coming here, he told me that I am very clever and should study hard. And I will. For him, and also for my parents.' Aishwarya's father has a knee injury. Yet he works hard to ensure that she is not denied an education. 'In our village, there is no school in our *basti*. Children, especially girls, don't study. My neighbour's daughter, Komal, is 13. She wants to study but has to stay home and do all the work. Another girl called Pratiksha lost her mother and her stepmother doesn't let her study. She doesn't even give her enough to eat. Babasaheb taught us to fight against atrocities. I want to follow in his footsteps. I want to be a good citizen, a good doctor. I want to save others, just like I was saved,' she explains.

Vaishnavi

'And while she saves their lives, I will teach their children. Give them a future.' I look into chocolate brown eyes, set in a round face with a warm tawny skin tone. The smiling face of 12-year-old Vaishnavi Venkat Pawar. Vaishnavi's family lives in Gopanagar Karve village of Karve Tehsil. Her parents get stationery from Mumbai and go from village to village selling it in their rickshaw. 'They have to go selling even when it rains. But the stuff gets all wet and doesn't fetch much money. We have built a small hut to store these things,' she explains. Vaishnavi's elder brother studied at the Ashram school, while she and her younger brother studied in the village itself. One day they accompanied their parents to visit their brother at the school. 'Our grandparents stay at home, but they didn't look after us. My parents were out for days selling their wares. There was no one to cook for us or give us food. When we saw this school, we requested our parents to send us here and they did.' Now Vaishnavi meets her parents whenever they come to Satara to sell their goods. Meanwhile she is studying hard to be a teacher. 'In my community, children are not sent to school. Even when they are sent, they never understand what is happening. Our language is different.' Vaishnavi belongs to a denotified tribe.'I want to grow up and teach the children in our language so that they can finish their schooling.'

Ganesh

The last story in this postcard is of 14-year-old Ganesh Arun Jadhav, a student of Class 8. Dressed in faded blue jeans and a full-sleeve light blue shirt, he sits quietly as the girls talk about their lives. Only when they head back to their classes does he begin to talk. 'My parents left me when I was one and a half years old. My *dada* and *dadi* raised me. Then suddenly when I turned five, my mother came to visit. She took me with her to her village in Ratnagiri district.' Ganesh's mother would make baskets and sell them to earn a living. She sent him to the Ashram school in Satara as soon as she was able. Ganesh enrolled in Class 1 and has been here ever since.

'Soon after I came here, my *dadi* passed away. Then when I was in Class 5 my *dada* died. They never told me who my father was. He never comes to visit. Till date I don't know who he is or what happened to him,' he tells me, his voice heavy with emotion. His anguish is palpable. As is his acute sense of loneliness. 'My mother remarried. My stepfather is a fisherman. They live in Rehmatpur near Koregaon Tehsil. I have a younger brother now. He is in Class 1 and stays with them.'

'Do they visit you?'

He simply shrugs his shoulder. I change the subject.

'What's a day like here? What's your routine?'

'We get up at 5:30 am, get ready, have breakfast and study on our own. Then at 10:50 am the school starts.' From 12:50–1:50 pm is the lunch break. There is another short 20 minute break at 3:40 pm. Classes end at 5 pm with *Vande Mataram* and attendance.

'The other children play cricket, kabaddi, etc., but those of us who are in the orchestra practise from 5–6:30 pm. At 7:30 pm we have our dinner.'

'And what do you do in the orchestra?'

'I play drums.'

'That's cool. Would you like to be a drummer when you grow up?'

'No, I'll become a Marathi teacher.'

'Wow, I wish I knew Marathi. It would make life so much easier. Right now, I am at the mercy of translators whenever I travel in your state,' I complain with a sigh.

'Don't worry,' he says, his face lighting up with a mischievous smile. 'I'll teach you. You can become my first student.'

'And I'll hold you to that.' I warn him as I get up to leave. 'I'll be back,' I promise as much to Ganesh as to myself. Back to this school that is filled with so much brightness, with the promise of so many young souls that are bruised but not broken.

POSTCARD 2: WELCOME TO SURAJ AND JAYASHREE'S FURNITURE SHOWROOM

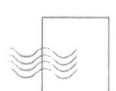

Sanand, Gujarat

Suraj (left) and Jayashree (right) working towards their dream of a furniture shop at the DSK campus Anand, Gujarat

Dear Reader,

Bang Bang Bang…I follow the sound of the hammer towards a building at the end of the campus. Like most other structures around it, it is single storeyed and completely at ease with the surrounding trees and plants; solid, yet unobtrusive. In front is a wide grassy patch, with a number of tables and benches engaged in cosy conversation under the cool shade of many trees—the dining area. Beyond, is a huge open field—empty now. But I know that as the clock reads 5 pm, it will be filled with hundreds of young boys and girls, running, exercising, climbing trees, playing cricket—in short, preparing their bodies and minds for the battle they are sure to encounter when they step out of this safe haven. Welcome to the Dalit Shakti Kendra Campus in Sanand, Gujarat.

Just 30 km from the traffic-choked, ever-expanding city of Ahmedabad, DSK is an oasis of peace and for the students who are enrolled here at any given time, of hope. Established in July 1999, as a joint initiative of Navsarjan and Jan Vikas, in the village of Nani Devti, DSK provides vocational training and life skills to almost 1000 boys and girls every year. Till date it has trained over 9500 children. Here, children mostly from economically weak and socially marginalized sections of society—often those who have been forced to drop out of school—learn to do secretarial work, bake, sew, photograph, prepare for police entrance exams, repair mobiles, create power point presentations, weld or even make furniture. More importantly however, they learn to read, think, question, reflect and introspect.

Furniture-making is one of the 23 odd courses offered here and so after the afternoon lunch break, I find myself gravitating towards the furniture workshop. It is easy to follow the sounds and find the place. What I see inside leaves me pleasantly surprised. A girl, she must be in her 20s, is busy hammering at what appears to be a door. A few feet from her, another young girl dressed in a green *kurta* with a Patiala *salwar* is sawing a piece of wood. In the last few years of my travel, only once before have I seen a woman sawing wood and making furniture. In Bangladesh, at the campus of the Gonoshasthya Kendra.

When the girls notice me, their hammer and saw come to a halt. We begin to chat. I learn that they are cousins from the district of Dwarka in Gujarat. They are also the first women to enrol in the furniture-making course being run by DSK. Till they came along, this workshop was populated only by boys. This despite the fact that half the students at DSK are female.

'So why furniture-making?' I ask them.

'Actually, we came here for the sewing course. Suraj here is my *mama*'s daughter. One of her cousins had studied at DSK. One day she called me and asked if I would like to come here with her. Since I was simply sitting at home, I said yes,' the younger, and later I realize, more garrulous of the two women tells me.

19-year-old Jayashree from Gatechi village is a young lady with a dazzling smile and a very sharp saw in her hand. She is also, in her own words, 'fearless and candid'. Her cousin Suraj from Varvala village is quieter. Her waist-length black hair neatly braided, she carries on working, her lips curving, perhaps unwittingly, into an indulgent smile as Jayashree continues with their story.

'After doing a course in blouse-making for three months and then sitting through dress-making for another 15 days, Suraj brought up the course in furniture-making. For some time, I had been yearning to do something different but when Induben from DSK had suggested furniture-making, I had recoiled at the suggestion. After all, it was a course for boys. In our state, girls don't make furniture. And even at DSK no girl had done this earlier,' the vivacious girl explains.

But when Suraj broached the subject, Jayashree started thinking. 'I asked myself, why not? Who says girls can't do it? Hadn't DSK taught us that men and women are equals? That we are as capable?' Her parents were horrified at the suggestion. They tried to talk her out of it and insisted that she 'wouldn't be able to do it'. That was all the push this headstrong young girl needed. She had to do it to prove to herself, her parents and everyone who thought that girls shouldn't or couldn't do certain jobs.

Now, seven months later, she sits in front of me, wielding the saw with ease and expertise. 'I have made doors, windows, cabinets and even chairs. When I go back to my village, I will start a furniture shop. We sisters will do what no one else has done before. In Gujarat the names of girls are not visible. We will launch a chain called Suraj and Jayashree's furniture shop. My dream is to see shops with our names all over Gujarat. Why just Gujarat, all over the country,' she laughs loudly as she shows me the beautiful canvas coloured with her dreams. Jayashree's father, I learn, has a grain shop in their village. She studied till Class 8 but dropped out after that as, 'I wasn't interested in books and studying further'. She started staying home and doing housework till that fateful phone call from Suraj. She has one brother and two sisters, she tells me.

When I ask Suraj about her decision to join furniture-making, she slowly puts down her hammer. 'I had initially wanted to do the course on videography but that needed English. While I had studied till Class 7, I knew I would be at a disadvantage there, so I decided to try my hand at furniture-making.' She explains. Suraj tells me that before she had come to DSK she would never have imagined taking such a huge step.

'But DSK has taught us a lot. It taught me girls can do anything. It gave me courage. I had faced discrimination all my life—my brothers were given *ghee ki roti* (*chapattis* made in ghee), while I was given *tel ki roti* (*chappatis* made in oil). When I would question my mother, she would say that you will get married and go away. The boys will be with us or that I only do housework whereas the boys go outside and so need more energy. Funny thing is that my mother who does so much work, does not value her own labour. DSK taught me that I should not accept this,' says the 25 year old, the steel behind her quiet voice evident.

When Suraj tried to explain this to her parents she was reprimanded with a, 'baahar jaake kuch jyada hi bolne lag gayi ho (you have started speaking too much ever since you stepped out of the home).' After all they had been used to a meek daughter. One who did not utter a word of protest when she was, at the age of 14, married off to a 24 year old. One who quietly endured physical and mental abuse from her spouse. 'I was confused and scared. I did not even tell my parents about it. Not even when my husband left me. But one day my parents got to know and they took me away. After that I filed for divorce.' The advocate advised Suraj to leave her little daughter with her in-laws and move ahead in life. But Suraj refused. 'Even now, everything I do is for my daughter. I want to give her a good life. Education is expensive and by working as a labourer, I won't be able to send her to any good school.' Pooja, Suraj's daughter, is in Class 5 and her current dream is to visit the DSK centre to see her mother and the place where she stays. 'I haven't been able to go home since we came here. It is far. But I speak to her every Sunday,' Suraj says fondly.

Returning to the story of furniture-making, she admits that neither she nor Jayashree had money to enrol in the course. Her father is an agricultural labourer. But once again DSK stepped in to help. They assured the girls that they could pay their fees by building furniture for the centre. While for the boys, the course finishes in a mere 2 months, for Suraj and Jayashree it will go on for 9 months—3 months of learning and 6 months of production work. They proudly tell me that they have made the doors and windows for the new hostel and they are also making the pieces for the new science laboratory being created at DSK.

This laboratory, that I had seen with Martin Macwan, the Dalit activist who runs DSK, is a story unto itself. It is designed as a human body. 'Seeing the body parts in textbooks isn't sufficient. The idea here is that children can travel inside the human body, observe every part, understand its functioning,' Martin had explained as I had looked at what appeared to be Goliath, lying on the ground and catching a nap.

'DSK has given us so much. It is not just about acquiring a skill. It made us question our actions, our beliefs. It made me realize that even though I was being discriminated against, I too was discriminating,' Suraj says in a low voice.

Both Suraj and Jayashree belong to the so-called upper castes. They tell me how they would never visit a Dalit household in their villages, wouldn't drink water from the same tap.

'Untouchability is all around us. The Harijans are made to sit separately in schools, given midday meals separately. If we touched them my mistake, my mother would purify me by pouring water on me. At that time I accepted it. My mother said it is a ritual. Now I know differently. This time when I go home, I will drink from a tap reserved for Harijans. Let me see who will stop me,' says Jayashree, a fierce glint in her eyes.

Suraj, in a much softer tone, concurs. She says that change has to begin with the self but adds that the other thing she would really like to change is the system of child marriages. 'I, for one, will never marry. See what happened with Suraj,' Jayashree adds heatedly.

'Parents don't realize what they are doing to their little girls. When you are married at 14, you are not equipped to handle the change, the demands. You accept everything that happens to you because you don't know otherwise. But if you are married at 25, then you have seen the world. You learn to manage and most importantly, you are stronger. Otherwise, you become like me, weak,' explains Suraj.

'You are not weak,' I protest bewildered. While she may not be as outspoken or confident as her cousin, I had witnessed an underlying reserve of strength in Suraj.

'I could not stand up to my husband. I could not tell anyone about the torture I was enduring. I could not stand up for myself,' she murmurs faintly.

'But you did. You walked out of an abusive marriage even when social norms dictated otherwise. You are raising a beautiful, young girl, ensuring a good life for her. You came so far away from your home. You are learning new things, moving into uncharted waters. That takes courage. It takes strength.'

Suddenly she smiles. 'Perhaps you are right. Perhaps I am strong. But more importantly, after this I can only become stronger. I will ensure that what happened with me never befalls my daughter. I will teach her to respect herself, to believe in herself, to dream.' And just like that I could hear the brick walls of the workshop applauding the grit and courage of this young woman.

POSTCARD 3: 'I WANT TO LIVE UP TO MY NAME'

Kanpur, Uttar Pradesh

Satyavrat Ambedkar at the Apna Theatre office in Kanpur, Uttar Pradesh

Dear Reader,

He is dressed in a full sleeve blue t-shirt. A thick black belt latches his blue denims firmly to his thin frame. A shy smile plays on his lips even as his dark brown eyes reflect conviction and determination. He is Satyvrat Ambedkar, a 13-year-old resident of GwalToli, Kanpur.

'To me he is more than God. He has done more for us than God ever did.' The 'he' little Satyvrat is talking about is none other than the man after whom he has been named—Babasaheb Ambedkar.

Satyvrat's given name, I learn, is Vishal. He is the youngest of five siblings. His father used to be a cleaner at a hotel. He also pulled rickshaws. Much of the money however went into his drinking He passed away earlier in the year. The family barely manages to get by. His mother, Shakuntala, and sisters work as cleaners in homes and offices. His brothers do manual work. None of them have been to school. But Satyvrat has decided he will not follow in his family's footsteps. He will not take up the profession that has been forced onto his community for generations—sweeping and scavenging. Satyvrat belongs to the Bhangi or Mehtar community that has traditionally been treated as untouchables not just by the upper castes, but by Dalits themselves. This community has through centuries been relegated to what are regarded as 'impure' professions—sweeping, collection of night soil, and playing musical instruments, especially those made from animal skins.

'Do you know earlier people from our community had to tie a broom behind them as they walked? They said even our footsteps would sully the earth. But Babasaheb changed that,' he tells me, respect and anger warring in his eyes.

'No, many people worked to remove that practice. But Babasaheb made sure that all forms of discrimination against us were stopped, not just the tying of the broom,' a colleague ruffles his hair affectionately and corrects him.

I look on in awe. We are sitting in a small one-room office of the Apna Theatre company in Kanpur's Gwal Toli *mohalla* that has over 150 Mehtar and Bhangi families. There are a few dusty chairs, a wooden table and a display case with a series of books that challenge the caste system, books that have been written by Apna Theatre's founder, Deo Kumar. On the wall behind Satyvrat's chair is a huge 24 inch × 18 inch poster of Babasaheb, his hero. I had come to this office to speak to Deo, whom, dear reader, you have met in the Gallery of Portraits earlier. It was Deo who introduced me to this proud, albeit shy little boy sitting in his office and I knew that you would enjoy the conversation that followed, almost as much as I did.

'How do you know about the practice of tying brooms?' I ask. I had only learnt of this obnoxious practice a few months ago during my travels to different Dalit *bastis*. I was amazed that such a young boy would know of it.

'I listen to Deo *bhaiyya* and the others when they talk of Babasaheb. Did you know, I recently did a programme with other kids on Babasaheb? I spent ₹50 from my own pocket to carry forward his message,' he says with pride.

'So how did you meet Deo Bhaiyya?'

'Oh, I used to saunter around the *mohalla* with other kids. Once I came to this office with some children. Deo bhaiyya normally organizes meetings here every evening. I attended one and I liked what he told us. So I came the next day and the day after. Gradually, the others stopped coming. But I didn't.'

'Why?'

'Because I understood what Deo bhaiyya and the others were saying and because I believe in Babasaheb.'

And it was this strong belief that convinced Deo and the Apna Theatre group to give Vishal a new name and to include him in their group.

'I sit and manage the office,' he beams with pride. He also sets up book stalls for the group and attends social meetings. Last year, Satyvrat participated in a rally that was held to inform the *safai karamcharis* (cleaners) and their children of pre-metric scholarships offered by the government.

'What about school?'

'I will join school next month.'

'Have you never been to school before?'

'No. I was enrolled twice but I never went.'

'Why?'

He simply shrugs his shoulders.

'What has changed now?'

'Now, I understand the importance of education. I want to be like Deo bhaiyya. I want to spread Babasaheb's message. I want to read his works. My brothers and sisters laugh at me and say who is Ambedkar? I want to explain his ideas to them and to many others like them. I want the world to respect Babasaheb. I want to live up to my name.'

Postscript: Much has changed in the year since I wrote this first postcard from Kanpur. Satyvrat enrolled in the Thakkar Bappa primary school in Gwal Toli in Class 3. He performed so well that within a couple of months he was moved to Class 4. A small step towards realizing his big dreams!

The Unbroken

When I am silent, I have thunder hidden inside
—Rumi

*The world breaks everyone, and afterward,
some are strong at the broken places*
—Ernest Hemingway

*What's the story of
the hidden daisies among the roses,
& the stars which break at the dawn,
or the littered leaves after the storm.
#Unsung*
— Saleem Sharma

Victory in defeat, there is none higher. She didn't give up, Ben; she's still trying to lift that stone after it has crushed her. She's a father working while cancer eats away his insides, to bring home one more pay check. She's a twelve-year-old trying to mother her brothers and sisters because mama had to go to Heaven. She's a switchboard operator sticking to her post while smoke chokes her and fire cuts off her escape. She's all the unsung heroes who couldn't make it but never quit.

— Robert A. Heinlein, *Stranger in a Strange Land*

POSTCARD 1[1]: THE UNBEARABLE AGONY OF BEING

Ranjangaon, Maharashtra

Hunting the Phaanse Pardhi way, 10 April 2015

Dear Reader,

The postcards I sent you thus far were about sunshine and music, about hope and *hunar* (talent), about the unsung, invisible heroes who are slowly but surely forging change, one life at a time. They inspire. Them, we cannot help but admire. Yet there remain thousands of others who have been unable to break free. Or perhaps, they are yet to pick up the cudgels, fight the good fight. Who are still being bruised and battered in the name of caste, religion and gender. Should their stories remain shrouded in oblivion? For a long time, I agonized over this. But tell me, till we see how the tea cups are steadily poisoning the brew, how will we rage, rage enough to break them once and for all?

This postcard and the ones in this gallery seek your anger and perhaps, even a healthy slice of your admiration, for those who continue to live despite their circumstances. Let this become an ode to The Unbroken!

Rani Bhonsale is a 10-year-old with pearly white teeth, long straggly brown hair and a dusky complexion. Dressed in a peach and green anarkali suit with metallic hoops in her ears and nose, a long stylish bindi on her forehead and a black string of beads that hug her neck almost carelessly, she tells me about her dreams. 'I want to make *rotis* and sweep the house.'

We are sitting inside my car, parked in front of her under construction house. It is a couple of kilometres outside Ranjangaon, the place where Sunita's father was murdered. Even today, a Pardhi cannot build a house inside most villages.' They say, we don't want thieves in our midst,' her *chachi*, a young woman barely out of her teens, tells me. In her arms is a little child—her son.

The Pardhi are a nomadic community spread across Maharashtra. Their name is said to be derived from 'Paradhi', literally 'to hunt' in Marathi or 'Paprathi' in Sanskrit (also to hunt).[2] Thus, people who lived by hunting were called Pardhi. They were notified as a Criminal Tribe by the British in 1871 and are still suffering the repercussions of that branding. Whenever there is a theft in the village, the first people to be questioned or picked up are the Pardhi, irrespective of their current occupation or economic status.

Rani's new house is being designed as a double-storeyed structure with enough room to accommodate her 22 member family. (Yes, the Pardhi tend to keep large families.) Right now however, all you see is a shell of the structure, partially laid roof and curtains that serve as doors. A few metres from the main building, is a single room that serves as the kitchen and receiving room. A cattleshed with two newborn calves suckling their mother stands in front of it. A hundred metres from the house stand four cubicle-shaped structures—toilets that are still under construction. On bushes between the house and the bathrooms, hang saris, suits, petticoats and sundry other garments worn by women.

'Looks like it is laundry day today,' I wonder aloud, pointing at the clothes. Rani giggles. Sunita, who has accompanied me on this trip shakes her head and explains, 'No. Among the Pardhi, once a woman is married, she is considered to be an untouchable even within her own family. Her clothes, howsoever fine or expensive they may be, cannot be kept inside the house.'

I turn my attention back to the shy girl sitting next to me. 'Don't you want to go out? See the world? Take a job? Become a doctor, engineer, teacher, sports person, artist, singer or even a policewoman?' I ask, foisting the typical 'urban middle class' aspirations on her.

She looks bewildered. *'Didi, yeh sab hum jaise logon ke liye nahi hai. Padne mei hamara dimaag nahi chalta hai,'* she admits quietly. (Sister, all this is not for people like us. Our brains don't work when it comes to studies.)

'Who told you this?'

'My teacher. When I used to go to school the teacher always said I don't have the brains to study. I always stayed in the same class. My classmates got promoted, but I couldn't even write an exam properly.'

Rani dropped out of school six months ago. Her initial enthusiasm for studies had died a quick death. Not only did she seldom understand what was being taught—the Pardhi speak in a dialect that is a mixture of Gujarati, Rajasthani and Marathi whereas the medium of instruction in schools is Marathi—every day, she would get a scolding from the teacher.

'I had to make *rotlas* (thick rotis made from bajra) for everyone in the house and wash my father's clothes before I could go to school. I used to get late. I got punished everyday.' Her school, I learn, was 2–3 Km from her house. The other students would also taunt her, call her names as she was a Pardhi. One day, someone threw food on her seat. When she asked them to clean it, they fought with her. That was the last straw. 'I didn't go to school after that day. What is the point anyway?' she asks with sigh.

Now she stays at home, looks after the kids, makes *rotlas*—'she makes them really well,' her 12-year-old *Bua* interjects—and watches Doraemon cartoons on television when she gets time.

I turn my attention to Pragati, the bubbly and bright-eyed 12-year-old who is Rani's *bua*. She is the daughter of Arcus Alshiram Bhonsale, the man who is head of this household of 22 and who had, some time earlier, demonstrated how the Phaanse Pardhi caught birds.

The Phaanse Pardhi are one of the many sub-clans of the Pardhi, so called because they hunt with a *phaansa* or a rope. With new wildlife protection laws coming up every day, the community is fast losing its 'art of hunting'. Arcus had insisted that it was an art, as he had spread out a 50-feet-long, finely crafted trap made from bamboo and horse hair. 'It took me two months to make this. See the carving on the bamboo. This was an art that only we knew but alas the current generation is not learning how to make the traps,' he said. They, however, still know how to use them to catch little birds, particularly the Lauhare.

I had watched in horrified fascination, as they set out to catch their next meal. First Arcus and his sons set the trap in the field, far away from the houses. Then, Arcus led his cow around it, all the while hiding behind a huge pink banner that was as tall as him. I heard a sudden chirping sound and saw that one of his sons had left his mobile near the trap. 'Earlier we used a bone whistle. It would attract the birds. Now these sounds from the mobile do the trick.' From a distance, the birds would see the cow in the open field, hear the sound of their companions and fly down to peck at the food grains. As they hopped across the field, their leg would get entangled in the fine trap laid by Arcus and his sons.

And thus, in a span of 5–15 minutes, the Bhonsale family would have arranged their supper.

Today, with hunting mostly restricted to small birds being caught for supper, cattle-rearing is the mainstay of the Bhonsales. That, and whatever odd jobs they can find. The stigma attached to their community makes employment a tricky business. Even when they do find jobs, they are always looked upon with suspicion. 'You know Arcus means cheat and Alshi means lazy. The branding of our community has become so institutionalized that until recently even the names our parents selected reflected our seemingly criminal tendencies,' Sunita says with disgust. It is only now that people have stopped naming their children Rifle, Shooter and Kaati. And perhaps it is this widely accepted social persecution of the Pardhi that has allowed lawmakers themselves to act with impunity. Impunity, that drove young Pragati to the railway tracks.

Angrily, this beautiful girl, on the cusp of puberty, narrates her story. 'There was a police officer here. He would often drop by and tell me that he liked me a lot. He would ask me to sit on his lap. I detested him and when I protested, he would say dirty things. He told me he would come at night and sleep with both my mother and me. I used to get so angry and one day I abused him verbally. Then the harassment started. They would arrest my brothers and even their little sons on false charges. We had worked so hard to buy cattle, build a home,' she says her eyes filling with hot, angry tears. Bit by bit the Bhonsale family had to sell their goats and cows on bribes and bail. They spent all the money they had saved to build a house. So now their home lies half-finished. 'We even took loans. The boys were so afraid that they stopped staying at home in the evenings. One day, my mother and I decided to end all of this. We went to the railway tracks to commit suicide.'

The very same day, Sunita was visiting the Bhonsale family. When she heard about what had happened, she rushed to the tracks to save mother and child. Thereafter, she took up the issue and has been fighting relentlessly to get the policeman punished.

I turn my gaze towards the young girl who till a few minutes ago had dazzled me with her bright smile and her chirpiness. It was difficult to imagine that but for Sunita's timely intervention, this bright flame would have been snuffed out forever. In her sky blue sari, with a small *bindi*, nose ring, earrings and a huge necklace, she was the very picture of innocence.

'Do you go to school?' I ask.

'No. I used to go to the Balwadi, but children would harass me, throw water over my slate, call me names. One day the fight got out of hand. I slapped a child who was troubling me and she threw a stone at me. It slashed my forehead. After that, I realized that there was no place for me in that school. So now I get up in the morning, collect sticks and take whatever goats we have left out grazing,' she explains, not a twinge of regret in her voice.

'But what do you want to do when you grow up?'

'Oh, I would love to be able to take my goats grazing. I have been doing it since I was 5 years old, you know. It's a good life. I leave around noon and come back by 5 pm. No housework for me,' she says smiling.

POSTCARD 2: I HAD A DREAM

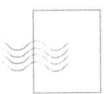

Kharda village, Maharashtra

Madari basti at Kharda village in Mahatrashtra, 11 April 2015

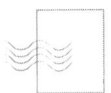

Kharda village, Maharashtra

Sardar Ismael Madari (extreme left) with Arun Jadhav (extreme right) at Kharda village in Maharashtra, 11 April 2015

Dear Reader,

When I was a child, snake charmers and *madari* (street performers with animals like monkeys and bear) were a common sight at public

The Unbroken

parks and picnic spots, especially when one stepped outside the four—yes, at one time not so long ago, there were just four of them—bustling metropolitan cities. Little children and grown ups alike would cheer them on as these men (I don't ever recall seeing any woman doing this) made the animals dance to their instructions. Now and then, the snake or the monkey would come too close and the crowd would quickly scamper with a collective shriek. At the end of an enjoyable 15–30 minute performance, the *madari* would go around collecting tips or in some cases, send his monkey out with a small bowl. Those days of the *tamasha,* as these performances were called, are gone. Jugglers and animal tamers no longer roam the streets of our towns and cities. Yet somehow, I never noticed their disappearance.

Kharda is a small village of about 9000 people, just off the Jamkhed-Umerga highway in the Ahmednagar district of Maharashtra. At its entrance lies the historic fort where the Peshwa of Pune defeated the forces of the Nizam of Hyderabad, in 1795. In the centre of the village is an open area with a series of raised platforms. This is the market square where the village bazaar is held every Friday night. Today is a Saturday. So instead of vendors trying to entice the villagers, the square is dotted by a series of *paals.* For six days every week, these huts are where the Madari community stays. It is here that they cook, eat, sleep and carry on with the business of living, under the aegis of the *Naag Devta* (Snake God) of the Hindus, whose stone idol lies between two *paals* at one end of the square. On market day, the *paals* along with the scanty belongings that are kept inside them are wound up and kept outside the village masjid. As the night awakens with a lazy stretch, the entire colony disperses to allow the village economy to flourish. After hours of haggling, of money and material changing hands, the vendors and villagers conclude their business when the soft rays of a sleep-tousled sun bid them good morning. Within a few hours, the *paals* and their owners reappear and life goes on, at least till the next market day.

I always thought that the term *madari* was a professional reference—anyone who tamed animals was thus called. Now I learn that the Madari is a nomadic community. In Maharashtra and Tamil Nadu (where they are also called Pambatti)[3] they are Muslim, while in Rajasthan and parts of Gujarat, they are Hindu.[4] In other places, their customs are a mix of the two religions. Traditionally, they have been working as snake charmers and street magicians. According to some legends they are the offspring of a Rajput father and a Muslim mother.[5]

The Madari are one of the 647 nomadic tribes identified by the Commission for Denotified, Nomadic and Semi Nomadic Tribes set up by the government in 2005. Along with the denotified tribes they account for 10 per cent of the country's population. These are the group of people who have no house, no land, and increasingly, no occupation.

Hussein Bhai Madari is dressed in a black *pathansuit*, a *tabeez* (talisman) on a black thread tied firmly around his neck and another on his wrist. At our request, he brings a small, round box, made of twigs, from his hut. Inside it resides a Cobra. 'Some days back, a villager came running for help. A Cobra had entered his home. We caught it. We have removed its poison sac and will release it in the jungle soon,' he explains.

Hussein tips the lid of the box back and a magnificent brown and beige Cobra stretches out. It moves its head around wildly and Hussein sprinkles some water on it.

'It is slightly disoriented with the heat, noise and light. Let him cool down a little,' he says. Then he explains how it is important to understand a snake, its moods and to care for it. He tells us that even when they did *tamashas*, they would never keep a snake for more than a couple of months. 'We would take out the poison sac, keep them for two months and then leave them in the forest. In some time, their sac would grow back.' he says.

'Unlike the other nomadic tribes, we have always been known for our honesty. Whenever a snake entered someone's house, a Madari was called. We saved people's lives at the risk of our own. And yet no one cares for our lives. With all the new wildlife and animal cruelty acts, we have lost our profession. No alternative was offered. They say this is cruelty, but we treat our snakes with utmost respect. What do we do now? Where do we go? Is this not cruelty?' The speaker is an elderly man with a snowy beard, dressed in a white chikan *kurta*, a small black comb tucked neatly into his pocket. Sardar Ismael Madari started catching snakes when he was barely 15 years old. 'Initially I used to be afraid, but then I realized it is all about intelligence and respect. You use your brains and treat the snake with utmost respect,' he explains. This was the education he received. His family never stayed anywhere long enough for him to join a school. The same is true for his eight children. Yet today, the man who has caught over 150 snakes in his lifetime is struggling to feed his family.

There are 60 Madari families that live in the Kharda village square. This village, they say, has been their *watan* (home) for over a century now. Even when the families did *tamashas,* they would travel through the year but come home for Muharram. 'Back then, we would travel all over with our donkeys and horses—Mumbai, Pune, Kolhapur. We stayed for 4–5 days in the bigger habitations and 2–3 days in the small ones. We got 10–20 rupees per *tamasha* plus food to eat. Young children would flock to us. I have been doing magic tricks since the age of 17,' Ismael says. Now however, the government has banned them from catching snakes or doing snake shows. And with television and mobile phones, children and adults no longer care for their jugglery and tricks. At our prodding, Ismael opens his *pitara* (bag) and shows us a trick or two—and I go back 20 years in time!

'You know in big cities people pay hefty fees to hire magicians for their kids' birthday parties,' I tell him.

'Yes, but who calls us? We are too uncouth for them.'

Over the last 5–6 years, Ismael and his community members have settled down. Their homes may still be temporary structures, but they no longer move around. Some people are forced to become *fakirs* and go begging. Others create some flimsy items to decorate the doors or windows of houses or hang on motor vehicles. There is no finesse to their work. Just a cut and paste job that they have taken up now that all other doors have been closed. They barely get by. Yet, most send their children to the government primary school in the village. Not to the madarsa, as popular perception would expect.

'Our life is over. We have no other skill to get by, but we hope our children will be able to have a better life. It is with this hope that we stay here. This and the fact that for the first time, Arunji has managed to get some houses sanctioned for us,' Sardar's nephew, Salim Ismael Madari says. Arun Jadhav is a young Dalit Foundation fellow from Jamkhed. He tells us that under the Yeshwantrao Chauhan Mukt Vasat Scheme, they have received 2.5 acres of land from the government to build homes for 20 Madari families.

Around me are the grubby faces of little children, boys and girls of all ages, bright, curious and a little shy. At the prodding of their parents, they begin to recite poems, sing songs. I ask them what they want to be and everyone says the same thing. '*Kuch achcha* (something nice/good).'

'What is *achcha*?' I ask.

After much mumbling and hurried consultations they come up with a collective answer. 'Teacher.' Thereafter, every child I meet in the *basti* expresses a wish to grow up and be a teacher.

I leave the gathering of the Madari men, women and children and walk around their colony—the village square.

'Where have you come from?' a lean, young girl, no more than 15 years, with bushy eyebrows and a curious smile asks me. She is dressed in a simple brown *salwar-kameez* with a multi-coloured *dupatta*. Her straight, waist-length hair is held back by an orange rubber band.

'Delhi.'

'What is your name?'

'Gunjan.'

'What do you do?'

'I travel and I write,' I answer in amusement. It is almost as if our roles have reversed.

'What do you write about?'

'Many things, but mostly about what I see and about people I meet.'

'Hmm,' she thinks a little, head tilting to one side.

'Will you be writing about us? About our village?'

'Yes. I will even write about you.'

'Me,' she appears startled. 'What is there to write about me?'

Then suddenly her face turns wistful.

'May I see your camera?' she asks.

I hand it to her but she shakes her head and asks me to show her the photographs instead. After browsing through some of them, she looks up. Then so quietly, that I almost miss it, she murmurs, 'You know, at one time, I too wanted to be like you. To see the world. To write.'

The look on her face, in her eyes when she said that; the stoic acceptance of a life she could not have and yet the fierce longing for it—I will never forget that. I can't describe that look and yet every time I close my eyes, I can see her, a young Salma (name changed), standing in the village square, under the scorching hot sun, reading an obituary to her dreams.

Shaken and a little perturbed by the sheer number of emotions I can see in her brown eyes, I say, 'That's great. I am sure you will do it.'

She gives me a sad smile and shakes her head.

'Why not? You are too young to give up. Which class are you in?'

This time the vivacious young girl who had stalled me with her questions has nothing to say.

By now a bunch of children have broken away from the main gathering in the village and are surrounding us. One of them, a young boy answers, 'Didi, she does not go to school. She stays home and looks after her siblings.'

'Why? Don't you want to study? To go to school?'

By now Salma has her emotions well in control. She looks me straight in the eye and says, 'I did study till Class 5.'

'What happened then?'

'I wanted to study further but *Abba* (father) said no. When I insisted, he beat me up. I guess I was being wilful. You see the middle school is far. Besides, *Abba* says it is not safe.'

'Let me speak to your *Abba*. There must be a way.'

'No didi, let it be. That was one and a half years ago. It will only create more problems now. Some things are just not meant to be.' With that she moves away. Salma's family, I learn later, is thinking of getting her married. They are therefore not amenable to letting her continue her studies now.

I don't know if Salma and the other DF fellows will be able to convince her *Abba*. I don't know if Salma will ever get around to travelling and writing her own stories. But this story I write for her, that little girl who once had stars in her eyes!

POSTCARD 3: BURN, MY BELOVED COUNTRY!

Lathor, Orissa

Malay Kumar Tandi at Ambedkar Colony, Lathor, Orissa

Dear Reader,

It was the morning of 22 January 2012. A young boy called Ganesh Suna went to a shop. The shopkeeper accused him of stealing a shirt and beat him up. The incident quickly took on caste overtones and before the end of the day, the entire Gandapara or Ganda colony of Lathor, a village of 5000 in Orissa's Balangir district, was burnt to the ground. 45 families lost not just their houses, but their life's work—money, goods and even educational degrees.

Three and a half years after the incident, Lathor's Gandapara is a site of frenzied construction activity. All around me, men—young and old—are busy ferrying bricks and laying them atop each other to build a shelter for their families before the monsoon sets in. Sounds of their hurried hands and feet are interspersed by the laughter of young children, scampering around the makeshift and half-built quarters. Some are trying to chip in by offering bricks to the adults, the rest are just playing.

I have travelled 85 km from the district headquarters of Balangir into what was once among the poorest and most backward areas of the country. As mentioned earlier in the book, this part of Western Orissa was the heart of the erstwhile KBK (Koraput-Balangir-Kalahandi) belt, infamous for malnutrition and starvation. Poverty is still ubiquitous; Naxal influence widespread. 'If someone stops the car, just say *Laal Salaam* (red salute),' my companion had joked on the way.

'How will they know I am here?'

'They hear of every newcomer who enters the area. But don't worry, they won't bother you if you don't mean any harm,' he said. 'Unless you are a big official, of course,' he added as an afterthought.

I had travelled to Lathor in search of two sets of people: the traditional *bajaawalas* from the Ganda community and the Birtia, who serve as the bards and the chroniclers for the Ganda. Often referred to as the elder brother of the Ganda or the Gana community, the Birtia act as their living and mobile history. They know the important events that take place in these communities and the legends surrounding their family and ancestral deities. At weddings, births and funerals, the Birtia recite these tales to ensure that the community does not forget its roots and beliefs.

As there is only one Birtia for a large number of villages and he keeps moving from place to place, locating him is not easy. I had learnt of one who lived in the Gandapara in Lathor. And this is how on a torrid May evening I find myself in this bustling colony.

I discover that Budu Suna, the 40-something Birtia I have come to meet is unwell. His tall, lean frame, draped in a brown *dhoti*, appears almost gaunt. His short bushy moustache has more white than black. The upper half of his torso is clothed in a white vest, covered with a yellow cotton *gamcha*. A sleek black watch strapped to his wrist helps him keep time. Lying on a cot outside his mud and brick dwelling at the edge of Gandapara or Ambedkar Colony, he apologizes for his inability to play the *damru* or recite the tales of the Ganda community. 'I know you have come from far away but I am too weak to speak much.'

Budu's father was also a Birtia. When he was 13, he started accompanying his father on his trips. 'My father played the *damru*. It is an instrument made of wood and the hide from the cow's stomach. All Birtias play the *damru* when they tell stories. My father taught me to play. He also taught me the stories. It wasn't just a source of livelihood, but it was tradition. We had been doing it for hundreds of years,' he explains. The *damru* is a small, hourglass shaped wooden instrument with two leather heads. These two halves or triangles of the *damru* are said to represent the male and feminine reproductive forms and its waist represents the place where the universe is created. Beads attached to leather cords are fastened around this waist and serve as strikers. When the Birtia shakes the drum using a twisting wrist motion, the strikers hit the leather heads producing sounds that are believed to be spiritual in nature. In fact, it is believed that the *damru* was created by Lord Shiva himself.

Every Birtia, Budu tells me, has 70–80 villages under him. People call him to recite ancestral stories at weddings and funerals. It is the Birtia who performs all the functions of a priest for the Ganda community. In fact, it is believed that whenever a birth or death takes place in the villages under him, the Birtia's *damru* automatically informs him.

'I go out for 7–8 days every month. My family lives on the *daan* (offerings and donations) that I get for performing my duties. Depending on the event and the family, we get gold, silver, utensils, money; at times, even a goat or a cow,' he rasps. Budu and his wife, whom he married when she was barely 13, have six children—three sons and three daughters. None of them have learnt the stories or the instrument played by their father. 'Only men can serve as a Birtia, but my sons are studying. I didn't teach them. I have spent my life in this profession but it has no future.'

Budu's 13-year-old son, Deva Suna, studies in Class 8 at the Shri Durgeshwari School. He tells me that history is his favourite subject and when he grows up, he wants to become a doctor. Deva does not know what a Birtia is. He does not understand what his father does. 'I only know that he goes from village to village, playing the *damru* and getting donations. I won't learn what he does,' he says with conviction.

By now Budu is visibly worn out. I turn my attention to my surroundings. A group of young men, mostly in their late teens and early twenties, has gathered around us.

'There seems to be a lot of new development taking place here,' I remark, pointing to the heaps of bricks and brambles around me.

They give me strange looks. A lanky youth with short, curly black hair, dressed in a green-and-white checked shirt, the faint shadow of a goatee on his face, answers. 'After the incident of 22 January, we didn't have much choice. It's been over three years. About time, we got a place to stay.' He is 22-year-old Malay Kumar Tandi, a student pursuing a Master's degree in English from the IGNOU centre at Balangir.

'What incident?' I ask.

'You don't know?' he fixes me with an incredulous stare followed by a deep sigh. 'Of course, you don't know. Back in the cities you never hear about these incidents, I guess.'

And then the youth of Ambedkar Colony tell me their version of the incidents of 22 January .

'My *chacha*'s son, Ganesh Suna, had gone to a shop to buy a shirt. He wears two shirts, one atop the other. It's fashionable,' the speaker is a stocky young man of average height, dressed in light blue denims and a black-and-grey striped t-shirt. His name, I learn, is Lava Suna.

'But the shopkeeper, a Meher, accused him of stealing the other shirt and beat him up. When Ganesh told me about it, I took him to the police station at Khaprakhol to register a complaint but no officer was present to lodge the case. The constable asked us to return later. So we headed to the hospital. The hospital is close to the shop. Ganesh and I went to the shop where two Meher youth were also present. We got into a fight,' narrates Lava. He tells me that all four of them got hurt in the ensuing fisticuffs. One of the Meher boys started vomiting. Both parties went to the police station in Patnagarh separately to lodge complaints.

'My in-laws live close to Patnagarh. There was a funeral and most men from the Ganda colony had already gone there. Ganesh and I also went to the funeral from the police station. A little later I got a call from a friend saying that an upper caste mob has come together and is planning to burn our colony. We headed back immediately but it was 4:30 by the time we came in. The houses were already on fire,' he says.

Malay was one of the few youngsters who was present in Gandapara at the time of the attack. 'There were mostly women and children in the colony and a few of us youth. The men had all gone for the funeral. Around 3 pm the mob came with petrol, kerosene and torches. I was home but we were severely outnumbered. We ran for our lives. We saved ourselves but our homes and all that we had worked for was burnt forever,' he recounts.

'Didn't the police or the fire brigade come?' I ask

'We tried calling the police and district administration, but no one answered their phones. At about 8 pm, the fire engines came in, but the mob torched them as well. When the police finally reached at 9 pm, they were not allowed in. Till 11 pm, the fire continued unchecked,' says Lava.

The affected families were later moved to a nearby school where they camped for a long time. The state announced an interim relief of 1 lakh rupees from the Chief Minister's fund and of ₹60,000 from the atrocity fund. 'But can money compensate for the loss of generations of work? Moreover while 45 families were affected, only 38 were given compensation. 118 people were charge sheeted and 52 detained,' says a visibly enraged Lava.

Both Malay and Lava strongly believe that the incident that took place on 22 January was a result of longstanding caste-based discrimination. 'Earlier, we used to play musical instruments in temples and festivals. Yet we were not allowed inside the temples. In 2007 we stopped playing. There was a huge hue and cry. The upper castes did not like our rebellion but we did not give in,' says Malay. He insists that he will never play the instruments again. Instead he will pursue a number of courses, including an MPhil and a degree in journalism. 'I want to sit for the JNU entrance exam. Later, I will become an English lecturer.' Meanwhile Lava wants to join the administrative services to fight for his community. He was pursuing a degree in law from Delhi University earlier but has dropped out of college now. 'These atrocities have to be stopped.'

Recent statistics from the National Crime Records Bureau show that crimes against Dalits (in this case, the nominal definition restricted only to the Scheduled Castes) rose by 17 per cent in 2013 and by 19 per cent in 2014. Incidence of rape rose by 31.5 per cent between 2012 and 2013; murder by 3.84 per cent. Uttar Pradesh, India's most populous state, reported the highest number of crimes against SCs, followed by Rajasthan, Bihar, Madhya Pradesh and Andhra Pradesh.

These numbers have genuinely perturbed many who had been basking in the euphoria of *Achche Din* with its allied Good News Networks. Caste, after all, is not a 21st-century phenomenon. It is true that untouchability and caste-based discrimination were shameful realities of our society at one point in time, the operative word being 'were'. That was a different time and era, a different generation. Surely, that is no longer the case. Of course, we have problems today and an increasing use of violence. But the modern-day miscreant is religion, not caste. How often have I witnessed these reactions, particularly in the last few years!

'But surely you've been reading the papers? The murder of two innocent Dalit children in Faridabad, the attack on a Dalit writer in Karnataka, the torching of Dalit houses in Villipuram district of Tamil Nadu over a temple procession, the fines imposed on four Dalit women for entering a temple in Karnataka, the burning of a 16-year-old tribal boy for playing loud music in Dhar district in Madhya Pradesh, the social boycott of a Dalit couple for raising a question in the Gram Sabha in Theni district, a Dalit boy being beaten by his teacher for touching the plates of other students in Rajasthan—all within a few months. The list is never ending,' I urge. Pat comes the argument. 'Yes, but that is because the media delights in pouncing on these stray cases and sensationalizing them.' Then slowly the first tendrils of doubt begin to unfold. 'Right?' A masked challenge is issued. 'Are you saying that caste is still a decisive factor in India?'

This naïve, almost complacent celebration of the demise of the caste system can perhaps be attributed to our school textbooks that lead us to believe that a slew of social reformers, independence and the ensuing development threw caste-based discrimination right out of our lives. The reality, as I discovered repeatedly throughout my travels, is very different. Caste and caste-based violence continue to be an integral part of our society.

What the media report are not aberrations. In fact, as I learnt in Lathor, most cases of caste-based atrocities are not covered by the media. Sometimes because of their location—they happen outside the bustling cities that are teeming with OT vans and cameras—and sometimes, because they are too common to be news.

Endnotes

1. In this gallery, we have changed the names of our heroes because they are too young and have already borne too much discrimination. Though we had their families' permission to write their stories and even use their pictures, we decided to protect their identity.
2. Anthropological Survey of India. (2004). *People of India: Maharasthra, Part Three, Volume XXX*. Popular Prakshan: Mumbai. pp. 16–55.
3. N. K. Singh and A. M. Khan (eds) (2001). *Encyclopaedia of the World Muslims: Tribes, Castes and Communities*. Global Vision Publishing House: Delhi. p. 859
4. Anthropological Survey of India. (2004). *People of India: Rajasthan, Part Two, Volume XXXVIII*. Popular Prakshan: Mumbai. p. 604.
5. To read more about Snake Charmers visit http://tribes-of-india.blogspot.in/2009/04/madari-tribe-or-snake-charmer.html

A Place to Remember*

> *All is as if the world did cease to exist. The city's monuments go unseen, its past unheard, and its culture slowly fading into the dismal sea.*
> **—Nathan Reese Maher**

> *I have reared a memorial more enduring than brass, and loftier than the regal structure of the pyramids, which neither the corroding shower nor the powerless north wind can destroy; no, not even unending years nor the flight of time itself. I shall not entirely die. The greater part of me shall escape oblivion.*
> **—Horace**

> *If our love of country is excited when we read the biography of our revolutionary heroes, or the history of revolutionary events, how much more will the flame of patriotism burn in our bosoms when we tread the ground where was shed the blood of our fathers, or when we move among the scenes where were conceived and consummated their noble achievements.*
> **—Committee of the New York State Legislature**

---

* This section draws on verbal commentary, corroborated through a series of online and literature sources that have been cited in the Further Reading section of the book.

POSTCARD 1: HERALDING A REVOLUTION, ONE HOSTEL AT A TIME

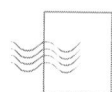

Kolhapur, Western Maharashtra

Miss Clark's Hostel in Kolhapur was started in 1908 for children from the Untouchable communities

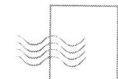

Kolhapur, Western Maharashtra

Dr Jaysingrao Pawar in his office

Dear Reader,

Come 2015 and newspaper headlines and editorials were once again screaming reservations. Hardik Patel and his violent demands on behalf of the Patels, followed by predictable reactions from the most unpredictable reactionaries of our times, once again resurrected a series of 'have' questions. To have or not to have? Further, for whom to have? When to have and in what to have? For how long to have?

These questions are important, not the least because they force us to go back to the raison d'être behind this much debated and oft maligned policy. Reservation, after all, was never an end unto itself. It was the means to empower a lot that had been disempowered, their self-respect systematically denuded. To strengthen communities that had hitherto been denied access to the very means that could enable them to build new lives.

Circa 1902. Chhatrapati Shahu Maharaj, the ruler of Kolhapur state, decreed that 50 per cent of the seats in his administration would be reserved for the *mulnivasis* or the depressed classes, that is, everyone excluding the Brahmins, the Parsis, the Prabhus and the Shenwis. While it was Mahatma Jyotiba Phule who had first raised the demand for reservation for the backward castes with the Hunter Commission in 1882, Shahu Maharaj's ruling became the first Government of India notification in this regard. The order created widespread discontent in a society steeped in caste-based prejudices, but Shahu was undeterred.

It is said that a clerk from Sangli province carried the protest of the Brahmanical classes to Shahu Maharaj. After listening patiently, the young ruler took him to his stables. There every horse was kept and fed separately. Shahu directed his grooms to free all the horses—strong and weak, big and small, healthy and diseased—and put them together in a single enclosure. A huge trough was put in the middle of the enclosure and the food given to each horse was collected and put into this trough.

After a while, the clerk noticed that the strong horses surrounded the trough, ate their fill, even dropped food around, but did not let the weak ones near. They kicked them away even when the food in the trough was more than enough for all the horses.

This, explained Shahu Maharaj, is why reservations were needed. Without them, the strong horses would leave the weak ones to die of hunger. It was about power and greed, not need. The caste system had weakened the 'lower' castes and the 'untouchables' beyond measure. They did not stand a chance when it came to competing with the rich and upper castes. If they had to be freed from the shackles of oppression, if they were to be empowered, then reservations were necessary. The promise of employment would incentivize the marginalized to study, despite the daunting odds. The power, prestige and economic freedom from the job would help their families to break free.

It was in Shahu's Kolhapur that I first heard this story. I was standing in Miss Clark's hostel—the first hostel that was built for the students from the 'untouchable' communities. The patron, of course, was the revolutionary Shahu Maharaj.

Shahu Maharaj was born to Radhabai and Abasaheb Ghatge in 1874. Due to close ties with the family of Chhatrapati Shivaji, he was adopted by the widow of King Shivaji IV of Kolhapur, when he was 10 years old. A decade later he acceded to the throne of Kolhapur and began a lifelong campaign to improve the lot of the 'untouchables' and the marginalized sections of society. He introduced free and compulsory primary education in his state, opened 22 hostels for students, introduced caste-based reservations, banned untouchability in public spaces, legalized widow remarriage and divorce, abolished the roll call and bonded labour system for the untouchables, encouraged inter-caste marriages and brought in laws against the devadasi system and the cruel treatment of women by their families.

Shahu's fight against caste-based discrimination started with his own experience of untouchability. Brahmanical supremacy was at its height at the time when Shahu ascended the throne. One day, he went to Satara. After having a bath, he went to the kitchen of his hosts to see how things stood. It was a Brahmin household. As he wandered in, he saw food being cooked in two separate vessels. A bare-chested Brahmin was walking between them with a cat curled in his arms. The minute he saw the king, he shouted, 'You can't wander in here like this. If you touch something, there will be havoc.' The statement shook the young king. He could not understand why a cat was allowed into the kitchen and not him. 'I am the king and yet I have to take these insults. What must be happening to the lot of the untouchables,' he thought. He decided to break social taboos and eat with the untouchables.

Gangaram Kamle, a groom in the government stables, belonged to the Mahar community that was treated as untouchable. One day, he was beaten up by the Marathas for drinking water from the palace well. When Shahu heard of this he was livid. Not only did he punish the culprits, he encouraged Gangaram to open a hotel in Kolhapur. Shahu Maharaj became the Satyasudharak Hotel's first patron. At that time, no one would even come near an untouchable, leave alone accept a cup of tea from him. But Shahu would regularly sit in the hotel, drink tea and offer it to those in his party. No one dared to refuse the king. Similarly, whilst travelling, Shahu would often stop at the house of a Mahar for tea and meals, breaking taboos and forcing his entourage to do the same.

Kolhapur is famous for its wrestling *akhadas* (training centres), another legacy of Shahu. Not only did he learn wrestling himself, he promoted it, both as a sport that ensured physical and mental fitness and as yet another tool to fight the oppressive caste regime. In Shahu's *akhadas*, men from all communities would live and practise together. However, when wrestlers from other regions came, they would not wrestle with an untouchable. So Shahu changed the names of his wrestlers. He would call the Maang Jat, *pahalwan*, the Chambar, *Pundit* and the Bhangi, *Sardar*. Thus no one would object to wrestling with them.

Shahu believed that no society could progress without education. He was appalled that the caste system had limited access to education to a single community. He dreamt of providing education to all his people. To this end he made primary education compulsory and levied a fine on parents who did not comply. He abolished caste-basted schools. Instead, he started common primary schools in villages and levied a small education tax to fund them. Classes were held in village offices, temples and *dharamshalas* (rest houses for pilgrims and tourists). For higher education, children had to come to Kolhapur. Yet they had nowhere to stay and no money to eat with. This was especially true for the untouchables. So Shahu started boarding houses that provided free lodging and food. On 18 April 1901, the first hostel named Victoria Maratha Boarding was started in Kolhapur.

'He was well ahead of his times. He began with cosmopolitan hostels that were open to children of all communities. But alas they did not work. Either the children from upper castes would ill-treat and make the children from other communities work, or they would simply not come.' The speaker is a bespectacled septuagenarian dressed in a white *kurta pyjama*. Dr Jaysingrao Pawar has spent his life studying Shahu Maharaj and his works. 'After all, I wouldn't be what I am today without Shahu. In 1958, I joined the Prince Shivaji Maratha Boarding House and stayed there till I finished my MA in 1964. Govind Pansare was my senior. I even studied at the Rajaram College, which had been patronized by Shahu.' By the time Dr Jaysingrao entered the boarding house, Western Maharashtra had become more tolerant and less discriminatory. The ideals of Shahu, Phule and Ambedkar had begun to seep into popular consciousness.

'There were six people in my room from Chambar, Mahar, Rajput and other backward communities. I was the only Maratha. All of us lived together. Then, there were no tiled floors. We cleaned the floor with cow dung, washed our own dishes. Initially, when I took my roommates home, my mother and other villagers were unsettled. But gradually they accepted it.'

But when Shahu started his boarding houses, prejudice was very strong. Ever the pragmatic, Shahu realized that he would need to empower the depressed classes before he could champion for equality. So, he built hostels for every community. There was Maratha Boarding, Muslim Boarding, Jain Boarding, Boarding for Mang, Mahar, Dhor and Chambhar. 'In all he opened 22 such boarding houses. But he never imposed them. He would encourage the communities to demand a boarding and then support them with land and money,' Dr Pawar tells me.

Today the Miss Clark's hostel, situated in Ravivar Peth, Lakshmipuri is a gated hostel with three storeys accommodating 54 students, studying in Classes 5 to 10. The compound also has a English-medium primary school, started in 2011, that is housed in the original hostel building—a single storey structure with four rooms, and a red gabled roof. In the early 1900s this was an area where stray cattle were kept.

Then, at a meeting in Jain Boarding, the need for a hostel for children from the Mang, Mahar, Chambar and Dhor communities was voiced. These castes were traditionally regarded as untouchables and had no access to education, lodging or food. When Shahu Maharaj shared his plan with Victoria Clark, the daughter of the Governor of Bombay Presidency, she decided to pitch in. She organized a charity dance programme in Bombay and donated the entire sum that was collected—₹5000—to Shahu's cause. This became the initial capital for Miss Clark's hostel and in 1908 it was started with four rooms and seven students from the Mang and the Mahar communities. By 1945, as many as 125 students were staying at the hostel. But after Shahu, no one gave any funds for its upkeep and maintenance. Eventually the Boarding closed down. It reopened in 1996 but struggled with funds and repairs.

In 2002, Kanshiram and Mayawati from the Bahujan Samaj Party visited the hostel. A programme was organized to celebrate the centenary of Shahu's reservation policy and the duo gave ₹10 lakh to revive this landmark that had provided many from the 'untouchable' communities an opportunity to study and build a life. Hindustan Petroleum also chipped in and a new hostel building was constructed. Today, the hostel runs with government money and houses children from all communities. Many from here have gone on to become police officers, district and state government officials fulfilling Shahu's dream.

Among the many beneficiaries of Shahu's vision is 48-year-old Tukaram Kamle from Kagne village of Chandragarh block. His parents were agricultural labourers. 'We belong to the Mahar community. So we could not study or wear new clothes. We had to clean the houses and cattle sheds of the villagers, feed the animals and work in the fields. We were not allowed into the temples and had a separate well. Our colony was outside the village. In fact, much has changed over the years, but we still remain on the outside. There were six of us, three brothers and three sisters,' Kamle tells me.

Kamle's parents and others in his village heard about Babasaheb and his efforts to end discrimination against the Dalits. One day they formed a group and tried to enter the Hanuman temple. They were insulted by the other villagers and sent back. But the group did not give up. They went to the police station to file a FIR, only to be sent back.

Kamle grew up seeing these struggles. 'Dalit children used to be beaten up badly for non-performance. No one ever examined why they didn't perform well. We didn't have books or clothes. I remember I had just one uniform. I would come back from school and wash it. One day, it didn't dry and I was forced to wear other clothes to school. I was in Class 9 then. My headmaster called me in front of everyone and asked me why I had broken the rules. I explained the reason but he didn't listen. In front of all the kids, he beat me up. I was so angry and humiliated.' But Kamle's father and elder brothers advised him to rein in his temper and study. That, they told him, would be the biggest slap on the face for the people who wanted to hold him back. So he studied.

'I decided that I would become a big officer and improve the lot of my community. I went to a boarding school in Kolhapur and completed my BA and MSW (Masters of Social Work).' It was during his MSW years that Kamle once again re-evaluated his options. A government job would provide economic security but working with an NGO would give him the chance to fight the discrimination he had grown up with. In 1994 he joined the Bhagini Nivedita Prathisthan in Sangli district. Gradually he realized the limitations of working with an NGO and joined the Mahila Rajsatta movement that had been started for the rights of Dalit women in Maharashtra. He trained with the National Campaign for Dalit Human Rights and in 2009 got selected for a Dalit Foundation fellowship.

'With DF, I learnt the meaning of atrocities. The fear I had of government and legal procedures went away. I learnt to engage with them and to use them in our fight for rights and dignity. Most importantly, I learnt to think beyond my community. I learnt that the term Dalit has a much wider application,' he tells me. Kamle started taking up cases of atrocities and helping them find legal recourse.

The fight has been a tough one. Most survivors or their families are unable to afford private lawyers. 'The government lawyers are not interested in winning cases. Besides, proceedings drag on forever. Eventually, most people give up. They need to get on with their lives, earn a living.' Now Kamle has become more selective with the cases he highlights. Resources are scant. After getting three years of support from the DF, he is on his own. He has had to move back to his village because he can't afford living in the city. Yet, he says that he will continue the fight, just like his inspiration—Shahu Maharaj! What better tribute could the revolutionary king have hoped for?

POSTCARD 2: A MIGHTY WOMAN

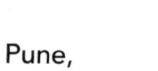

Pune, Maharashtra

The country's first school for girls lies crumbling opposite the rich Dagdusheth Ganpati temple in Pune

Dear Reader,

As I travel across the country, visiting Dalit communities, one name keeps recurring in our conversations: Savitribai Phule. Just like Babasaheb Ambedkar, she is the role model for many Dalit girls. Yet, to my shame, I know little about her. So, I decide to find out more about this brave woman, who is remembered with so much love and admiration.

My quest brings me to Bhide Wada in Pune. I am standing right across the famous Dagdusheth Halwai Ganpati, one of Maharashtra's richest temples. My destination is a small school that was run by Savitribai Phule and her husband, Jyotiba Phule—a school that was perhaps the first school for girls in the country. The annual *Ganeshotsav* has just finished and the street is still littered with signs of the festivities. The main idol of the Dagdusheth Ganpati is said to be insured for a sum of 10 million rupees. Every year lakhs of devotees visit and offer all kinds of conceivable riches.

Meanwhile, just across the road the double-storey monument I seek lies crumbling, bit by bit, every day, with nary a backward glance from the thousands who pass it by in their spiritual ardor. I cannot go in. It's too dangerous, not to mention illegal. Shops run on the ground floor of the erstwhile school. A narrow flight of steps that led to the first floor has been blocked. It is full of debris. This monument to the fight against gender and caste-based discrimination is disintegrating little by little. Yet no one seems to care. It is not on the Cultural Heritage list. A small board on the footpath, just outside the building proclaims its historical value. It goes unnoticed. The building is under litigation, I am told. Some time back, the *wada* owners sold this 2,500-square- foot property on 257 C, Budhwar Peth to the Pune Merchants Co-operative Bank. The bank sold it to a real estate developer who wants to demolish it and build a mall, just like the two that flank it. Dalit and gender activists have been fighting to preserve it. A few years back the Pune Municipal Corporation announced it would compensate the shopkeepers and develop the property. The shopkeepers were unhappy. They obtained a stay order. The case is now in court. But the commercial interests are content; some are already celebrating. They know that soon the structure will collapse and with it, all obstacles to a swanky new mall.

It was in this dilapidated and decrepit building with its peeling paint that Mahatma Jyotiba Phule and his wife Savitribai Phule started the first girls' school in the country in 1848—one year before Iswar Chandra Vidyasagar started the Bethune school for girls in Kolkata. The property belonged to a friend, Tatyarao Bhide. It came to be known as Krantishala (Kranti meaning Revolution) because at a time when the education of girls was regarded a sin and women were not allowed to step out of the four walls of their houses (unless they were cleaning house or working the fields), the school marked a radical shift. In 1848, when the young Phule couple started the school with Savitribai as the headmistress and teacher, there were just nine students. By 1853, they ran three schools with 237 girl students—a remarkable feat. The journey however was a tough one.

Savitribai was born to a farmer family on 3 January 1831 in Naigaon village of Satara. At the age of nine she was married to 13-year-old Jyotirao Phule, the son of a vegetable vendor and florist. It is said that the young, uneducated girl went to her new house clutching a book that the missionaries had gifted her. When Jyotirao saw this he decided to educate his bride. Jyotirao himself had only managed to complete his primary education before he was forced to drop out of school and help his father run the family flower farm. In fact, it was their flower business which had earned the family the name, Phule. But seeing his intelligence and keen desire to learn, his neighbours convinced his father to let Jyotirao join the Scottish High School in 1841. Thus, the young boy would go to school, work the farms and also teach his new bride. Later, he supported Savitri in going to the village school to complete Classes 3 and 4. Jyotirao's father was worried that this would incite the ire of the villagers. During those times, even men from the 'lower' caste—they belonged to the Mali community that was considered untouchable—were not allowed to study. A woman stepping outside the house to go to school was unheard of.

But Savitribai and Jyotirao persisted and had to leave their house to move to Pune. Savitribai took formal training from Ms Farar's institution in Ahmednagar and Ms Mitchel's school in Pune. Thereafter, she, along with Jyotirao, formally took up the cause for the education of girls. Two women are believed to have helped them with the school—Fatima Sheikh, Savitribai's friend from the training school and Saguna Bau, Jyotirao's maternal cousin.

Every day, a 17-year-old Savitribai would walk from their home in Ganj Peth to Bhidewada. On the way, an outraged society would sling insults, stones, sticks, mud and cow dung at her. But she did not give up. She simply kept an extra sari. Once she reached school, she would change her clothes and teach the girls. The harassment grew to such an extent that one day Savitribai had to slap an upper caste youth. It is said that such was the social taboo associated with the education of girls that a few fathers would hide their daughters in sacks and carry them to school.

Savitribai did not limit her activities to teaching. She would visit the families of girls and encourage them to let their daughters study. If anyone was ill, she would arrange for doctors and medicines. In her classroom, she applied new and innovative methods of learning. She would use short stories, poems and examples from everyday life to teach her girls. At the end of the day she would reward them with sweets.

An excerpt from an anthology of Marathi poems by Savitribai, published in 1854, reads,

Awake, arise and educate,
Smash traditions, liberate.
We will come together and learn
Policy, righteousness, religion.
Slumber not but blow the trumpet
O Brahman, dare not you upset.
Give a war cry, rise fast
Rise, to learn and act.[1]

Due to Savitribai's efforts, before the end of the year, her school had 25 pupils—10 Brahmins, 6 Marathas, 2 Chambhar, 2 Mahar and one each from the Gadaria, Julaha, Matang, Sali and Mali castes. The very composition of this school is remarkable in a caste-based society. After all, even half a century later, Shahu Maharaj was forced to close his cosmopolitan boarding schools because children from different communities would not live together.

Encouraged by the response from her students and undeterred by the insults that came her way, Savitribai shouldered on. Within a year, the Phules opened another school in Usman Sheikhwada for adults. In 1852, they opened a school for Dalits, yet another first in a society where the right to education was limited to the Brahmins and the upper castes.

As mentioned in the beginning of the book, it was Jyotirao who first used the term Dalit, meaning broken, to describe the 'untouchables' and the lower caste. Immediately after he finished studying at the Scottish school, Jyotirao had gone to the wedding party of his Brahmin friend. There he was insulted and thrown out because he belonged to the lower caste. This infuriated Jyotirao and he began a lifelong crusade for the rights of the oppressed. He advocated universal and compulsory education and asked for reservation in schools and jobs for the Dalits.

Through all this, Savitribai stood by his side, quietly and efficiently taking his crusade forward. When her brothers objected to her stepping out of the house and teaching, she chided them for their orthodoxy. In a letter she captures her discussion with her brother, 'Bhau, your point of view is extremely narrow, and moreover, your reason has been weakened by the teachings of the Brahmins. You fondle even animals like the cow and goat…but you consider the Manga and Mahars, who are as human as you, untouchables…. Learning has great value…. Jyotiba confronts the dastardly Brahmins, fights with them and teaches the Manga and Mahar because he believes they are human beings and must be able to live as such. So they must learn. That is why I also teach them. What is so improper about that? Yes, we teach the girls, the women, the Manga and the Mahars. It is a pleasant task and I feel immensely happy.'[2]

In 1852, Savitribai started the Mahila Seva Mandal to educate women about their rights and other social issues. In 1873 when Jyotiba Phule started the Satyashodhak Samaj to fight for the rights of the oppressed, she was right beside him and became the leader of the women's wing. Together the couple opposed idolatry and promoted rational thinking. They opened their personal well for people of all castes and served food to thousands during the droughts. They fought ceaselessly for the rights of women, particularly the widows. At that time, young girls were married off to elderly men and on their death forced to undergo great hardship. Their heads were shaved. They were sexually exploited by family and society. Any children born of such dastardly acts were killed. It is said that the couple once met a young Brahmin widow who was about to commit suicide. They took her home, cared for her, helped her deliver and adopted her child as their own son. Yashwantrao went on to become a doctor and stood firmly by his parents in their crusade.

The Phules started a campaign for the remarriage of widows. Savitribai convinced the barbers to not shave the heads of women and opened a centre where the widows could stay. Later, along with Jyotirao, she established a Balhatya Pratibadhak Griha (Home to stop foeticide and infanticide) where widows could give birth to the children and leave them, if they so desired.

In 1890, Jyotirao Phule, who had been given the title of Mahatma, passed away. Once again breaking with tradition, Savitribai decided to lead her husband's funeral procession. She carried out his last rites—an act that few women brave even today—and once again immersed herself in what had been their lifelong crusade. In 1897, when Pune was reeling under the onslaught of the bubonic plague, she along with her son Yashwantrao, started a clinic to provide succour to those afflicted by the scourge. Savitribai would herself carry patients, especially children to the facility and administer medicines. In the process, she caught the disease and succumbed to it.

It is the legacy of this brave and courageous crusader that stands in shambles today, on a busy street in Pune. Perhaps the state of the first school for girls in the country is reflective of just how we treat our women even today, 170 years after the Phules embarked on a campaign to get them their due. Our plummeting sex ratio and the barrage of incidents of violence against women—sexual, physical and mental—are a testimony to that.

RAMBLINGS: WHO DID IT FIRST?

We humans seem to have a unique obsession with firsts. Coming first in class, being the first to come up with an idea or simply commemorating our firsts—school, job, friend, love, trip. I too am guilty. I do it all the time—my first experience of snowfall or my niece's first Diwali, first day at school, first dance—everything is duly noted and celebrated. There is no doubt a sense of achievement and exhilaration that accompanies the first; a novelty, a challenge and often, a leap of faith and courage. And yet does it deserve the disproportionate attention that we lavish on it? Does not being first make the subsequent achievements any less special?

While writing these postcards, I spent a lot of time corroborating facts, especially when they concerned historical figures. I became obsessed with verifying things like: Was Shahu Maharaj indeed the first to introduce reservations? Was the school at Bhidewada the first girls' school in the country? Was Gulab Bai the first female *nautanki* actor? Yet, the more I dug, the more blurry the picture became. For everything there seemed to be more than one pioneer. In some instances, historians or sociologists who identified these pioneers built their cases well. In others, there were no supplementary documents, no references. Just a powerful, if unsubstantiated claim. Yet it was enough to send me into a tizzy. It shouldn't be that difficult to verify these facts, I reasoned. After all, they are not perspectives. They are events and while how people view them may differ, the date and time shouldn't. So, I ploughed on.

One author claimed that contrary to popular perception reservations were first introduced in 1850 by the King of Mysore. He sought to fight the growing influence of Tamil Brahmins in his administration and reserved seats for the Kannadiga Brahmins, Lingayats, Shudras. Another claimed that the first school for girls was in fact opened in 1820 by David Hare. I spent a lot of time searching and researching these bits of information—looking for definitive answers. I wanted to ensure that every fact in the book was represented correctly. In my earlier work too, I have struggled with similar problems. The fort administrator at Kumbalgarh Fort in Rajsamand district of Rajasthan had claimed that it is the longest wall in the world, after the Great Wall of China—a claim reiterated by the district administration. Yet there are many others that claim the distinction. Who is right? At one time, I even contemplated visiting the various candidates and verifying for myself.

But then I asked myself—to what end? Does it really matter? Or is it simply my own obsession with numbers that is driving me?

Perhaps Shahu Maharaj was the first person to officially introduce reservations. Perhaps he was not. Yet the fact remains that the policy he introduced was a landmark step. It changed the lives of many generations. It changed attitudes and perspectives. It was brave and bold and it tells us a lot about the person who promulgated it. Perhaps it was his own idea, perhaps it was inspired. But the courage and the initiative were his alone, and they cost him a lot. That is undebatable and undeniable. That is the truth and perhaps that is the only truth that matters. What he did, why and what it achieved. The rest is mere arithmetic.

The abuse that Savitribai braved daily to educate the girls, especially from the untouchable communities is true. Her dedication and determination to the cause inspires thousands of Dalit children even today. Perhaps, it is this fact alone that is pertinent.

And so, dear reader, I humbly seek your indulgence. Let us celebrate these heroes and their actions for what they are—monumental, life and country altering. Let historians debate the order and the dates. Perhaps someday they will reach an agreement. Till then let us celebrate each one of these heroes, be they first or not!

Endnotes

1. S. Phule (2012). *Kavyaphule, Poetic Blossoms: A Collection of Poems in Marathi by Savitri Jotirao Phule (1854).* Translated by Ujjwala Mhatre. Dr Ambedkar College of Commerce & Economics: Mumbai
2. Sabrang. To Jyotiba, from Savitribai Phule: These aren't Love Letters, but tell you what Love is all about. *Scroll.in.* February 14, 2016. https://scroll.in/article/801848/to-jyotiba-from-savitribai-phule-these-arent-love-letters-but-tell-you-what-love-is-all-about

The Sacred Feminine

What didn't you do to bury me
But you forgot I was a seed.
—Dinos Christianopoulos

They point at my body or face,
They argue about how I look-
I feel like a garland-seller, my wares examined,
Tested for quality, coldly.
I loiter alone amidst them all,
Each day hangs so heavily.
People here are like worms crawling between bricks
There is no love, there is no gaiety.
What of you, mother, where are you?
You can't have forgotten me, surely?
When you sit outside on our roof beneath the new moon
Do you still tell fairy-stories?
Or do you, alone in bed, lie awake at night,
In tears and sickness of heart?
— **Rabindranath Tagore,** *Bride*

POSTCARD 1: EARLIER THEY CALLED ME A *JOGINI*, NOW THEY CALL ME LEADER

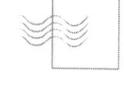

Mahabubnagar, Telangana

Disparate tales: Hajamma (left) is scripting a change in Telangana while Manneyamma (seen with her jemkiya on the right) clings to tradition

Dear Reader,

This time I write to you from the town of Jadcherla, located 80 km from Hyderabad in Mahabubnagar district of the newly formed state of Telangana.

I am standing in the shaded courtyard of a modest, single-storey, under-construction cement house, under the watchful eye of Dr Ambedkar. The temperature outside is 48 degrees Celsius and the newspapers are full of reports of the heat wave. Clad in a simple cotton sari, with a small black bindi, her well-oiled hair neatly parted in the middle and tied in a plait, Hajamma has travelled 105 km from the village of Utkoor to meet us. Tall, with a rotund face and stout build, Hajamma shares her story in slightly broken Hindi. A story that began some 40 years ago in a small village located just 10 km from the border of Karnataka.

'My parents were agricultural labourers. They had three daughters. Their only son had died when he was seven. I was the middle daughter, born when my mother was 40 years old. My elder sister had polio and had already joined the ranks of the 60 *joginis* in our village. The man who employed my parents was from the upper caste, an astrologer. He convinced them that if they dedicated me to the Goddess, it would be good for them.'

'And your parents agreed?'

'In our community, the Madiga, this is a very old practice. Not only would it please the Goddess, since they had no son, this would ensure that I look after my parents in old age,' she shrugs.

Known as the Mang or Matang in Maharashtra and the Chakkaliya in Tamil Nadu, the Madiga as they are called in Karnataka and Andhra, are the most populous Scheduled Caste community of Telangana. Found in large numbers in other states (according to the 2001 census there were six million Madiga in the undivided state of Andhra Pradesh), they face widespread discrimination, and are regarded as untouchables. In ancient times, they were the leather workers—people who cleaned carcasses, tanned them, made *chappals* (shoes), the drum beaters and the village messengers. In 1920, George Weston Briggs in his book, *The Chamars*, wrote, 'The great leather-working caste of the Telugu country is the Madiga. He lives on the outskirts of the village.... He works in leather, and serves as a menial and as a scavenger. Many Madigas are practically serfs. Most of them are field labourers. They beat drums at festivals.... Their girls are often dedicated to temple service (basavis).'[1]

As Briggs noted, the Madiga girls are often dedicated to temple practice, married to the Goddess Yellamma and known by various local names—Matamma, Renuka, Parvati, Basavi, Jogini. To the outside world, they are all devadasis, literally 'servants of the Goddess'.

Hajamma explains how the making of a devadasi is a communal practice. 'Once their employer broached the subject, my parents went back to our community and a consultation was held on whether I should be made a *jogini*, a *basavi* or a *renuka*.'

'What's the difference?'

'In actuality, very little. Our lives are all condemned, but some practices differ. We go to beg on different days, the *taali* (*mangalsutra* or neckpiece that is tied around the neck of a Hindu woman by her spouse) varies a little as do some rituals. In some areas, girls are allowed to marry despite the dedication, but not so in our district.'

While the community discussed her fate, a confused 11-year-old Hajamma sat weeping. 'I did not understand what was happening. The other *joginis* in the village told me of the life that awaited me, the hardships. Two *joginis* in our village had developed mental problems due to the trauma. They asked me to run away unless I wanted to beg throughout my life. But I was 11. Where could I go? I was so confused. My friends had begun to tease me. It was a nightmare,' recalls Hajamma.

Soon, the 11-year old found herself sitting in front of the entire community, bedecked in flowers, jewellery, and a red-coloured sari for her engagement to the goddess. 'I felt like a princess or a goddess.' The previous day, she had been made to fast and conduct a series of rituals that involved praying to the various goddesses revered by the Madiga—Yellamma, Lakshamma, Poleramma, Mashamma, Gajamma, etc. A design with rice and turmeric was made on a black towel and she followed an older *jogini* around it, a *diya* (country lamp made out of mud) in hand. Other *joginis* sang traditional songs. Hajamma explains that the dedication rituals are much akin to the celebrations at any Brahmin wedding. Only the bridegroom is missing! 'My parents took a loan of ₹10,000 for the various ceremonies. After the engagement, they served *tari* (local liquor made from mahua, a tropical tree found in South Asia) to the entire community. A wedding date was set for three days later.'

So once again, little Hajamma found herself fasting and going through a series of rituals before she was prepared for her wedding with the Goddess Yellamma. 'I was not allowed to wear clothes made of any fabric. Five joginis dressed me up in a sari of neem (margosa) leaves that had been made by the community. Only after that was I allowed to put on a white sari with green bangles for the *taali*-tying ceremony.' In Hajamma's area the *taali* of a *jogini* has three coins. In parts of Andhra, the *taali* is made of red and white beads whereas in Tamil Nadu, it has nine types of symbols. Depending on the local practice, the *taali* can be tied by an older *jogini*, a priest, or any upper caste man, including the one who wants to reserve the right to 'deflower' the girl when she attains puberty.

'They asked an old man to tie my *taali*, but his daughter used to study with me. So he refused. Another one refused. Finally, my uncle's son, who was already married with three children, tied my taali,' says Hajamma, a catch in her voice. 'I wept through the ceremony. I was given a pot with yellow rice, *kumkum* (vermillion), turmeric and neem leaves. I had to make a *rangoli* and circumambulate the temple with the pot. Thereafter, I was sent to the village to beg, with the pot on my head.' It was an ingenious plan. Not only was the young girl taught to beg and become completely dependent for the rest of the life, but as she went from one upper caste house to another, the men got to 'examine the new goods'. By the time she attained puberty and was ready for her initiation or deflowering ceremony, the willing upper caste men would have already expressed interest and negotiated the rights of consummation with her family and community.

After her wedding, Hajamma's life changed. 'I was taught the rules—I was not allowed to marry, to say no to any man and to work. I had to go begging every Tuesday and Friday and survive on whatever I received. I used to love school but within three months, I quit as everyone had begun to make fun of me.

Those days, I used to cry a lot. I didn't want to go begging to my friends' houses, to be the butt of jokes. I wanted to study. But my parents told me that if I did not follow the rules, I would die. The irony was that eight days after my wedding, my father passed away. Till the age of 13, I lived the life of a devadasi. I went begging, I sang at weddings and funerals, carried out rituals like fasting and breaking bangles when someone died. In the midst of all this, I also worked in the fields. Often men would come home and proposition me. They offered a bag of paddy or half a kilogram of silver in exchange for a night. At that time, I didn't understand what was happening. I just felt humiliated and frightened.'

Then one day, Hajamma decided to follow the advice given to her by the older *joginis*. Before her virginity could be auctioned off to the highest bidder, she went away to her birthplace. 'My parents had both been construction workers in Mumbai. I was born there. When I turned seven, I was sent to the village to look after my elder sister's baby. When at 13, I decided enough was enough, I went back to Mumbai and started working as a construction labourer.' But life is never easy for a woman who has been made a devadasi. One day someone from her community saw her *sindoor* and *taali* and realized she was a *jogini*. After that Hajamma had to face constant harassment. People thought she was 'available' and kept trying to back her into shadowy corners. 'My husband, you know God, he wasn't with me to protect me,' she says. Life was a nightmare and Hajamma shared this in a letter with her friend Lakshmaiah, another Madiga who lived in her village. He was pursuing his intermediate (higher secondary) education at that time. Within three months he joined Hajamma in Mumbai. In 1989, the government announced houses for *joginis*. So Hajamma and Lakshmaiah returned to the village and took up jobs as agricultural labourers.

'Twenty nine joginis were given houses in a colony. All around me there was sex work going on. Men came and assumed I too was available. I was living with Lakshmaiah. He would drive them away. In 1992, my son was born and in 1994, my daughter. Till then I stayed with Lakshmaiah like a *jogini*.'

Change came in the 1990s in the form of Grace Nirmala and her NGO, Ashray. For two years, they alternately observed and counselled Lakshmaiah to marry Hajamma and treat her with respect. Gradually Lakshmaiah saw the wisdom behind their words. He agreed, but the whole village, especially his family, rose in opposition.

'You cannot marry a *jogini*, the villagers said. His family called me a sex worker. But his mind made up, Lakshmaiah stood by me. The villagers even threatened us. At that time LV Subramanium was the district collector. He said that he would take us elsewhere and get us married.' But that was not to be. The villagers did not let them go. Finally, in 1995 when Hajamma's daughter turned six months old, Anita Ramachandran, then the local revenue division officer (at the time of writing, Director, Panchayati Raj and Rural Development in the Government of Telangana) intervened. She threatened to arrest anyone who stopped the wedding. Raymond Peters (at the time of writing Principal Secretary, Panchayati Raj & Rural Development, Telangana), who had come in as the new District Collector, also supported them. The villagers were scared enough to let the wedding take place and yet they were angry. 'I was the first devadasi in the district to get married. They worried that others would follow suit. The community issued a diktat that anyone attending the wedding would be fined ₹1000. The only guests at my wedding were government officers.'

Even after the wedding the harassment did not stop. For the next couple of years, the villagers blamed Hajamma and Lakshmaiah for every problem in the village. But by now Hajamma had joined Ashray as a teacher. She was stronger. She had also decided it was time to act against the practice that had nearly ruined her life. 'Three months after my dedication, Lakshmi, the 5-year-old daughter of a relative was also made into a *jogini*. When she turned 12, she was forced to have a defloweing ceremony. I used to see her cry and could do nothing to save her from the life of a *jogini*. Luckily, she met someone who loved her and married her. But not everyone is this fortunate. Most are forced to have sex repeatedly, at the whim of the villagers. You can't even call it sex work. They are not paid. When the upper caste patrons are happy, they gift them saris or a few rupees. By the time the *joginis* turn 40 and are of no interest to the villagers, they become *bidi* workers or agricultural labourers, that is, if their body is not destroyed by disease, alcohol and malnutrition.'

For the next 15 years, Hajamma worked with Ashray, teaching children and also fighting for the rights of other *joginis*. 'You know what the biggest tragedy of a *jogini*'s life is? Even her children disown her. They are so ashamed of her that they abuse her publicly. I am lucky. My children have always stood by me. If they had called me names, I would have died.'

Within a few years of Hajamma's marriage, Lakshmaiah passed away. She went on to become a district co-ordinator for the Jogini Vyatireka Porata Samithi. When the Ashray programme wound up in 2010, she began imparting gender training for government programmes at ₹300 a day. In 2012, she was selected as a fellow by the Dalit Foundation. This provided her with an opportunity to travel, to broaden her horizons, and to focus on atrocities and fact-finding. 'The law abolishing the practice of devadasis was formulated in 1988 and yet till date rules have not been framed in either Andhra Pradesh or Telangana. Meanwhile the practice continues. Recently, I filed four FIRs against the dedication of girls. There is so much to be done. The practice has to be stopped, existing *joginis* have to be rehabilitated, provided with houses, pension. We have to encourage their marriages. Also, caste-based discrimination continues. The Madiga still have separate colonies, wells, even temples. The dedication happens not at the village temple, but in our community temple. Yet, the upper caste people have no qualms in exploiting our girls.'

But it is not just the upper castes who have been protesting against the marriage of *joginis*. Most people, including those from Dalit communities, are unhappy with the change that Hajamma is bringing. One such person is Manneyamma, the 55-year-old from Dhanwara village who has accompanied her. Dressed in a multi-coloured cotton saree, with a big red *bindi*, nose rings on both sides, multiple earrings, an array of bangles and a string of orange flowers draped around her bun, she presents a sharp contrast to the simply dressed Hajamma. Manneyamma does not wish for the devadasi practice to end. 'How will we earn otherwise?' she complains in Telugu. Hajamma plays translator. Manneyamma belongs to the Baindla community. A sub-caste of the Madiga, they are the priests who carry out the rituals and preside over the dedication ceremonies. And for every such ritual they get money, clothes, food grains and sometimes, even cattle.

Manneyamma's 30-year-old sister-in-law is a *jogini*. Her in-laws had long been overseeing the dedication of *joginis* in their village. After she had kids, at the age of 30, Manneyamma too joined the profession. 'One dedication ceremony takes two days, and the parents of the newly made *jogini* gift us with a sari, foodgrains and ₹2000–3000,' she tells us. They also get money for conducting funeral rites for the Dalits or for making *rangolis* in upper caste marriages. The rest of the time the Baindla women go from house to house with their *Jemkiya*—a small, barrel-shaped drum made of bamboo and goat skin—and ask for food. Manneyamma plays her *Jemkiya* and sings a few songs for me.

She is angry with Hajamma. 'She stopped the dedication ceremony of my niece and got her married instead. Since then my sister has been keeping unwell,' she complains. Manneyamma also says that she will continue with her profession and keep creating devadasis till she dies. It is partly because this is the only life that she knows and partly because of community pressure. 'I have five children. Two daughters and my youngest son are still studying. One of my sons is a teacher, another a salesperson. The children did not learn our ways and because of that we have to face the wrath of the community, especially of the upper caste. We were lucky, but in some cases, the villagers don't even let our kids study saying who will perform our rituals if your children go elsewhere,' she explains as she wraps her *Jemkiya* in a white cotton cloth.

Nonetheless, Hajamma is undeterred. She is convinced that the Baindla can find other jobs, but the practice has to stop. This is the third and final year of her DF fellowship. The change, she says, is palpable. 'At 11, I didn't even have a place to run away to. Now, I have been as far as The Hague, telling people my story. Earlier people called me a *jogini*, now they address me as a leader,' she smiles.

POSTCARD 2: I CHOSE MY OWN NAME

Tirupati,
Andhra Pradesh

Vijay Kumar at the Yellamma temple in Tirupati

Dear Reader,

About 552 km from Hyderabad, at the foothills of the Seshachalam hills, in the Chittoor district of Andhra Pradesh, sits the bustling temple town of Tirupati. Every day (and night), undeterred by the heat or humidity, up to one lakh pilgrims, from all over the country, brave the dangers of a stampede to queue for long hours in narrow, stuffy corridors to catch a half-minute glimpse—the temple authorities ensure it is no more—of their beloved Lord Venkateswara, who sits in a temple at the heart of the seven hills. If you live in India, you have probably heard of the Tirumala Tirupati Devasthanam, the devotion it inspires and the much sought after laddoos that it sells, albeit in a rationed manner. It is the richest and the most visited temple in the world.

Yet what brings me to this pious town is a different kind of pilgrimage. I chase not the divine, but those whose lives have been repeatedly mutilated in the name of the divine—the devadasis. I am attending the two-day National Conference on the Eradication of

The Sacred Feminine

the Devadasi System, organized by MESRO (Mother's Educational Society for Rural Orphans).

I had heard about the devadasis, even read the occasional stray report about their plight but quite frankly, before meeting Hajamma, they were never a part of my consciousness. Perhaps, I knew of them, but I never really knew them. My abiding love for classical Indian dance notwithstanding, I never knew that it was the legacy of this group of much maligned and exploited artists. Even after over a decade of involvement with the women's movement, I never really understood what life entails for a devadasi.

In a 12×18 sq. feet room, packed to the seams with devadasis from the four southern states, and activists who work with them, I began to understand that Hajamma's story is different. She has not only wrested control of her present, but she continues to define what tomorrow will hold not just for her, but for her community as well. Most of the estimated five lakh devadasis in the country, however, have no say in their today or tomorrow, just like they had no say in their yesterday. These numbers are of course, not official. The National Commission for Women estimates that there are 450,000 devadasis in the country. The Karnataka Devadasi Mahileyara Vimochana Sangha maintains that the state alone has 100,000 joginis.[2] A recent report submitted by Justice V. Raghunath Rao says there are 80,000 devadasis in Andhra and Telangana alone.[3] Activists and field workers allege that the Act notwithstanding, young girls continue to be dedicated even today. A living proof of this is the 15-year-old with *mogra* flowers in her hair and a big *bindi*, seated at the back of the room—the youngest devadasi in our midst. In fact, most of the devadasis in the room seem to be quite young—in their 20s. Dark complexioned, their lean bodies dressed in saris with golden yellow borders, many have little toddlers in their arms; children who will probably grow up without a father. Luckily for them they will now get admission into government schools.

'In 2009, the government modified the school admission forms. Now you can put your mother's name and get admitted. Earlier most children were denied education as they didn't know what to put under their father's name. Somehow, the authorities were not thrilled when we wrote God,' says a former devadasi, dressed in a simple cotton sari, a line of *kumkum* prominently displayed in the middle of her neatly oiled and braided hair.

The modification of the school forms may have paved the way for school admissions in the southern states, but access to education still remains a distant dream for many. 'I recently visited schools in Chittoor district and realized that while the modification of the school form under GO139 had brought many into the schooling system, only two children had received scholarships. The online application form for scholarships still need a father's name,' explains Vijay Kumar, Founder Secretary of MESRO.

Sitting in the room, listening to the status of devadasis across the four southern states, I realize how widespread the practice is, and how old. A journalist from Kerala informs the group that evidence of temple girls is found in many engravings and texts from the 8th century onwards, and that the practice itself can be traced to the 3rd century AD! In fact, devadasis were present across the country, in temples in the western, northern and the eastern regions. A similar tradition was prevalent in Nepal wherein young girls were offered as Deukis to the temple. Gradually, frequent invasions from West Asia and the consequent erosion in the wealth and status of temples in North India led to a decline in the practice in this region. In Orissa, as well as the Southern states, however, girls continued to be married to various gods and goddesses.

According to the participants, today devadasis are present in 14 districts out of 30 in Karnataka, more than half the districts in Andhra Pradesh, all districts in Telangana and 4 districts in Tamil Nadu.[4] But the exploitation of Dalit girls through a system of caste-based prostitution is much more widespread. Bharti Sonkar, a young (former) Dalit Foundation fellow from Bhopal, who runs the Daksha Ambrose Empowerment Society, talks about the plight of the Bednis of Madhya Pradesh. 'Earlier the eldest daughter among the Bedia community was forced into prostitution. Now, there is no such rule. Any girl can be sold into prostitution under the garb of the Rai dance that is performed by this community,' she informs the group, triggering off a discussion on whether caste-based prostitution, where there is no definitive set of rituals and no co-relation to the temples, can be included under the ambit of the Devadasi system. I am reminded of the Kolatti community from Maharashtra who perform the Lavni and a discussion I had with some Dalit scholars and students in Pune. 'It is all right for you to talk of cultural heritage and art forms, but do not push us back into the same mould,' they had urged.

As cultural activists or people who value art, as women who have had the privilege of paying hefty fees to learn various dance forms in city schools, it is easy for us to seek the art (at times without paying due regard to the artist and what the art has cost him or her). But for these communities, who created and nurtured these art forms, their very talent has become a symbol of exploitation. Ironically for them, as long as they practise their art, they will continue to be seen as sex objects, and respect will elude them and their families. If they want to get married, if they want to tell the people that their bodies are not available, if they want their children to be able to go to schools, then they will have to dissociate themselves completely from these art forms, these dances that were once their life and livelihood. Not only do they have to stop dancing and singing, they have to even denounce these art forms as debased.

Do you remember my first postcard to you, dear reader? The discussion regarding facts, figures, and the power of stories? Perhaps nothing drives that point home for me as strongly as this conference. As I listen to the participants tracing the history of the practice and the problems faced by the devadasis today, my mind keeps returning to the look on Hajamma's face as she recounted her story. Hajamma, who is also sitting in this room, compiling a list of measures that need to be undertaken to ensure a life of dignity for the devadasis. As soon as the discussion draws to an end, I find myself seeking out the devadasis or the former devadasis, to hear their stories.

Saroja is a thin, cheerful 27-year-old who speaks only Telugu. Dressed just like the other devadasis, she is accompanied by her six-year-old daughter. And she is in a hurry. It will take her over an hour to reach her home in SBR Puram village. Nonetheless, she shares her story while another NGO worker, who knows English, plays translator.

Saroja's parents were agricultural labourers. When Venkatamma, her mother, was pregnant with her, her father fell in love with a *matamma*. He went away, leaving his pregnant wife heartbroken and scared. There was no hospital in the village. So she did the only thing that had been taught to her. She went to Yellamma, the patron goddess of the Madiga, and prayed for herself and her unborn child. 'Protect us and I will dedicate him or her to you,' she promised.

'Dedicate him?' I ask intrigued.

'Oh yes, in our community, boys are also dedicated to temple service. They are called *Matayyas*.[5] They do temple work and play instruments that accompany temple dances. But unlike the girls, they are allowed to lead normal lives—study, work, get married,' Saroja explains.

This is how when young Saroja was born she became the first *matamma* in her family. She went to school and seemed to have a fairly normal childhood till she reached Class 3. That year there was a flood in the village, and as compensation, the government gave them some land. Saroja moved there with her *nana* and *nani* and her mother. But there was no school close by. So, she had to travel by bus. One day, the bus conductor remarked, 'Even now you are so beautiful. When you grow up, do come to me.' The eight-year-old was confused. She didn't understand why a grown-up would say something like that to her.

'Everyone called me *matamma*, even in school. At that time, I thought it was my name. I knew of no other. When I was in Class 4, an organization came to our school and explained that *matamma* was not my name. Why should you be called that, they asked? You are just a little girl. That day I decided to call myself Saroja. I chose my own name,' she smiles, displaying a set of evenly spaced pearly whites.

In sharp contrast to her delicate form, little Saroja was full of determination and strength. She refused to acknowledge anyone who did not address her by her new name.

By the next year, she had attained puberty. She was taken to a temple and a series of rituals were conducted. When she asked her mother what was happening, she was told that this was a part of their culture. So during the Pottukattu or *taali*-tying ceremony, she simply did what was told to her.

Unlike in Hajamma's village, here the *taali* is made of cowries and tied by elderly *matammas* or married women. Three older *matammas* put the *taali* on Saroja. Her tongue was blessed (touched) with a *trishul* (trident) and her forehead with a *katti* (a knife that is called the *khanjar* of the Goddess). Thereafter she was asked to dance.

'*Matammas* are supposed to dance at the annual festival each year, in addition to other occasions. The practice begins on the day of the wedding ceremony. The older *matammas* dance and the newly dedicated girls follow them.'

But once again young Saroja was defiant. She did not like the idea of dancing in front of complete strangers and refused to do so at the annual festival. Some time after her dedication, RISE, an

NGO that rescued newly dedicated *matammas* and the children of *matammas*, sent her to a hostel in Tirupati.

'The first thing they did was to remove the *taali*. Initially, I protested. I had been told never to remove the necklace and I was worried that I would be punished at home. Also, there was the fear of the goddess. I was only in Class 5. But the organization insisted that if I wanted to stay and study, the *taali* had to go. So it went. I didn't realize this then, but they had saved my life,' Saroja says lost in her memories.

Thereafter, her course was set. Saroja stayed at the hostel and studied till class 12. She would go home for holidays, but not follow any of the rituals that were designed for *matammas*. In the village, she fell in love with Munaswamy, a Madiga boy who was self-employed. Much to the consternation of the villagers and her mother, they decided to get married as soon as her studies were completed. Gradually Saroja's mother came around but her husband's family remained adamant. They would not accept a *matamma*—even if she had not lived the life of one—as their daughter-in-law. But Saroja was lucky. She had found true love. Munaswamy refused to budge. He stated that he would marry no other. They married on 14 July 2004. Munaswamy's parents threw them out and they began to stay with Saroja's mother. Today, they have two beautiful daughters—Akshara Shwety Priya and Gunapriya. One is nine, the other, six. Both are studying, while their mother has started working with Vijay to bring change into the lives of other *matammas*. It was Vijay, who first introduced Saroja to DF and convinced her family to let her go to the training in Ahmedabad. Six months later, in December 2014 Saroja became a DF fellow and for the first time, stepped out of her own world and her own state.

'Though I had never lived the life of a *matamma*, I was always worried about the repercussions of angering the goddess. The DF fellowship changed that. I am no longer scared. I know that no religion sanctions such a practice; no god encourages it. I was rescued by an NGO and now it is my turn to rescue others. With the fellowship, I am learning to conquer my own fears and to motivate others to do the same. Now I stop dedications, support and motivate the rescued matammas,' Saroja explains. Currently, she covers 10 villages in Chittoor district, ensuring no new dedications take place and rehabilitating the women who have already been dedicated.

'When you have been taught something your whole life, stepping out is difficult. You are full of doubts, insecurities, not to mention the societal pressure. I have been through it. Now I help others make the journey. After all, this practice has to stop,' she says with a determined glint in her eyes.

POSTCARD 3: THE MANY SPOUSES OF GODDESS YELLAMMA

Thimmayigunta village, Andhra Pradesh

Renuka inside her hut at Thimmayigunta village, Andhra Pradesh

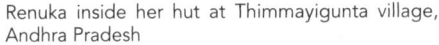

Dear Reader,

Perhaps by now, you too are wondering about the Goddess in whose name so many lives are destroyed. In every region and state, the names and forms of the Divine bridegroom differ. However, in Karnataka, Telangana and the parts of Andhra Pradesh that we visited, most dedications happen in the name of Yellamma or Renuka.

According to legend, the great sage Jamadagni fell in love with a beautiful woman called Renuka. He married her and they had five sons together, the youngest of whom was Parshurama. Every day Renuka would carry food to the forest where the sage was meditating. In order to test his wife, Jamadagni demanded that she bring him water in a pot made out of sand. 'If you are chaste, the sand will automatically turn into a pot in your hands,' he said. So every morning, Renuka would faithfully go to the river bank, make a pot out of sand and carry water for her husband. The sage was extremely pleased with his wife and his life. Then one day, while Renuka was making the sand pot, she saw a pair of lovers frolicking in the water. She admired the Gandharva (male celestial being of great beauty) and her pot broke. The sage saw this through his third eye and in his rage ordered his sons to kill their mother for the sin of coveting another. Parshurama thus set out to kill his mother. A frightened Renuka ran from village to village, asking for shelter but no one wanted to incur Parshurama's wrath. Finally, a tired Renuka reached the Madiga colony. The Madiga decided that they could not deny protection to a woman and so fought Parshurama. They were butchered. Parshurama finally severed his mother's head and took it to his father. A pleased Jamadagni granted his son a boon wherein the clever Parshurama asked for his mother. Jamadagni told him to put his mother's head back on her body and she would come alive. So Parshurama went back to the site of the massacre and put his mother's head on the body of a Madiga woman. (Some versions of the tale maintain this was a mistake, while others say that he did this as his mother's body was long dead). Renuka came back to life. When she saw the dead bodies of the Madiga who had died trying to protect her, she revived them and promised to forever protect them. Thus Renuka, literally meaning a fine grain of sand in Sanskirt, became the patron goddess of the Madiga.[6] While some say that Renuka is just another name for Yellamma, others insist that she is the goddess with Renuka's head and the body of the Matangi.

The most famous temple dedicated to Yellamma is in Saunditti in the Belgaum district of Karnataka, where almost half a million people gather twice a year—in January–February and in October–November—for the Yellamma festival. But the festival is almost five months away when we visit the Goddess Yellamma in her local temple. Vijay Kumar, the Founder Secretary of MESRO and my translator for the day, informs me that there is a Madiga *basti* right next to Reddy Bhawan, where the two-day conference had taken place. 'And every Madiga *basti* will definitely have a temple dedicated to Yellamma. She is one of nine sisters and all of them are revered by my community,' he explains.

This temple is a tiny, albeit clean, one-room structure, that shares a wall with the neighbouring house. Inside, much of the green walls are covered with white bathroom tiles. The floor is made of patterned brown tiles. The space is divided into two parts—a sanctum sanctorum at the back with a decorated statue of the Goddess Yellamma and a space with two idols outside it. Inside the sanctum sanctorum, protected by ornate curtains and adorned in a red dress with gold borders and ornaments, the black stone statue of the goddess presides over offerings of fruits, sweets, coconut and neem leaves. Just outside, there is another idol of a fair-skinned goddess, with four hands, dressed in yellow. This is a new rendition of the Goddess Yellamma in wood. She holds a bowl of *sindoor*, a musical instrument, neem leaves and a lemon. A turbaned male deity, dressed in a white *dhoti* and wielding a severed head in one hand and a whip in another, sits in front of her. 'That's Pothuraju, her brother,' Vijay informs me. Considered to be an avatar of Vishnu, Pothuraju is revered as a fierce warrior who will protect the community.

There are no devadasis or *matammas* who live in this temple. So we travel to Thimmayigunta in Renigunta taluk. In the middle of the Madiga colony stands a temple with concrete walls and a shaded courtyard. Here, the entry is barricaded by iron grills, and we just manage to peep into the dark interiors. Inside a fairly spacious room, sits another adorned idol of the Goddess Yellamma.

'Till a few years back, I lived inside this temple. Of course, back then it wasn't this huge concrete structure with proper walls and a roof.' I turn to see a dusky, young woman in a pink nightgown with a blue *dupatta* draped across her chest. A dab of *sindoor* sits on her forehead and a yellow thread with a coin and six red and black beads hangs around her neck. Meet 24-year-old Renuka, a former *jogini*.

Renuka's story is like that of a girl child in many Dalit households in this part of the country. When she was born, she was unable to suckle. Too poor to visit the hospital, her mother went to the upper caste men in the village for a loan. What they gave her instead was advice. 'Offer the girl to the temple and the goddess will save her life.' And thus the tiny infant was promised to the almighty Yellamma. When she was barely five, Renuka started sweeping the temple premises. Two years later MESRO came to her village. When the organization learnt of the little girl who used to stay at the temple and keep it clean, they sent her off to a hostel. But Renuka's parents kept trying to bring her back. 'Every time someone in the family fell ill, they attributed it to the Goddess' curse and blamed me for it. Then they would bring me back to appease her by resuming my duties. During my holidays too, they would keep telling me how it is my duty to serve the goddess and accept the life of a *matamma*. You see, they hadn't even given me a name,' she recounts sadly in Telugu. Ironically, when MESRO got her admitted into school, she chose a name after the very goddess to whom she was married—Renuka.

Despite MESRO's intervention, Renuka could not lead a normal life. Whenever she would come home for holidays, the other village children would not play with her. Finally, her parents' persuasion wore her down. She dropped out of school in Class 10 and returned to her family. She began to learn dance from a senior *matamma*. Once again MESRO intervened and managed to make her finish Class 10. But just as she turned 15, she finally accepted her fate and the life her family had charted out for her. The formal dedication and initiation rituals were carried out and Renuka became a practising *matamma*. She no longer had a home. She stayed in the temple. Whenever the men wanted her, they would take her to some nearby hut. When their sexual appetites had been sated, they would leave her with food, at times even clothes and a few rupees. 'I was young and had been taught that this was my fate in life. I began to enjoy sex. I thought this is a good life. I am invited to dance at temple festivals and paid for it. Everyone wants me. Other people from our community are treated as untouchables, but upper caste men line up to sleep with me,' she recalls with downcast eyes.

During this time, a man from her community, who had also been dedicated, began to chase the beautiful *matamma*. For three years he wooed her with promises of love and marriage and finally, Renuka too fell in love with him. She left her practice to be with him and gave birth to two daughters in quick succession. Prachi (name changed) is now six years old and Rashmi is five (name changed). Their mother still remains unwed. Soon after she left behind her life as a *matamma*, Renuka realized that like many others of her ilk, she had been fooled. Matayya, who had promised to take care of her, only wanted her body. He abused her, physically and verbally, and refused to acknowledge or support his children. But by then it was too late for her. Renuka had begun to realize that she did not want the life of a devadasi, did not want to be available for any and every man. And because of this she no longer had the temple roof over her head or the food and clothes offered by patrons. Her six siblings—two brothers and four sisters—wanted nothing to do with her. 'This is your fate, your life. Stay away from us and our homes,' they said. Even the parents who had forced her into this life, refused to support her.

'What choice do I have now? I work as an agricultural labourer and during the good months, I barely manage to make ₹5000. When Matayya's family refused to allow me into the house, I worked painstakingly to build a hut in front of their home. It was burnt down. My in-laws (she considers herself married to Matayya) don't want me to stay here. But where will I go with two young girls? Men in the village still proposition me,' Renuka says, misery writ all over her tired face. She has erected a thatch next to her 'husband's' concrete house. Inside it, she lives with her two little girls. 'I need 30 Kg of rice in a month for the children and me. If I had a ration card, I would get it at ₹1 per kg but now I have to buy it at ₹10. The government gave some plots of land to former *matammas*, but not to me. All I got was ₹10,000 in my account. How long would that money last? How do I educate my children? Give them a home?' she asks.

Renuka's children, two bright little girls dressed in green school shirts, run around us as we talk. Her mother-in-law, who is lying down on a charpai (cot) in front of Renuka's hut, eyes us with suspicion but does not utter a word. In fact, that is the other reality of Renuka's life—overwhelming silence. No one speaks to her children and her, not her in-laws, not her parents, not her siblings and definitely not the villagers.

'What about Matayya?'

'He only comes to my hut when he is drunk and wants to have sex. And then he doesn't even wait for the children to go out. If I refuse or plead that the girls are watching, he beats me up,' she says.

Renuka's story alas is not unique. This is the lot of *matammas*, including the seven others in her village. Renukamma, a stout 50-year-old lady with beautiful brown eyes set in a round face, is one of them. Like Renuka, she too is reluctant to talk of her former life—MESRO has ensured that there are no practising devadasis in Thimmayigunta. After much hesitation she describes the *taali* ceremony.

The family of the girl who is to be dedicated has to obtain the consent of their community and shower them with money and *tari*. Most take loans for this. On the day of the dedication, the priest comes with wedding materials. The girl's family reaches the temple where a small drawing with four Matamma idols around it has been made. Garlands of betel leaves are put on the idols and the girl is made to sit in front of the *rangoli*. The priests and the parents of the girl then ask the community, 'Do you have any objection to her dedication?'

'No,' they reply as one.

'She will provide sexual pleasure to one and all. Do you object?'

'No, we need it. Dedicate her.'[7]

After this farce seeking community consent, the ceremony proceeds. The *taali* is tied. Once the girl attains puberty, the date of her initiation is decided in consultation with the village leader and the priest. It is these two men who tie the *taali* on the girl, but the first night is shared by four people, one after the other. As the frightened girl, who is not even informed about what is to transpire sits in a room, the *pinapedda* or the community leader, the peddakappu or village elder, the *pujari* (priest), and the *pedagolla*, a man from the backward castes, take turns to consummate her holy union with the divine. Then they declare her a *matamma*, a village asset to be used by one and all. 'They even encourage the Madiga youth to copulate with the *matammas* so that none of them protest against the practice,' Vijay explains.

But the ordeal of the young girl does not end here. 'For the next seven days, we are sent to neighbouring villages to satisfy the demands of their village elders and community leaders. We do not have the right to say no.' By now Renukamma is openly sobbing, assailed by memories from her own past, crying for the innocence that was brutally murdered the night of her initiation.

'Don't ask me anymore, it's too painful,' she urges, tears in her eyes.

Today Renukamma lives with the man who tied the *taali* around her neck (and around that of many other young girls) in 1996. He never married her, despite MESRO's intervention. But just like Renuka, Renukamma regards him as her husband. She shows us a picture of her husband tying a *taali* around her neck. 'Do you know the extent of people's insensitivity? Often when a man wants to keep a woman, wants something longer than a night, he will repeat the *taali*-tying ceremony. Take off the previous *taali* and tie one on his own as if by removing that piece of thread, he will also remove all memories from the *matamma*'s head. When she is with him, he will stake absolute claim and then when he is tired, he will move on without a backward glance or a thought to the memories he has given her,' says Vijay, shaking his head in disgust.

Perhaps Renukamma is lucky then. Her 'husband' is still with her. Eight years ago, she finally had a daughter with him. Most devadasis in their prime abort children to ensure that their patrons do not run away. That, and because they have no place to house the children or look after them. It's one of those things that no one will tell you openly but everyone knows about. Renukamma and her husband live in a small house on the tiny plot that was allotted to them by the government. Katamma, another *matamma* also got a piece of land and built a house on it. Now, the villagers are harassing her. 'The plot is surrounded on all sides by land belonging to the upper caste. They are saying they want to build a compound wall. How will we enter or exit our house?' she questions as she shows me her house. From Katamma, I learn that while the villagers are only too happy to sleep with the *matammas*—after all, they are manifestations of Yellamma herself—and share her body with men from all castes, they haven't stopped caste-based discrimination. I had already noticed that the Madiga colony was built way outside the village. Even the plots of land given by the government were outside the main village. 'Not only are we not allowed to enter their houses, but if we ask an upper caste family for water, they only give us water from the bathrooms. That is what the Madiga are fit for,' she chuckles ruefully.

POSTCARD 4: GOD'S OWN CHILDREN

Mehboobnagar, Telangana and Tirupati, Andhra Pradesh

Narshima with his *dappu*

Dear Reader,

I no longer have the strength to listen to the story of another devadasi. Each time I think of an innocent 13-year-old being sent to a room to have her body ravaged by four men, men she has grown up calling *chacha* or *dada*, I am filled with anger and revulsion. Each time I imagine the confusion and pain of the little girl as the parents she trusts send her from village to village to flaunt her 'goods' and sate the appetite of different men, my heart breaks a little. Each time I picture the gloating faces of the men who consider it their right to sleep with any and every child, even those that are as young or perhaps younger than their own daughters, I lose a little more of my already diminishing faith in humanity.

And then I see the as-yet-innocent faces of their children. In the conference room in Tirupati I had heard of the practical difficulties that these children face—in admissions, in getting scholarships. But what is their life like? The children of the temple, born to the goddess; treated not as little gods, but as social pariahs. Children, who never have a childhood because they grow up seeing a trail of men using and abusing their mothers. Do they ever laugh? Do they ever dream? And if yes, of what? What do they think about women, about marriage? This postcard, dear readers, is about two Madiga boys born to the temple.

After spending two days at the conference and visiting the *matammas*, I ask Vijay Kumar, my translator and guide, about his interest in the devadasis. Behind his black rimmed plastic glasses, the eyes of this 50-year-old activist dressed in a simple jeans and white half sleeve shirt, fill up. In a barely audible voice he admits, 'I too am from this community.' And then, I hear what it means to be the child of a *matamma*.

Vijay's mother was a *matamma*, but he has no memory of her. She died when he was very young. His sister was also a *matamma*. So he grew up as an orphan, running amok on the streets of Nindra, his village located in Chittoor district. His grandmother, while she was alive, put him in the village school where he studied till Class 7. When she passed away, he dropped out of school and began to work as an agricultural labourer in order to ensure that he had food to eat. One day, a teacher who had taught him in Class 6 saw the bright little boy working in the field and agreed to support him. Thus, he completed Class 8 but was once again forced to drop out and clean tables and dishes at a restaurant. This he continued doing, till another former teacher agreed to support him for another year of schooling. 'I dropped out six times between Classes 7 and 12. Each time I would have to work till I found someone who would support my education. By the time I finished Class 12, I was already 20 years old,' Vijay tells me.

When he was in Class 11, the young boy was filled with aspirations. He worked hard to support himself and dreamt of becoming a doctor. He sat for the medical entrance exam and secured a seat at the Medical College in Sri Venkateshwara University. But he had no money to pay his fees. Once again he was forced to take up a series of jobs. 'From working in limestone quarries to chopping wood and breaking stone, I have done it all. Alongside these, I would offer tuitions. That ensured that I got a meal at the student's house.' All this did not dampen his quest for higher education and through sheer perseverance, Vijay managed to obtain a Master's degree, albeit through a correspondence course.

While in college, Vijay was no different from the other Madiga boys in his pursuits. He drank, had relations with *matammas*, attended the Yellamma festivities in his village. Then one day while he was standing at the bus stop, he saw a beautiful girl. She was a *matamma*. 'I remember that day so distinctly. It was drizzling. Five youths came and started pulling the *matamma* into a rickshaw. She was crying, but no one stepped in to help her. I followed them and asked the guys what they were doing. They simply said that the girl had no right to refuse them as she was a *matamma*. At that moment I realized that I too had been following in their footsteps, treating women as public property,' Vijay recounts. After that day, Vijay carried out a survey on the condition of *matammas* but soon he became involved with the business of living. He started looking for a life partner.

Marriage for the children of a *matamma* is never easy, not even for the boys. People want to know their father's name, family credentials, property details. Vijay had none to offer. So seven times he approached people and seven times he was turned down. Gradually, he collected enough money to purchase a house. During that time Vijay used to work at a coaching centre. He often visited police stations to get support for *matammas* or to stop dedications. During one of his visits, an inspector he had become friends with asked him if he was interested in marriage. He introduced Vijay to Priya, a relative of one of his colleagues. Initially, the family was reluctant but in 1991, the couple was married.

Soon after marriage, Priya began to express her unhappiness over the work that Vijay did. She worried that he might be having relations with the *matammas*. One day she was walking on the road with her friend, sister and sister-in-law. Two guys on the road came and started propositioning. They asked her sister-in-law, who was a *matamma*, about the new *matammas* who accompanied her. 'People assume that all Madiga girls are *matammas*. They started passing lewd comments. I didn't sleep for many nights after the incident. I knew I had to do something,' says Vijay.

In 1995, Vijay started MESRO (Mother's Educational Society for the Rural Orphans). He began going to villages, trying to convince the villagers and devadasis to give up the practice. Finally, Priya was moved by his dedication and began to support his work. In August 1999, they opened a residential school for the children of *matammas*.

Located in Srikalahasti, the school began with 25 children. Getting money was tough, so Vijay hit upon an ingenious solution. Instead of money, he asked for supplies. He got trunks, medicines and money from doctors; vessels, bedsheets and mats from banks; and vegetables and food grains from the shopkeepers. The manager of a local bank used to conduct magic shows. When Vijay approached him, Siddaiah Rajkumar decided to help. He performed magic tricks at five schools and colleges and collected ₹12,000. This became the seed capital for the hostel. Thereafter, his wife put 12–15 collection boxes in different streets across the town. 'She would tell people to put in a fistful of rice into the box, every time they were cooking. This again was very successful,' Vijay tells us with a smile. So for more than a decade, a few children of *matammas* continued to find shelter and education. Thereafter, Vijay decided that he needed to focus on advocacy, on forcing the government to take care of its responsibility. After all, how many children could he support with donations? What would happen to the rest? So in 2012 he closed the hostel.

'About four years ago I heard about the Dalit Foundation at a meeting. A colleague who worked on manual scavenging (lifting of night soil manually) in Tamil Nadu made the introduction. Since then I have felt that I am not alone in my struggles. Not only has DF enabled me to make many connections, they have also provided a space where I can share ideas and experiences. Now, I think nationally,' says Vijay. This is perhaps what prompted him to convince Saroja, a former *matamma*, to take up a DF fellowship and go to Ahmedabad for training.

Today, MESRO, which started with 20 *mandals (talukas)* of Chittoor district, operates in 14 districts of Andhra Pradesh, creating awareness, stopping dedications, arranging marriages of dedicated girls, and securing admissions for promised girls and for the children of devadasis. At the same time, it has started an advocacy campaign to demand government support for those who are trying to leave this life behind. The conference in Tirupati, where Vijay's three smiling daughters had been actively helping their father was a step in this direction. With the support of partners like the Dalit Foundation, Vijay now wants to take up issues at the national level.

Through sheer grit and hard work, Vijay has managed to create a life for himself. He is also ensuring the future of many others. The first *matamma* he rescued was his own sister, but most children continue to be trapped in the course that was set for them the day their mothers were dedicated. 26-year-old Narshima is one of them. He lives in the village of Danwara in Mahabubnagar district of Telangana, the same village as Manneyamma whom I introduced you to in an earlier postcard. A well-built young man with blood shot eyes, curly black hair and the beginnings of a short black beard, Narshima is dressed in a pink shirt and white *pyjamas* when I meet him. Strapped to his torso, with a thick belt that lightly straddles his shoulder is a flat drum—the *dappu*!

I had become so engrossed in the stories that I had encountered, so inspired, angered and moved by them that I had forgotten the reason that had originally brought me to Telangana and the Madiga community—the *dappu*. Known as the *Thappu* in Tamil Nadu, this percussion instrument which can yield 40 different kinds of sounds, is the Madiga's big contribution to society (alongside Bharatnatyam and the art of tanning). I had first heard its rhythmic beats in a 2004 documentary on the Madiga made by Lelle Suresh. So powerful was the music that my limbs had begun to move of their own volition. And I understood why the Madiga with his *dappu* had become an essential part of all 'upper caste' festivities. Yet ironically, neither the instrument nor the artists who bring it to life have received any recognition.

Before we begin chatting, I request Narshima to play the *Dappu*.[8] This he does with two wooden sticks, one thin and long, the other, short and thick. While doing so, he supports the one-sided flat drum with his torso and left arm. Gradually, the *dappu* weaves its spell; its clear sounds reverberate in my veins, my very being. Every beat resonates through me and once again my feet start tapping of their own accord. By the time the music draws to a close, releasing me from its spell, I have been side-tracked.

'Who taught you how to play?' I ask when he keeps his drum aside.

'Nobody. On Holi and other festivals, I saw people playing and learnt from them.'

'Did your parents also play the *dappu*?'

'No, but my grandfather used to make *dappus* and sell them.'

'Can you also make one?'

'Of course, I made this one,' he says with a smile.

Through my interpreter's patient translation, I learn that making a *dappu* can take up to a month, unless the leather is bought from the market. But that is expensive, taking almost ₹1500 to make the instrument. So normally, the *dappu*-makers find the carcass of a cow and take its skin. The Madiga are expert tanners. The hair is removed and the skin cleaned thoroughly. Subsequently, it is alternately dried and wetted. Once the leather is ready, it is cut into the right size and threads are made from the rest. After this it takes 3–4 days for the instrument to be completed. The trick lies in warming the skin just enough. The metal frame is bought from the market. If handled carefully, a *dappu* lasts for 3–5 years. Thereafter, the skin of the drum has to be replaced and the frame is reused.

Ironically, the very profession that earned them the label of untouchables also opened new avenues for the Madiga. As they dealt with carcasses, especially cow skins, the Madiga were treated as 'untouchables' and 'impure'. They cleaned the villages of filth but were themselves treated as filthy. Perhaps, it was in the course of handling leather that someone tried putting it on a metal sheet and discovered the joys it could provide. The Madiga *Dappu* was born. And while the upper caste denounced the Madiga for handling the dead, it did not stop them from enjoying the talent of the *dappu* players. The drums became a pre-requisite at all ceremonies and rituals.

'We play at weddings and funerals, at temple festivals and when children are born,' says Narshima.

'How old were you when you started playing?'

'I started learning when I was nine, but it is only in the last three years that I have begun to get money for my performances. Before that I worked as agricultural labour earning up to

₹250 a day. During the season—playing the *dappu* is a seasonal occupation—I make up to ₹300 per performance.'

'What about school?'

Silence. Then haltingly, the story of this man who fills people's lives with beautiful beats, begins to emerge. Narshima's mother was a *jogini*. He never knew his father. His grandfather also passed away when he was very young. So there was no one to put him in school, guide him, take care of him. The little boy went around bewildered as others in the village mocked him, asked about his father. When he was barely six, he understood he was different from the other children. A stream of men would visit his mother. Few would come back. That is when he realised that unlike the other village children, he did not have a father, one who would come home every day and indulge him. He began to stay away from his mother so that her profession ceased to bother him. He had to fend for himself. School was out of question. He began to learn the *dappu*, do menial jobs and partake of generous amounts of toddy distributed at temple festivals and on other occasions. By the age of 10, he had become a *coolie* (manual labourer). Narshima denies drinking but Manneyamma is quick to take him to task.

'I have seen you grow up. You have been drinking since the age of 10,' she remonstrates and he acquiesces with his head bowed.

Hajamma explains that alcohol addiction is common among the *joginis* and their kids. The women drink to lessen the pain and humiliation. Children are put on *tari* (local liquor) at a young age to keep them from disturbing the patrons. 'I escaped as I grew up in Mumbai. I was eight when I would take my sister's one-year-old daughter to the shop and feed her some *tari*. This would make her sleep through the day and her mother could work in peace. By the time they become teenagers, most children are thus addicted,' she says sadly.

'When we play *dappu* at the festivities, beat the drums all night, especially when someone dies, we are given copious amounts of *tari*. We can't say no. It is considered an insult. So we drink and we play through the long hours ceaselessly,' Narshima adds.

This is why he is not teaching his son the *dappu*. 'He has to study. I don't know what he will become, but I will keep him away from this life, these bad habits.'

Narshima wants to change his own life as well. When a night school started in his village, he attended the three month course. He can now sign his own name, he tells us proudly. But alas, society does not let these children lead normal lives, despite all their attempts. When he was a teenager, Narshima fell in love and married. He had four children, of whom only two survive. Yet even today, nine years after his marriage, his wife continues to abuse him. 'You have so many fathers. I don't feel good being with such a man,' she frequently taunts him.

As Narshima recounts his story, his head is bowed, his voice a soft mumble. That he is ashamed of his life is easy to see. And somewhere, he blames his mother for this—for a lost childhood, for a lifetime of taunts and abuses, for the indignity he is subjected to every single day. So, he has not kept in touch with her, the only parent he knew. He may not beat her up like the children of other *joginis*, but he has little regard for the woman who gave him life. Perhaps because it is a life where he has only known pain. He, the son of the temple!

POSTCARD 5: INNOCENCE LOST

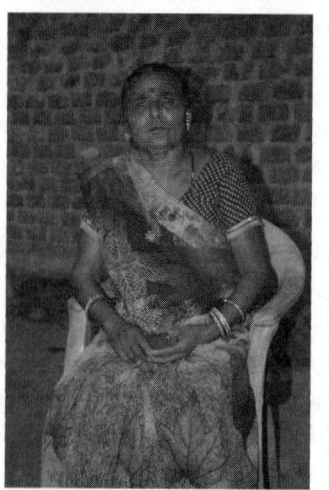
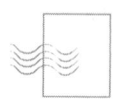

Sukha Karar, Madhya Pradesh

Krishna bai, the former Pradhan of Uncher who started a movement to stop Rai

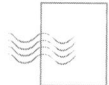

Sukha Karar, Madhya Pradesh

Radha and her family

The Museum of Broken Tea Cups

Dear Reader,

When I started writing this book, I set out to explore stories of hope. Everyone, if and when they could be bothered to engage with the Dalits, spoke about the discrimination they faced or became entangled in the debate about reservations. No one talked about the immense contribution of these communities; their talent, especially in the field of music, dance and theatre. This book, I decided, would be a celebration of the Dalit way of life, or rather of the various people who are Dalits. It would look not at the exploitation they face, but at their food, their lifestyle, their talents, be they in the field of hunting, tanning, taming of animals, playing musical instruments, dancing, storytelling or weaving. Yet, in the last few months, as I moved from one invisible lane to another, I realized how naïve my intent had been. You cannot talk about Dalits and ignore the exploitation that they face. Their connection with pain is almost organic. Behind every art form that they have nurtured, every skill that they have developed, hides a story of untold misery and an enviable ability to make the most of an untenable situation.

Today, we cannot but admire the paintings they have created, albeit anonymously. Yet, look closely and you will notice that the only colours in their palette are their own sweat and blood. For every stroke that goes into the making of that masterpiece that you and I so admire, their brush dips into their own bloodstream. Even as life ebbs out of them, drop by painful drop, the strokes never falter. And when the last drop in their veins has been exhausted, another takes its place, quietly. The brush never stops. As long as people continue to admire it, the painting is never left incomplete.

A week after I heard about the caste-based prostitution that happens behind the veneer of the Rai dance, I find myself on the road to Sanchi with Bharti Sonkar, the DF fellow who has been fighting against caste-based atrocities for almost a decade now. Sanchi of the Great Stupa and the Ashokan pillars built in the

3rd century BC. Sanchi of the Bodh *viharas*, of learning, of enlightenment and history. Sanchi, 46 km from Bhopal in the Raisen district of Madhya Pradesh. Our destination lies just 7 km from this UNESCO World Heritage Site, across the railway crossing—the village of Sukha Karar. When our cab driver realizes where we are heading, his anxiety is palpable.

'Madam, have you been there before?'

'No.'

'It's not a nice place. This is a bad idea.'

'Why?'

'Something is not right there. Don't ask me what. But dusk is gathering, we should turn back,' he advises, even as he maintains that he has never been to the village, only heard of it.

We, Bharti and I, ignore his advice and continue with the journey. There is no *pucca* (paved) road to the village and definitely no road signs. At every fork in the muddy lane, we stop to ask for directions. Many stares come our way. Sukha Karar is a popular destination with car owners; only the passengers who seek the village are seldom women.

There is a huge *maidan* (empty field) outside the village where children—only boys—are playing. In most villages across India, children often stop and stare when a car arrives. Not so here. No child spares us a look. They are used to cars coming and going from the village at all hours of the day and night. The adults are another story. We see a few men on the street. Curiosity is writ large on their faces.

Finally, we stop in an open area. Immediately, a young man—tall, lean, he must have been in his 20s—approaches us. He greets our driver and asks our business, even as his eyes rove over us. He is clearly drunk. We begin to walk away. On a *charpai* (cot) outside a house, we notice a man and finally, a woman. Thanking our stars, we rush towards them. The young man hangs back to quiz our driver, whose anxious gaze we feel even as we approach the strangers.

'We are looking for Krishna Bai. Can you tell us where she lives?' We ask.

'Is she expecting you?' The man, tall and well built, questions us.

'No, but we have come from far to speak to her. I have met her before,' Bharti says.

A phone is whipped out and the man, no more than 40 years old, speaks to Krishna bai.

'She is on her way. You can wait for her here,' he says, clearly curious.

'Thanks, but we will just walk around,' we say, backing away.

'Not a good idea. Stay here,' the woman, dressed in a cream *kurta* with a turquoise *salwar* says, but Bharti and I have already turned around.

As we move inside the village, the drunk young man approaches us once again.

'Do not go in there. It isn't safe,' he warns.

'It's okay. We are only walking around,' I say and hurry away. Our driver comes running.

'Madam, it is evening time. Be careful. Take my number and keep your mobile handy. If you feel any unease or there is any problem, please call me,' he requests anxiously.

We assure him that we would do so and once again walk towards the village, clutching our mobiles firmly. As the drunk man starts to follow, the man who had called Krishna Bai shouts at him to back off. Thankfully, he obeys.

On both sides of the street, there are rows of concrete 7 × 9 sq. ft structures with thatched roofs. A few houses are bigger and even have an additional floor. Shops and vendors with carts are doing brisk business. Groups of men are sitting and chatting outside the tiny shacks selling cigarettes, tea, pan masala and other knick-knacks. We see a young girl, no more than 16 or 17, dressed in capris and a top, walking down the street, hips swaying as she combs her long hair. Outside another house, four men and a woman sit on a cot engaged in deep negotiations.

None of the people seem particularly welcoming, so Bharti and I head to a group of children that surround a vendor selling some savouries. After a few minutes of general chitchat, we ask one of the boys where his home is. He points to a tiny lane that leads away from the centre of the village. We learn that he lives with his *Bua*. At our request, the seven-year-old agrees to take us to his house.

Enroute we encounter several questioning glances but hurry on before someone can stop us. There is something in the air, something unfriendly and mildly threatening, that has us on the edge. Or perhaps it is just our hyperactive imagination reacting to the many warnings that have come our way. As we move farther away from the village centre, our nervousness increases. The mobiles we have been clutching turn out to be useless—there is no signal in this area.

Finally, we arrive at a wooden fence with a door. Our guide runs inside to get his *bua*, while we look around. A small house with concrete walls and a small concrete courtyard sits before us. The roof is thatched. Inside the wooden fence chickens are running around with a few children. A rabbit keeps trying to scurry outside the house, only to be caught by the kids and put back in. Two slightly older girls are also there. Just as we are asking them about their schools, the man and the woman who had called Krishna Bai for us, walk into the compound. Turns out that this is their house!

As plastic chairs are put out for us, they jump into the discussion. The lady we had come to meet is more retiring. Of slight built and dressed in a printed synthetic saree, she emerges from a hut behind the concrete house, nods and heads back in. So we are left with Radha, Iqbal and a bunch of giggling, albeit clearly curious children. Women do not visit their village, especially ones who carry cameras and notepads.

We learn that there are about 200 houses in Sukha Karar, all belonging to the Bedia community. A few decades ago, the village was at a place called Sukha. Radha points in the direction where our car is parked. 'See those fields in the distance, that is where we lived. But there was no access to that place. So we shifted here, some 30–40 years ago. The government gave us a little land here. We still grow wheat and rice in the fields there.'

Radha is a corpulent woman with a wheatish complexion and a round face. In her late 30s, for the last two decades she has been married to Iqbal, the well built man who had called Krishna Bai for us. Iqbal is not a Bedia; his family owns a shop in Vidisha. Perhaps this is why Radha and he are happy to tell us about the lifestyle of the Bedia and the life that Radha left behind.

'We were seven sisters and two brothers in the family. Two of my sisters were married when they were young. The rest of us were sent for Rai, when my father died,' she tells us, sitting on a *charpai* inside the wooden fence. Rai is the traditional dance of the Bedia community. Girls, as young as 13, are sent to perform in upper class houses and functions. They see the older Bednis and learn from them. There is no formal system of training, no *guru* (teacher), no *sishya* (student). They dance at weddings, childbirths, village functions. Thereafter, many sleep with the men. They know that once they start doing Rai, no man will marry them. These days, the young girls get up to ₹1500 for a night, plus all the money that people throw at them. Hence the big, concrete houses.

Radha and her sisters were lucky. All of them found men who loved them and today, they are all married with children. But this is not the fate of most Bednis, as the women from the community who perform the Rai, are called.

'I used to go to perform at someone's house in Vidisha. Iqbal was his relative. We fell in love and eloped. His family did not want him to be with me, so they disowned him. After a while, we came to Sukha. We built a hut here,' she says pointing to where her home stood. 'We had two children, Aman and Khushi. I had given up Rai and this was a source of discomfort for my family, a loss of income. For two years, my mother and brothers kept trying to send me to men's houses to dance. But I refused despite the harassment. Then, 20 years ago, 1100 Bedia couples tied the knot in Sagar. We were one of them,' she adds.

As always, the details of the courtship and marriage are blurred. I tried reconciling dates and events but realized that they were not important. The crux of the matter was that these two people had the courage to fight a system that otherwise condemned Radha to a life of humiliation and perhaps even disease. Perhaps their story wasn't exactly as they had narrated it—some of the jagged edges had been smoothened. Perhaps, Iqbal had vacillated a little—he married Radha well after the kids were born. Perhaps the land promised by the then district collector to the marrying couples had sweetened the pie. Sitting on the outside, it is easy to pass judgement. And yet, to stand up against an entire community is not easy. To give up your family, your home and everything that you have been taught your entire life is not easy. To become a social pariah overnight is not easy.

'Till today people in the village don't speak to us. Being a Muslim, I can't eat in their homes. Many don't even let me enter. We only stay in this village because we don't have to pay rent and electricity bills. Firewood is readily available. I work as a DJ. Radha rears chicken and sells eggs. We make do,' he explains.

This is why when Krishna Bai, another Bedni, started a movement to stop Rai and the prostitution that is carried out in its name, Radha was the first woman to join her.

By now, Krishna Bai, the 55-year-old we had come to meet, has joined us. Dressed in a brown synthetic saree, with a black and white polka dot blouse, a big red *bindi* and a black *mangalsutra* clearly proclaiming her married status, Krishna Bai, in 2009, became the first Bedia sarpanch of Uncher Panchayat. Not just that, she fought and won from an unreserved seat. A blue mobile in hand, this former sarpanch with reddish-brown, henna-dyed hair, is quick to launch into her story.

'My mother was a Rai dancer. We had no land or assets. It was just my mother, my sister and me. My sister died. When I was 10, I was sent for Rai. I went a few times, but when the men surrounded me and began passing comments, I didn't like it. So I quit,' she explains.

Unlike Radha, Krishna managed to get an education. She went to school in Dhania Khedi. The man who had fathered her, never married her mother but Krishna claims he took care of her. In school, a young Krishna fell in love with a Yadav boy. Much later, she had a daughter with him who currently studies in Class 12 in Uncher.

'Just recently, her daughter has got engaged to another man from the Yadav community,' Iqbal tells us.

We learn that the person in whose name Krishna wears a *mangalsutra* did not marry her. He had been married off to another as a kid, way before he met Krishna and fell in love. 'But I visit him and his family. He gave his name to my daughter,' Krishna explains. After school, Krishna decided that Rai has to stop, not because there was something wrong with the dance, but because it had become synonymous with prostitution. For 25 years now she has been trying to wean women and young girls away from the dance. 'About two decades ago, we had a collector who was very supportive. He promised 1.25 acres of land to people who would marry Bednis. 25 couples tied the knot. Alas, most of them never got the land and so some of the men deserted their wives,' she recounts.

Due to her work, Krishnabai came to be respected by one and all. In 2009, she became the sarpanch of Uncher panchayat, which covered the four villages of Sukha Karar, Uncher, Madaa and Anosi. 'Of this only Sukha Karar is a Bedia village. Anosi is a village of Pandits, while the other two have mixed populations. Yet she won,' Iqbal says, pride evident in his voice. And after that Krishna worked hard for her panchayat. She built 51 toilets in Sukha Karar, installed tubewells, got a road sanctioned. Iqbal is confident that had she stood for re-election she would have won. 'But she got carried away by what the Pandits told her,' he exclaims in dismay. As a result, the road though commissioned is yet to be laid, and the tubewells have stopped because the electricity bills were not paid by the panchayat.

'Who is the new sarpanch?'

'A pandit from Anosi, Rama Maharaj.'

'So why did you vote for him?'

Iqbal shrugs. 'Actually we voted for his wife. This seat is now reserved for women.'

'So who is the actual sarpanch?'

'I don't recall her name. Anyway, she is sarpanch in name only. Rama Maharaj is the one who runs the show.'

By now it is pitch dark. Krishnabai has to run to Uncher to fetch her daughter but before she goes, she leaves us with a strange request. 'Currently there are at least 50–60 Rai dancers in this village. If we have to end this practice, the government has to allow us to marry the girls young. You see, these days 14–15-year-olds are sent to do Rai. If we marry these girls off, then they won't be prostituted.'

Appalled, we watch her leave. Iqbal takes off from where she left. 'About 30–35 girls have entered the profession in the last two years alone. Earlier, girls were forced by their families into Rai, now many opt for it. They get good money. Their families are happy. Besides, it is not as if they have much of an alternative. Even if they manage to study, who will give them a job?' Once again. I am reminded of the Lavni dancers, girls who studied up to Class 12, only to get back to dancing because whenever they went looking for a job, they would be propositioned.

'Not that studying is easy.' Radha's statement drags me back to the present.

'Why do you say that?'

'The term *Bedni* is used as a *gaali* (expletive). The children, when they go to school, are teased and harassed by all. Many have changed their surnames, started calling themselves Lavariya to escape the taunts,' Iqbal explains. But it doesn't help. We learn that two young boys from the village dropped out of their school in Sanchi because they were being abused by their classmates. When they complained to the teacher, he too taunted them. For 18-year-old Ram Ratan and 16-year-old Shivam, this was the last straw. Six months back they stopped going to school and started working in the fields.

'18-year-old? Which class were you in?' I ask confused.

Ram Ratan bows his head. Once again Iqbal steps in to explain. 'That is the other problem. They don't promote the kids. Imagine being 18 and being stuck in Class 5 or 7?'

I learn that 18-year-old Ram Ratan was in Class 7, 16-year-old Shivam in Class 6, 15-year-old Khusboo in Class 5. While Ram and Shivam left their studies all together, Khusboo moved to the school in Uncher when the taunts became unbearable. The village of Uncher is just a kilometre away. 'Now we have good teachers. Earlier, at the government school in Sanchi, the teachers would not come. When they did, they never paid any attention to us. Once I found an insect in my food and complained about it. But to no avail,' the bright 15-year-old—she could recite tables of all numbers up to 20, Math being her favourite subject—dressed in a bottle-green salwar suit tells me. Even at this age, she is an obvious beauty and I worry about her.

'What do you want to become when you grow up?'

She simply gives me a shy smile. When I put this question to Radha's children—Aman who is in Class 9 and Khushi in Class 10 at a private school in Sanchi—I once again get no answer. After chatting with them for a few more minutes I realize that it is not shyness which is keeping the children from answering. They have just not thought about it. Unlike us in the cities, who grow up with a new ambition every year, these children only aspire to get away from the deprivation and degradation they have seen in their short lives; education seems to be their one-way ticket out of the morass of their lives. That itself represents a big, bold step to many. Beyond that, they are yet to explore.

We say our goodbyes to the children and get up to walk into the village. Radha and Iqbal stop us. 'Please don't go there. It is dangerous. By now everyone would be drunk and the pimps will be prowling with customers in tow,' they inform us.

Intrigued, I ask them how the system works. 'Are the women taken to brothels or do they have separate rooms in the village itself?'

'Oh, there are no separate rooms. Everything happens in the house,' Radha says.

'The family does not object? Throw them out?'

'Why will the families throw them out? They bring in hard cash. No, they stay at home and being the earning members, they have full control over the household, at least till the time they hit 35 and are unable to find customers. Then they chase the pimps and are willing to work for as little as ₹50 or 100.'

'But how do the men know where to go? I mean not all households here engage in this profession, do they?'

'Well, most houses have a girl in this *dhanda* (trade). People know of this village through word of mouth and through the Rai performances. Throughout the day and night, you see cars arriving and leaving. When customers come, the *dalals* (pimps) accost them, like the man who stopped you when you got out of your car. These are either the relatives of the Bednis or men from outside who had initially come to the village as labourers. For a bottle of alcohol and ₹50–100, they take customers to the houses of the Bednis,' Iqbal explains. Sometimes, the men come and take the women away for the night.

'What about the Rai dances?'

'Earlier they were restricted to the houses of the upper caste men. But now increasingly, it is the Dalit households who call the girls. And with demand for Rai going down, they agree. Though they don't eat or drink in any Scheduled Caste household. They demand food grains instead.'

Bharti notes that times are indeed changing. She recalls an incident a few years back when a teacher from the Dalit community had tried to arrange a Rai performance at his place. 'The upper caste men told the Rai dancers that if they went to his household, they would be considered spoiled goods and would not receive any patronage from their community. So the dancers never turned up,' she recalls.

'And what about the children?'

'Every household has 5–6 children and they grow up seeing all this. This is perhaps why when they grow up, the girls don't protest against this lifestyle. This is all they know.'

Besides most, I learn, are too drunk to care. Here too, children start drinking very young. When they are ill, when they cry, alcohol is pushed down their throats to make them sleep.

'Shopkeepers from the town come here and go house to house, selling liquor. The women drink to hide the pain—because many men are abusive; the men, to while away the time. This is why we don't let our children step out of the house. Next year, we will put them in a hostel in Sanchi. While they are here, I am always scared,' Radha confesses.

And so, we find ourselves bundled into our car and speeding away from Sukha Karar. Just like Iqbal and Radha, our driver is not taking any chances.

POSTCARD 6: FATHER'S NAME? PAISA

Pathariya, Madhya Pradesh

Umedi Bai

Pathariya, Madhya Pradesh

Satya Shodhan Ashram in Patharia, Madhya Pradesh

The Sacred Feminine

Dear Reader,[9]

In the early 1980s, a disciple of Acharya Vinoba Bhave, from Dehradun embarked on a *padyatra* (walk) from Delhi to Bhopal with the Bhoodan movement. At the gathering in Bhopal, Champa Ben, a gentle Gandhian in her late thirties, met a woman from Pathariya village who told her about the plight of women from the Bedia community. Champa Ben promised to visit their village soon.

True to her word, a few months later she visited the village of Pathariya located in Sagar district of Madhya Pradesh. Here, she went from house to house speaking to the women and understanding their condition. Appalled by the caste-based prostitution, wherein girls as young as 12–13 years were sold off to the highest bidder, she began a lifelong crusade to bring them succour. In 1984, the foundation of the Satya Shodhan Ashram was laid in a 2.5-acre plot of land donated by the villagers. This Ashram soon became the place where young boys and girls from the community would receive shelter and more importantly, education. They would move away from homes where sex work was a way of life. The Ashram became their passport to the outside world, to employment and success.

Today, 31 years later, it is in this Ashram that I stand, under the shade of an old tree. Champa Ben is no more. She passed away on 21 January 2011 at the age of 76 and was cremated in the very village that had become her *Karambhoomi* (place of work).

In the second week of June, the sun is merciless and the Ashram is closed for summer vacations. The campus, normally abuzz with the mischievous laughs and screams of over 100 young boys and girls, is enjoying a quiet two-month siesta. Located just outside the village, the Ashram stands opposite a tiny temple. For an outsider, it is difficult to say, which predates the other. On one side are the series of rooms where Classes 4 to 8 are held. The benches and chairs lie neatly stacked against the bare walls of the classroom. On the other side is a tiny garage with a car, the kitchen, bathrooms, storage room and the dormitory for the boys. In the centre of the campus is a huge tree, the one under which I presently stand. In front of it, separated by a shaded courtyard stands the prayer room, the office and the spare rooms where Classes 1 to 3 are held. On the wall, just outside the office is a plaque that commemorates the date on which the foundation stone for the Ashram was laid by Nirmala Deshpande, another renowned Gandhian. Behind this is the hall where 50 female students stay.

Bharti and I sit on a bench inside the shaded courtyard as we wait for the *chowkidar* (gatekeeper) to call some Ashram functionaries. Samrat, Bharti's four-and-half-year-old daughter, who has travelled the 200 km from Bhopal with us, gets busy exploring the Ashram. Soon, two elderly men join us. Mehtab Singh, the *sachiv* (secretary) of Shakti Shodhan Ashram is a 65-year-old man who has studied till Class 8. At that time, it was a huge achievement because children from his community did not generally make it to school. 'I was with Didi since the day she entered our village. At that time, I was the ward member from Bhainsa panchayat. Even before Didi came to Pathariya, we had been raising our voice against the prostitution,' he says. His companion, Ram Narayan is the teacher and the *Lipik* (government clerk) at the Ashram. A Bedia from Gondia village of Banda tehsil, he has been with the Ashram since 1989.

Together, they recount the story of the Ashram and its courageous founder.

'When Didi came here, untouchability was rampant. The Pandits kept different glasses for us. Such was the level of discrimination that when an upper caste man visited a Bedni, he brought his own food and drew water from the well for his own use. He would not touch stuff made by her.' At that time, Rai was only performed in upper caste households. Dalits didn't have money to call the dancers home. They were also afraid. Champa Ben took out a *padyatra* (march) in Banda and Rahatgarh blocks of Sagar district against the scourge of untouchability. People would call her names, attack her, but she would just smile and ask, 'Did their foul words leave a wound? They just bounced off me. See, I am still unhurt and unfazed.' The men told us how even when Didi was shot, she did not give up her crusade.

'I remember that day so vividly. The upper caste people were angry as she had successfully made many girls give up Rai. We were coming back from Sagar and suspected trouble. So we suggested an alternate route but Didi refused saying everyone has to die some day. Nonetheless we forced her and changed course. Still, someone fired at her. As soon as news of the attack reached the village, a mob began chasing the attackers. They went and hid in a neighbouring village but the people found them and handed them over to the police. At their trial, the judge asked Didi to give a verdict. She simply said that the attackers were keeping an underage girl in the village. She requested that the girl be sent to the *Nari Niketan* (women's shelter) and the men freed,' recalls Singh.

It was these gestures as well as her compassion that won the hearts of the villagers and Champa Ben became a familiar name in every Bedia household. The Ashram functionaries insist that thanks to Didi's efforts, there is no untouchability in their area now, though the practice is still widespread across Bundelkhand.

'We have four teachers, two *adhishikshaks* (assistant teachers), four cooks, two chowkidaars (guards), one *chapraasi* (peon) and five *karyakartas* (social workers) at the Ashram. Approximately 50 boys and 50 girls study in Classes 1 to 8 here. Almost 60 per cent are from Pathariya. The rest are Bedia children who come from various districts. Today this village, which at one time did not educate its children, tops the Rahatgarh block on education indices.'

The duo informs us that almost 20–25 kids from the village are now in government service. 'Unfortunately, once they step out, they want nothing to do with their earlier lives. They dissociate themselves from the village, their community and consequently, from the Ashram itself,' Singh laments.

This is perhaps why the Ashram has been unable to attract donations from its alumni and add Classes 9–12. The original buildings were made with donations. Now the Ashram runs with money that they receive from government schemes, especially the Jabali Yojana, and from donations, mostly foreign. They also grow crops in two acres of land—this they either consume internally or sell.

The Jabali Yojana[10] was initiated by the Government of Madhya Pradesh in 1992 to rehabilitate the girls from the Bedia, Banchara, Sansi, Kanjar and Bedia Nut communities. It was a direct result of a petition filed by 65-year-old Ram Sanehi from Morena. Sanehi, also a Bedia, spent his life fighting against the practice of caste-based prostitution. He rescued over a thousand girls and finally filed a petition in the MP High Court. The Court ruled in his favour and the government responded with the Jabali Yojana. This led Sanehi to establish the Abhyuday Ashram, a residential primary and middle school in Morena. Like Champa Ben, Sanehi is a household name in these areas.

'But adding the other classes is important. You see, most children, especially girls, drop out of school after they leave here. One, they have to travel to go to school and two, in outside schools they face widespread discrimination. Given that this is the age at which they are most vulnerable, it is imperative that they be kept in schools and hostels,' Narayan explains.

'But hasn't the practice ended here?' I ask.

'After Didi came here, for 14 years, there was no Rai and no prostitution. Bit by bit, she won everyone over. The girls also began to resist when they saw their friends studying. It was a movement. Girls began to get married. But their families had no way of sustaining themselves. The women who left the profession also had nothing to do. There is no occupation here and most didn't have land. The government did nothing to help. Didi helped some of them learn alternate occupations. They started weaving, making pickles, papad, *diya* (oil lamps), mats. But there were no buyers,' Singh says.

So gradually, between 1995 and 2000, the women went back to prostitution. Girls once again began to do Rai. 'Then the government started calling Rai dancers to their annual festival and giving them money. That became an added attraction,' the elders complain. Today, according to Ashram officials, almost 70 of the 100 families in the village do Rai. About 10 per cent of the girls have been taken to red light areas in other cities.

In Pathariya, the business was carried out differently than at Sukha Karar. Men would come and take the girls, usually two at a time, for dance programmes. Each village had their own groups of singers and musicians. The girls would perform with them through the night and receive up to ₹5000 for one such programme. Thereafter the men would 'keep' the Bednis that they liked. When they tired of the girl, they would leave them and the Bedni would look for a new protector. Earlier some men would look after the children born to the Bednis but things are changing now. Long-term patrons are becoming rare. Increasingly customers looking for a 'quickie' are finding their way into the village.

'You know during our grandfather's time if you asked a child his father's name, they would say Paisa. The practice was so deeply entrenched. There was no shame associated with it. With the Ashram here, at least that has changed. These days no one wants to admit that they do Rai,' Narayan says.

But is it necessary to ban the dance to rescue the Bedni? I wonder.

Narayan and Singh both say no. 'Don't ban it. But promote it as an art form done on the stage. Currently, that is not the case. These women have to deal with lewd comments, groping and a lot more. See the video of a Rai programme and you will understand.'

By now, a few more Ashram functionaries have joined the group. This set of people claim that there is no Rai and no prostitution in Pathariya. A verbal tussle ensues. Singh and Narayan are livid that the Ashram functionaries are covering up the very practice that Didi fought against her entire life. As matters escalate, we decide to leave. How would Didi have felt to see her successors, men she had trusted to carry forward her crusade, squabbling?

I am truly curious about Rai, the dance form which seems to be blamed for the life of abuse, humiliation and exploitation thrust upon little girls by their own families. Dance has always been about sensuality, about emotion, and yet here was a dance that is seen not as a form of expression but as a means of soliciting—even by the community that performs it.

I decide to seek out some traditional dancers in the village to learn more about this dance form and its genesis. Both Iqbal and the Ashram functionaries had told me what they believed to be the history of prostitution in the community. But they knew little about the actual dance form. According to them the Bedia were a nomadic tribe. They used to move from place to place singing and dancing. When they came to Bundelkhand, the local landlords gave them land to settle. Their girls would go and perform in the houses of the landlords. If the landlord liked a girl, he would simply keep her and maintain sexual relations with her. Thereafter, no one would marry the girl and she would be forced into a life of prostitution once the landlord turned her away. Gradually this system became more institutionalized and families began to pledge at least one girl child to this profession.

As we enter the village, we are greeted with hostile stares. Having been forewarned by the Ashram functionaries, we are not disconcerted. We simply look for a woman who could perhaps guide us. Most houses are concrete structures. They are also bigger than what I have seen in Dalit *bastis* in general. From a few, we hear the sounds of raucous music. Once again, we find a little boy and urge him to take us to his home. We explain our quest to his mother. 'In my house, everyone is in service. We don't do Rai. You can ask anyone in the village and they will corroborate this. Most households here have women who do Rai. They are however very uncomfortable when strangers approach them and quiz them about customers,' she tells us.

'But we are not looking at the sex work dimension. I only want to meet some elderly lady who can perhaps tell me a little bit about the dance itself,' I explain. This time, after a quick consultation with her husband, the lady instructs her son to take us to meet a few people. 'Don't tell them we sent you though. They won't like it. You understand?' she cautions.

The first house we visit is locked. Inside the second, a woman in her 30s meets us. As soon as she hears our request, she pleads ignorance. 'I know nothing about Rai. Who sent you here?' she queries with narrowed eyes. We tell her that we have been going door to door in the village. Once again, I repeat that I am only interested in learning about the dance form but she is reluctant to talk. Bharti and I try to persuade her and gradually she answers some of our questions. She tells us that traditionally Rai was performed mostly at Holi and as a *Badhai* dance (congratulatory dance) when a child was born. Every village has a troupe of local musicians and it is to their music that the girls dance. The men sing Suvaang, Dadra and Phaag and play the *nagaria*, the *dholakia*, the *mridung*, the *jhoola* and the *tare*. For every performance the dancers get approximately ₹5000. They wear bright, jazzy *lehenga cholis* and cover their faces with a *dupatta*. Underneath their *lehengas* they wear slacks and on their feet are *ghungroos* that weigh up to 1.5 kg. The dance involves a lot of whirling, she tells us.

Suddenly she realizes that she has spoken more than she should. Once again she informs us that she really has no idea about the dance and shows us the door. As we walk around, looking for someone to enlighten us, a man in his 30s walks out of his house.

'What have you come here for?' he asks abrasively.

'I am looking for traditional Rai dancers. I am researching the history of the dance form.'

'We all know about people like you. You will go out and say that the Bedia make their women have sex with strangers. Go away. No one will speak to you.'

By now, a few people have gathered around us. None of the glances are friendly.

Once again, I try and explain that I am only interested in the Rai as an art form. I begin a discussion of different dance forms, how they began and what they mean. Gradually, the hostility abates.

'Madam, you are mistaken. Rai is not like these other dances that you talked about. It is hardly even a dance and definitely not an art form. No one teaches it. Women just learn to do it on their own. And these days, they all dance to Bollywood music. People don't even remember the traditional songs. No one here will be able to help you,' the youth who had initially tried to shoo us away offers sympathetically.

Just then another young man walks up to us. 'I once heard that when Luv and Kush were born, Sitaji brought women from Kareela village to dance. Their dance is called Rai,' he says. The others simply shrug. 'Maybe. I have never heard anyone talk about the origin of the dance. Anyway, these days the children are all studying and taking up jobs. No one does Rai any longer.' Finally, after much consultation a name emerges, Umedi Bai. The crowd tells us that she is one of the oldest Rai dancers from the village. If anyone would know about the history of the dance, it would be her. With much hope we trudge down to Umedi Bai's house, which is right next to the Ashram.

It is a double storey house and we walk up a steep flight of stairs to get to the first floor, where Umedi Bai, her daughter and granddaughters are all having their lunch. There has been a bereavement in the family, we learn, and so the grandchildren, both of whom are married and stay in Morena, are visiting. Umedi's daughter is unwell and while Umedi eats in another room, we speak to her grandchildren. Both women seem to be in their 30s. They tell us that their grandmother was a Rai dancer, but neither their mother nor they ever entered the profession. In fact, just like them, their mother also married. They tell us that Rai takes place in this village, but no one will openly admit to it.

By now Umedi has finished her lunch. She doesn't remember her age but is able to rattle off the birthdays of all her relatives. Her grandchildren speculate that she must at least be 70 years old. She denies doing Rai. She tells us that she ran away at the age of 10 to escape the dance and everything it entailed. She found herself in a Rajput village where she fell in love with a man and married him. Her granddaughters look surprised. 'You were married?'

'Of course, I was. And I also studied on my own by watching other people read. I know more than the people who have done MA today. I was the woman who opposed Rai in our village. I got many girls married way before Champa Ben arrived,' she says in a wobbly voice. By now, I know that I will learn nothing more about the Rai here. I have no way of knowing whether Umedi Bai, sitting on a beautiful carpet she has made from old plastic bags, is narrating her true story or making it up to earn the admiration of her grandchildren. The facts do not seem to tally with what the villagers and her own grandchildren have said. Many discrepancies crop up in the narrative—for instance, she says that she never did Rai, but also adds that when an ascetic came to their village, she was so inspired that she burnt her Rai dress. But I let it slide. After a lifetime of struggle, is one not entitled to rewrite one's life story, if only on paper?

At the hotel, I follow Narayan's suggestion and google Rai. The YouTube videos and recordings that come up make me understand what the Ashram functionaries were trying to say. Mayhap, at one time Rai was a sensuous dance form performed at specific occasions. But today, Rai performances are little more than a series of bust and navel shaking moves to provocative songs, performed in the midst of raucous males. Somewhere along the way the art got buried under the weight of exploitative patriarchal systems. In Madhya Pradesh, I went looking for a dance. What I found instead was the story of the dancers.

POSTCARD 7: BIRTHDAYS? THEY ARE ONLY FOR SCHOOL RECORDS!

Tirupati, Andhra Pradesh

29-year-old Manjula Telegade

Dear Reader,

It's been an interesting journey, travelling with you. These last few months have been like no other. Every person I have met, every story I have heard has somehow changed me. I have met enough heroes to never lose faith in humanity; seen enough villainy to never completely believe in it. Encountered enough courage to face a million lifetimes; experienced enough distress to dread every single one of them.

Each postcard in this book has taken something out of me; it has given me a lot more. And yet, there is one story that moved me like no other.

The Sacred Feminine

I have often asked myself what was it about the bespectacled 29-year-old from a small village in northern Karnataka that up-ended my world. What was it about her story that made it extraordinary even among all the other extraordinary stories I had heard. Her circumstances have been no more appalling, her life no more distressing, her valour no more pronounced than the others I encountered. And yet, whenever I think of the Museum it is with this story that I end; with this story that I begin.

I met Manjula Telegade at a gathering comprised mostly of unsung heroes—the National Conference on the Eradication of the Devadasi System—in the pious temple town of Tirupati. She was in the same crowded 12 × 18 room as Vijay, Saroja, Bharti and many others whose stories I could neither hear nor tell. And she clearly stood out from the rest. Manjula was just like any other young professional that you encounter in the conference room of the metros. Smart, confident, dressed in a black and white *salwar kameez* with a small nose ring. Articulate and multi-lingual—she was fluent in English, Hindi, Telugu and Kannada with a working knowledge of Tamil and Marathi. In a room where there were two marked groups of people—the sari-clad devadasis with prominently displayed *Kumkum bindis*, *sindoor* and a wreath of mogra in their hair, and the s*alwar-kameez* and shirt-pant-clad activists and reporters who espoused their cause—her place was clear.

I didn't pay any attention to her—she was after all, just like me, minus the flair for languages. And then she spoke, in crisp, clear sentences, not a catch in her voice. 'I fell ill when I was young. That was when I was promised to the Goddess Yellamma, just like my mother and my aunts.' My world was upended. I realized that I had once again fallen into the trap of stereotypes. I was judging books by their covers, shelving them by the kind of binding they came in. Manjula was nothing like me. Or rather I was nothing like Manjula. I had neither her courage nor her tenacity.

And so dear reader, this is the one story that I will not write as a postcard. Instead I will let Manjula, the girl who caught me, red-handed and even more red-faced, in my act of unwittingly boxing people into Styrofoam cases, do the talking. This is her story in her own words:

My mother's family lived in Sanganatti village of the Mudhol *taluka* in the district of Bagalkote. My *nana* and *nani* had nine children—six boys and three girls. All three girls were made into devadasis and sent to brothels in Pune. The system is pretty well developed. One or two years after a devadasi attains puberty, the pimps come to the village and offer good money to take her to the city. Parents invariably agree—the income is better. Of course, by the time they leave for the brothels, these teenage girls have generally become mothers. The children are left behind in the village with grandparents and the girls send money for their upkeep.

My mother was the middle girl child. She was barely 13 years old when my elder sister was born. She didn't survive. Within a year I was born, followed soon after by my younger sister.

Date, you ask? We don't record birth dates. But yes, I did need one when I went to school. Officially I was born on 8 June 1986. My *nana* died soon after I was born. My mother went to the city to join her sisters. At home, it was just *nani* and five of us children. Me, my sister, my *Badi Ma*'s (mother's elder sister) son and my *Choti Ma*'s (mother's younger sister) two children. I remember, when Sheela, my *Choti Ma*'s daughter who was older than me, turned six, she was put into school. But she refused to go. So I would go along with her. I was just four. They didn't admit me, but nonetheless I started to learn alongside. Then when I was five or maybe six, my mother returned to the village. *Nani* was getting on in years and unable to manage five kids on her own.

In our village, the government gave some land to the poor families. We were allotted five acres. But this was unacceptable to the Lingayats and the Brahmins as we were devadasis. In our village, when there is a wedding in an upper caste household, a Madiga has to clean the utensils, sweep the floor and participate in many derogatory rituals. If it is a son's wedding, we have to make a pair of chappals for him. They say it is a gift, but funny how we do not even have the right to choose what we gift. The villagers were afraid that once we had our own land, we would not work for them. And why should we? My uncles were already beginning to say no. They bought 10 buffaloes and we started thinking of tilling our own land. But the villagers intervened. They did not let us keep the land. My *Badi Ma* took the case to court. Both she and my *Choti Ma* would send money to fight the court case. But how much do you earn in a brothel? It wasn't enough. We didn't give up. We took loans. Before we knew it, we had a debt of three lakh rupees on our heads. Then one day my uncle lost the land deed and the court papers. It was all over. All the six brothers decided that the sisters could pay off the loans and went away. We stayed on the land—my cousins, my *nani*, my mother and me, but the villagers constantly threatened us. My *nani* decided it was better to leave the land than to die.

One day we moved to the nearby town of Mahalingapur. We sold the buffaloes and rented a house. Some time later, we took another loan of ₹50,000 and built a small one-room house in the Dalit colony. Somewhere along the way, my *Choti Ma* stopped sending money. She had her own expenses to meet. Everything my *Badi Ma* sent went towards repaying the interest on the loans.

When we were in the village, my mother was with a Lingayat man. Normally, when a girl is made into a devadasi, an upper caste man negotiates with her family for exclusive rights. He keeps her for a year or so, till the kids are born. Then he moves on. But this man, whom I considered my father, was always there, at least till I was in Class 7. He even visited us in town. But the ₹200–300 he gave my mother every week was not sufficient to run the household. So my mother started bringing customers home. This led to a fight between them. My mother told him, 'I can't just rely on you. I have to raise my kids, pay off the loan. I am a devadasi. This is my fate.' After that, he stopped coming.

In the colony, some people used to give tuitions at ₹10 a month. I started going there. During the holidays, we used to visit our aunts at the brothel house. I didn't understand the place, didn't like going there but my cousins used to tell me that we would get good food. So I went. I used to be so full of questions. Why do the girls get ready at night? Who are these people who visit the brothel? Why do they come if they are married? What happens inside the rooms? I would keep badgering my *Badi Ma* with questions. One time, she got so angry that she hit me. Gradually, customers at the brothel house started noticing us. They began asking *Badi Ma* to send us to them. That year, *Badi Ma* decided that we would no longer visit her. Instead, she and *Choti Ma* would come to the village to see us.

I remember, during my last vacation at the brothel house, I noticed a girl applying lipstick. I was in Class 7 then. My discussions with my tuition teachers had emboldened me. So I asked her, 'Who do you think you are? You apply lipstick and stand like a heroine. Aren't you ashamed of yourself, of what you do?' The girl calmly turned around and told me that I would do the same when I grew up. I was shocked. 'What are you saying? Why? I will never do this. I don't like the people who come here. I don't like what you do.' Again she told me that irrespective of my likes and feelings, I would do it too.

I came home and started questioning my *Ma*; telling her that I wanted to study. You see, till then I had no idea that my family was planning to dedicate me. In the devadasi system, the girl who is to be dedicated is pampered till the *taali* ceremony. I too was pampered, my every whim pandered to. I always thought it was out of love. Among the devadasis, there is a ritual. During Muharram, a band is tied on the hand of a male child or a girl child promised to the goddess and they are sent out as *fakirs* (beggars). I was in Class 7 when I was sent out as a *fakir*. I did not understand what was happening. My family told me that this was for my own good. That I was unwell and this ritual would help. I believed them. But that day there was a showdown at home. My *nani* told me that as a child, when I was unwell, the family had sought the blessings of Goddess Renuka (Yellamma) and had promised to dedicate me. 'Besides, your mother's generation is almost over (over professionally as most devadasis stop earning after the first couple of decades). Who will look after your mother?' she asked. My mother was silent. I kept pleading with my *nani* to not do this. 'I will die the day you make me a devadasi. I will commit suicide.' That scared her but she did not relent. At that time there was a man who visited my mother. He would often sit and talk to us as well. I called him uncle. He spoke up on my behalf. He reasoned with *nani* that times have changed. What would she gain out of forcing me into this profession if I committed suicide? But *nani* was simply looking out for herself and her daughters. 'If we let her study, who will look after us? She will marry and go away. What about us? Will her mother beg for food?' That day I made a promise. 'I won't marry. I will study and take a job. I will run the family, look after all of you. Just don't make me a devadasi.' Finally, *nani* agreed.

So I started studying. After Class 10, I also took up a part-time job as a receptionist at a nearby hospital. From 7–11 am I would attend classes and then from noon to 10 pm, I would work at the hospital. I made ₹700 a month. My mother used to get ₹50 from a customer and ₹300, if he spent the entire night. So, my job helped. But that wasn't the only reason I took it up. Fact was, I didn't like staying at home. We had a tiny room with a side entrance where my mother did her business. Us children were kept in a small, matchbox-sized space next to it. The walls were so thin that we could hear everything. I used to put cotton in my ears to study, to block out the sounds. There was no ventilation as the main door was kept locked at all times. My mother didn't want any of her customers propositioning or even noticing the children. The job provided an escape along with much needed cash.

You know I wanted to become a doctor. But there was no government school in our area and the admission fee for Science at a private school was ₹5000. We had stopped drinking tea in the evening, because there was money only for one thing—dinner or tea. Yet despite saving meticulously, I only had ₹2000. And in any case, I may have required tuitions for Science. Where was the time and money for that? So I opted for the Arts. When I was in Class 12, my cousin Sheela got married. She had a daughter but her husband was abusive. He burnt her with cigarette butts and accused her of not being 'chaste'. He would taunt her saying that you are the daughter of a devadasi. Who knows where all you have been? What all you have done? One day she gave up and committed suicide. Her mother, my *Choti Ma*, went into depression. Right about this time she also found out that she had HIV. She refused to take medication and within a year, she too passed away. Then *nani* died of a heart attack. I was in the second year, of my BA at the village college. In two years, the environment at home changed completely. *Badi Ma* also came back.

In my final year, Shri Gautam Gram Kalyan Kendra, an NGO that provided tuitions to the children of devadasis contacted me. They had heard that I taught children for ₹30 per month and offered me a job at ₹1000. This was the turning point in my life. As I worked with the organization, I understood the extent of the discrimination we faced. I realized that I had to do something to change the system that had ruined my family. Initially I had thought of pursuing a BEd (Bachelor of Education) degree to become a teacher, but again I didn't have any money for it. Now I started to see other possibilities. The NGO asked me if I would be interested in pursuing a degree in MSW instead. Till then I didn't even know that such a degree existed. My world was so limited. I liked what I heard and appeared for the Tumkur University Government College entrance test. I secured the fifth rank but unfortunately, they just had one seat for students from other universities. When the Head of the Department called me for an interview and asked me why I wanted to pursue this degree, I told her my story. I explained to her how I needed to make a difference. She told me that everyone came to the college for a degree, for a job, but I had come for a cause. So she would help me. She put me in touch with her friend at Udipi College in the University of Mangalore. When they heard my story, they even waived my fee. But I needed money to get there and to live, to eat. Once again, the NGO stepped in. For two years I did sundry projects for them and paid my expenses. At that time, I barely slept for two hours a night. I had come from Kannada medium and here the course was in English. In the end, all those sleepless nights were worth it. I graduated with a first class and during campus interviews got recruited by Prajwalla, the Hyderabad-based organization run by Sunita Krishnan. I worked as a counsellor at their shelter for a year before returning home. I wanted to work in my village for my community. So I took up a NIMHANS project on child psychology and in 2013, I applied to the Dalit Foundation for a Fellowship. That was the second turning point in my life. DF sent me to Madurai, Orissa, Delhi, Pune, Gujarat, Mumbai, among other places. I travelled across the country, I met different people and I became stronger. When my fellowship ended in September 2014, I joined Samvada, a Bangalore-based organization that works with the youth.

Today I work there as a youth mentor and earn ₹25,000 a month. I live alone but I love my work. I have also been able to support my family. My mom and aunt have left sex work. They still follow some of the devadasi rituals like fasting on festivals, breaking bangles and visiting the Yellama temple. Some things are hard to change but I did get my younger sister married. She has an adorable son. Both my brothers are also married. I still have to pay a portion of the loan off but I am confident I will do that soon. And then, I have just one dream. To become a policy-maker and ensure that this dreadful system, the one that destroyed my family, that took away so much from me, is abolished forever. That no more innocent lives are wrecked.

By the end of her story, Manjula's eyes are full, as is her voice. Yet, just like her neither bows. The tears do not flow, the lips quiver but hold firm. Nary a sob escapes them. I don't have the courage to look at her and yet I can't stop looking at her. This young girl, who has gone through so much in life, who has had the courage to not just break the tea cup that had threatened to relegate her to a lifetime of misery, disease and exploitation, but to also recount her story to me, a complete stranger. Most people in her position would have tried to deny their past, or at least to not talk about it. After all, it is painful. 'Oh I was no different. I used to be so afraid. You see the minute people find out that you are the daughter of a devadasi they think you are available. When I started Class 11, someone found out about my mother and propositioned me. After that day I never went out with my mother. I did not want to be seen with her. A few years back, my college selected me as the best alumnus. That day, for the first time, in my speech, I narrated my story. My former classmates and teachers were shocked. But now I am stronger. I take my mother everywhere. I am not ashamed to tell my story. And I don't care what people think.'

'You spoke of your siblings getting married. Do you want to get married?' I ask.

'Of course.'

'Then why don't you?'

This time her eyes are sad. 'First, it was the promise I had given my *nani*. Now I know that I can get married and still look after my family, but who will marry me? After all, I am the daughter of a devadasi. And remember what happened to my older sister. At times, I am so scared. '

'How did you learn such good Hindi?'

'Now that's a story,' she replies, a twinkle finding its way into her still moist eyes. 'I was in Class 8. My teacher asked me to read

The Sacred Feminine

a poem in Hindi. I couldn't. He started insulting me. Who sends people like you to school? He shouted. So I decided to show him. I went home and studied. There was no money for tuitions or classes. But I started watching Hindi serials, movies, songs. Everything. They became my tutors. I learnt Bharatnatyam the same way—through TV, and now, with the internet. And you know what, in Class 12, I topped in my school in Hindi! I owe it to the serials, but let me tell you a secret, I hate them. I have watched more than my fill and I think my Hindi doesn't need much brushing up now. Don't you agree?' She laughs.

'Definitely. I took you for a native Hindi speaker. So you like dancing. What else?'

'Oh yes, dancing is fun. I just choreographed a dance on *Mann ke Manjeere* for the youth group that comes to our centre. I also enjoyed sports at one time,' she says, her voice turning wistful. 'It was our Sports Day. I was playing long putt and won the first prize. My teacher was writing my name on the certificate. Suddenly he turned, and in front of everyone, asked me my father's name. I said I had no father. He looked at me and laughed. Then all the kids also started laughing. After that I never participated in any sports. This was in Class 8. Gosh, that was one eventful year, wouldn't you say?' She says with a forced laugh.

'But you see this is why I get angry when people talk about the status enjoyed by devadasis. They have not lived our lives. They don't understand our pain. You know what they call devadasis in our village? *Sule*. It's a slang for prostitute. When my sister was getting married, I went to the village to invite my father. My biological father, the man whom I had looked upon as my real father. He never visited or supported us after his fallout with my mother, but it was his daughter's wedding. He came outside, took the card from me and never showed up. But that wasn't the worst of it. His sister made me sit outside the house and offered refreshments from a distance, like I was an untouchable. My own father and his family! That day I decided I didn't have a father, and I didn't need one. But it hurts. This is a spectre that continues to haunt us at every step. You need a father's name not just in the scholarship forms, but even for things like the Provident Fund. When I got confirmed at my NGO, they filled an online PF form for me. It was not accepted. The reason: there was no father's name. It just never ends,' she says with a sad smile.

Normally when I see something so powerful, my pen moves of its own volition. But with this book, it took me days to put down a single word. I had broken the cardinal rule that had been drilled into me since my days in journalism college—I had become too involved with my subject. And so I couldn't write. I was afraid that I would not be able to do justice to the people who had trusted me with their pain, with their struggles and their brave little smiles. Would I be able to convey the depth of all that I had seen, heard and experienced? Have I been able to do justice to their courage, their hopes, their aspirations? I wonder.

**

P.S. While to us these are stories of inspiration, of success, to the people whose tales they are, these are full of painful memories. Memories that they have shared because they felt someone else could benefit from their story. And yet revisiting the darkest corners of your lives and recounting its horrors to strangers is not easy. In that moment, it is easy to skip over a few details, to forget a few dates. It is possible that the dates in some of these narratives do not match. And yet, I did not try to force people to reconcile them. The content, the act of speaking itself, is much more important than the figures here. So, please accept my sincere apologies for any inconsistencies that you find in the timelines of these narratives. The facts still remain the same, only they happened a few months before or after the time mentioned. Is that really so important?

BLACK, WHITE AND EVERYTHING IN BETWEEN

There has been a lot of debate on the institution of Devadasis. Some see it as a symbol of empowered women, others as a symbol of oppression. Yet others, and this typically is a line of thinking propagated by the colonialists and the reformists, as the hallmark of degenerate women. Of late there have been two kinds of writings on the subject—both equally passionate. One, primarily by journalists and activists, talks about how the devadasis today are little more than sex workers who suffer from poverty, disease and sexual exploitation. This group criticizes the institution as an oppressive patriarchal and caste-based strategy to exploit women from particular communities. The narrative here is made up primarily of interviews conducted in dingy brothel rooms, or at the Yellama festivals. It looks at the here and now. The other seeks to remove the taint that has been foisted on this ancient practice. This group of writers, primarily Indians and often, dancers and cultural activists, seek to establish the Devadasi tradition as a matriarchal system that gave women the freedom to learn, to maintain property and to run their own lives. Here again there is lack of consensus on the sexual freedoms enjoyed by the women. While most suggest that these women had the freedom to choose their consorts and enjoy physical relationships without being bound by prescribed wifely duties, some argue that these women remained chaste. In these writings, there is often no mention of the caste dimension of the practice, either because it was indeed not a feature of the ancient tradition or because it takes away from the narrative of empowerment. That aside, what this stream of writing seeks to do is establish the devadasis as artists who created and kept alive some of India's best-known dance forms, a contribution that is seldom recognized. Present-day Bharatnatyam is a 'sanitized' version of the Sadir dance performed by devadasis in Tamil Nadu; Odissi can be traced to the dance of the Maharis in the temples of Orissa and Mohiniattam (literally the dance of the enchantress) to the Tevidichiyattam of the devadasis or Tevdichi of Kerala. These writings do acknowledge the current condition of the devadasis, but lay the blame squarely at the feet of the colonial administration that viewed 'nautch' as amoral and sought to ban not just the dances, but even their practitioners, effectively robbing them of their art and means of livelihood. They use historical references to bolster their case.

The truth perhaps lies somewhere in between. Perhaps the Devadasi system, to begin with, was about women willingly dedicating their lives to the pursuit of art and culture. Perhaps it did provide them with much needed freedom—social, economic and sexual. Perhaps it was not overtly caste-based, and a few kings did send their family members into the practice. And perhaps these women were indeed respected—they were invited to important ceremonies, unlike their caste brethren. Many claim that a new bride was made to wear a *mangalsutra* made by a devadasi, or one which had a bead from her *taali* as she was regarded as *nityasumangali*, a woman eternally free from widowhood. I have no evidence that proves or contradicts these statements. Nor is my concern with finding this evidence or exploring the genesis of the system. I only know what my interactions with these Wives of God, and these fatherless Children of God revealed. The fact is that today, the practice is largely caste-based. Today, women, or rather little girls, do not willingly become devadasis. Today, they enjoy no respect, no freedoms. Today, they are sexually exploited, their bodies marauded, constantly. They are not prostitutes because they are seldom paid for the copulations, forced or otherwise, but today, they are often sold into prostitution. Today, the practice stipulates that they beg for their sustenance. Today, they languish while the art form that their community created, and painstakingly nurtured, has been appropriated by others. Today, they, and their plight, are invisible and when they are seen, it is not as artists, contributors, cultural ambassadors, but as victims, prostitutes and emblems of shame for leading a life they never chose.

History is important, but is it more important than the living? Is its re-appropriation critical for reclaiming the respect due to this group of much-maligned people? And is it possible to retain their position as teachers and artists, even as the practice that once led to the nurturing of their arts (but also subsequently, to the organized exploitation and 'othering' of these artists) is permanently eradicated?

Endnotes

1. G. W. Briggs (1920). *The Religious Life of India: The Chamars*. Associate Press: Calcutta, p. 31.
2. These numbers were given out during the conference. Media reports also seem to quote similar numbers. However, I have not seen any actual report that gives these numbers to understand the basis of calculation, the scope, etc. Also see Neeta Lal, Indian girls sexually exploited in the name of religion. *The Star Online*. 21 April 2011. Available at https://www.thestar.com.my/lifestyle/features/2011/04/21/indian-girls-sexually-exploited-in-the-name-of-religion
3. S. Vadlapatla, Devadasi system still exists in Telangana, AP, says report. *The Times of India*. 23 February 2015. Available at https://timesofindia.indiatimes.com/india/Devadasi-system-still-exists-in-Telangana-AP-says-report/articleshow/46337859.cms
4. Again quoted at the conference with similar references in media reports, S. Parthasarathy, Slaves of circumstance. *The Hindu*. 17 August 2013. Available at https://www.thehindu.com/features/magazine/slaves-of-circumstance/article5028924.ece
5. *Matayyas* seem to be different from *Jogappas*—the men dedicated to the Goddess at her annual festival. According to various reports and studies, their genital parts are often mutilated, they dress up as females and beg from house to house. They definitely do not lead a 'normal' life. However, no reference to *Jogappas* came up during my interactions with the joginis and their children.
6. There are many versions of this tale. In the story narrated by Vijay Kumar, the woman was called Arundhati and was a Dalit. That is the version that I have used here. Another popular version of the tale, floating on the internet, does not identify the woman as a Dalit. According to this version Renuka, Jamadagni's wife, was always accompanied by a faithful Matang woman servant. The arrow that Parshurama used to severe his mother's head also severed the head of the Matang woman who was following her. It was night when Parshurama, came to revive his mother with his father's blessings. In the darkness, he attached the head on the body of the Matang servant instead.
7. As described by Renukamma, verbatim.
8. 'The *dappu* is the simplest of the traditional percussion instruments. It contains a wooden frame, fixed at three places, made of either *udisa* or *vēpa* (neem) planks with 6" to 8" width. This frame is called "palaka" in Coastal Andhra and "gundu" in the Telangana area. To one end of this frame is tightly tied skin of a young male buffalo. If such a skin is not available,

the skin of either a lamb or a goat will be used. The preparation of the leather to be used in the making of the *dappu* is by itself an art, as it is in the case of preparing the skin for making a puppet. The drummer uses two small sticks to beat the *dappu* to produce varying types of sounds. The round stick in the right hand is about 9" long (called *sirre*) and ¾" in its diameter and at the tail end measures ½". This is the main striking tool. The other stick (called *sitikena/chitikena/pulla*) is thin and is a little longer. The drummer controls the sound by placing his left palm on the upper edge of the frame and uses the stick with the left hand to control the rhythm.' As noted in M. Nagabhushana Sarma, 1995, *Folk Performing Arts of Andhra Pradesh* Telugu University, Hyderabad, pp. 50–51, available at: http://www.simoncharsley.co.uk/perform1.html

9. S. Pathak, New life for Bedia girls. *Pioneer*, 19 November 1999, p. 10. Available at http://www.womenstudies.in/elib/girl_child/gc_new_life.pdf; A. Pateriya, Winds of change sweeping through Madhya Pradesh's Bedia community. *Hindustan Times*. 20 December 2014. Available at http://www.hindustantimes.com/india-news/winds-of-change-sweeping-through-mp-s-bedia-community/article1-1298324.aspx

10. Bedia. Back to basics. *Hindustan Times*. 3 December 2000. Available at http://www.thehindu.com/2000/12/03/stories/1303061s.htm; Special Correspondent. Rabri sets price. *The Telegraph*. 17 August 2000. Available at http://www.telegraphindia.com/1000818/national.htm

Epilogue: Confessions

This chapter has been in the making for as long as the book. It was nine months ago, on a hot summer afternoon when Arpita, the publisher of Yoda Press, first suggested it. I had met her to discuss the book and after the initial introductions and logistics about timelines, design and processes, we got to talking about how the book happened. The discussion spiralled into the personal journey this Museum has been for me, how it has forced me to confront my own blindspots.[1] Of course, at that time, the term 'blindspots' had not been added to my lexicon. We used the more mundane 'bias'.

'Why is this not in the manuscript?' Arpita asked. I remember my defence well. There is nothing special about it. We all have biases and prejudices and one day, we realize them. Why would people care? It is the stories here that are important. I am just a curator.

I had always believed untouchability to be repugnant. How could one human being do this to another? How could the act of humiliating another person bring joy, power or contentment? Yet, at the same time, I harboured the naïve conviction that it was a thing of the past. That apart from a few isolated rural pockets and practices (manual scavenging), we were over this shameful phase of our culture and history. Laws had been put in place, affirmative action had been taken and while a lot more was needed to undo the damage caused by systemic violence and discrimination unleashed over centuries, we were on the right path. It is only when I started working on this Museum that I realized how ubiquitous this malaise is. It is everywhere, in our cities, in our localities, in our very homes, only now it is more subtle. Over, the years we have rationalized it, found the most reasonable explanations for our own practices of discrimination, cloaked them with rich arguments about health, hygiene, dignity of labour. Yet it is still everywhere around us and within us.

This realization was not just painful, it shattered every belief I held about myself. All of us have a notion of who we are and who we aspire to be. We manage perceptions all the time—for friends, family, bosses, acquaintances, neighbours, but most importantly for our own selves. How principled we are, how fair, how just, how generous, how equitable, how amusing, how stoic, how honest! Whether consciously or sub-consciously, we have a set of characteristics that we aspire to. Over the years, aspirations turn to convictions. We no longer want to have a great sense of humour, we possess one! We care deeply for our fellow human beings. We are non-judgemental. We are excellent listeners. One by one, we keep adding the layers, hiding the blemishes, not because we are bad people, but precisely because we aspire to be better! If intent is what matters, then ours is a perfect score.

As I type these words, I can almost see the Professor of my Leadership class shaking his head. 'Work Avoidance.' In my head, I hear him loud and clear. 'Stop taking cover in this intricate maze of stories and counter-stories. You know what you need to do.' I do and it is not easy.

'I care,' Arpita had said. 'Pointing fingers is easy. Acknowledging that you are part of the problem is not. Does your honesty end where your own story begins?'

Over the last nine months I have gone over the conversation a hundred times in my head. I moved from dismissing her suggestion to realizing its value. But I never had the time to actually pen down these few pages. There was just too much to be done—exams, problems, classes or simply research on the book itself. I was in a new country, new town, with a new life—that of a student. In 2017, I moved to Boston for a mid-career programme at Harvard. Not only do I now have a vocabulary to explain my actions and reactions, I am armed with an arsenal of incredible texts that expound on the hidden biases of good people, 'good' being the operating word. I have accumulated enough excuses to counter any judgement you may pass on the solitary glass that sat in my home all these years, till the time I embarked on this journey and realized what it meant.

At home, there had always been a separate glass to serve water to the domestic help, labourers, plumbers, electricians, or the postman. Till I heard the story of the tea cups, I never thought about it, never questioned the underlying assumption that the oral hygiene of a group of people was questionable due to their financial circumstances, and hence called for a separate set of glasses. It seemed reasonable enough. Toothpaste, toothbrush, even clean water is a luxury!

But the day I began to understand the significance of the tea cup or in this case, the separate glass, I oscillated between sheer disbelief and disgust. How could this be? Caste had never been a factor in my life. I never heard it mentioned at home or in family gatherings. I had been a part of the human rights movement—both on the streets and in the hallowed halls of Yojana Bhawan. Disbelief gave way to anger and I began to look for a scapegoat. I stormed home and asked my mother about it. She was shocked. 'What has caste got to do with it? I don't even know what caste anyone is from. Do you?' she reasoned.

'Why a separate glass then?'

Momentary silence. 'I never thought about it. It has been there for as long as I remember. We even had separate utensils at one point. It was the hygiene factor. Why do you think this is about caste?' Till a few months ago that would have sounded perfectly reasonable. Reasonable to the extent that I had never noticed it. None of us did. Just like the fact of not being able to accept that glass of water from the Kudmude Joshis who lived under a pal near Ahmednagar in Maharashtra. The dirty glass, the floating debris in the water. It sounded perfectly reasonable to not drink it. But was it? Was it simply hygiene that stayed my hand? Why did I not trust water from any source apart from my own home and the bottle sold in motley shops that I had time and again read about and seen in documentaries? Water whose source was unknown—it could be from washroom taps (and in India, that is not safe for drinking) or from leaks in a pipeline. Why did I trust it more? Was I also discriminating? Over the course of the last couple of years I have often asked myself this question. I don't yet have an answer.

All this I explained to my mom. I could see my own shock reflected on her face. Gradually, it gave way to conflict and then resolve. She got up and threw the glass into the dustbin. 'This won't be easy. It's something I have believed in for as long as I can remember, but it is obnoxious. I am sorry I never questioned it,' she said with a sigh.

Neither had I. Not once. Not even when I had my own house and kept the very same glass in it. That wasn't my mother's decision. It was mine. I was as much to blame. Perhaps more. Suddenly, I began to question all my actions and explanations. My water bottle is an extension of myself. 'She never drinks water anywhere. Such chua-choot (untouchability),' a friend had once joked in school. Perhaps, it hadn't been a joke. Perhaps he had been trying to tell me something. Perhaps I hadn't wanted to understand. It is easy to ascribe motive or reasons in retrospect. Does one ever truly know? And does it matter? The hundreds of houses where I had politely refused a glass of water during my field visits, did it matter to them what my reasons or excuses were? If they belonged to a certain caste, then my actions were another rejection, humiliation. In their much-acclaimed book, Mahzarin Banaji and Anthony Greenwald say, 'Implicit bias may operate outside of awareness, hidden from those who have it, but the discrimination that it produces can be clearly visible to researchers, and almost certainly also clearly visible to those who are disadvantaged by it.'[2]

I have struggled with this for months. Acknowledging your own prejudices is not easy, but exposing them to others is even more difficult. What would people think of me? It's not that I haven't talked about it. I have—with friends, family, colleagues, and eventually classmates. But these are safe audiences. People who either know me or believe in my values. Who know my story. Who would attribute the best intentions to it. People who would not judge me because they would see that these were simply my blindspots. They may even make excuses for me, commend me on my ability to face my own prejudices.

But acknowledging them to strangers? To people who know nothing of me. Who would see my actions just by themselves, without the benefit of a backstory. To people who would definitely judge me as they would have every right and reason to. I know now why this chapter took me a year to write. A year of constant reminders and excuses.

Why is it not in the manuscript? Arpita had asked. Because I was scared, because I was ashamed.

Why is it here now?

Am I no longer worried about your opinion of me?

I am.

Do I no longer seek your respect?

I do.

But this chapter is to remind myself and to reassure you that in this Museum, you will not be judged. All these years, I have been part of the problem myself. If I raise a finger, it has to first point at myself. This Museum is not about ascribing blame. No one else needs to know. But if you too have a chipped tea cup lying somewhere in your house, it is time to break it. Because sometimes breaking is a good thing!

Endnotes

1. M. R. Banaji, and A. G. Greenwald (2013). *Blindspot: Hidden Biases of Good People.* New York, NY, US: Delacourt Press.
2. Ibid.

Further Reading

The Gallery of Portraits

Read more about the origins of the term *Bhangi* in the book *The Bhangi: A Sweeper Caste: Its Socio-Economic Portraits, With Special Reference to Jodhpur City* by Shyamlal

Read more about the Handloom industry in Bargarh at http://www.navratnanews.com/hand-loom-handicraft/

Theatre of the Invisible

Here are some resources that will help you to know more about the Naqqara and the Nautanki http://www.Devnautanki.com

K. Toomey (Spring, 2014). *Study of Nagara Drum in Pushkar Rajasthan.* Independent Study Project (ISP) Collection. 1816. Available at http://digitalcollections.sit.edu/cgi/viewcontent.cgi?article=2836&context=isp_collection

K. Hansen (1991). *Grounds for Play: The Nautanki Theatre of North India.* University of California Press: Berkeley.

Rana Siddiqui Zaman, Nautanki again, *Frontline*, Vol 29 (16), 11–24 August 2012. Available at http://www.frontline.in/static/html/fl2916/stories/20120824291610700.htm

M. L. Varadpande (1992). *History of Indian Theatre: Lok Ranga, Panorama of Indian Folk Theatre.* Abhinav Publications: New Delhi.

J. Blade (2005). *Percussion Instruments and Their History.* The Bold Strummer Ltd.: London.

D. P. Mehrotra (2006). *Gulab Bai: The Queen of Nautanki Theatre.* Penguin Books India: New Delhi.

Want to get better acquainted with the Lavani? Try some of these resources.

Rupali Bansode. The linked caste slavery of the Kolhatis and the Bedias, *Savari*, 28 April 2014. Available at http://www.dalitweb.org/?p=2556

Shanta Gokhale. Disrespect of dance. *Mumbai Mirror*, 4 September 2014. Available at http://www.mumbaimirror.com/columns/columnists/shanta-gokhale/Disrespect-of-dance/articleshow/41632072.cms

Mridula Chari. There's more to Maharashtra's bawdy Lavani dance form than Bollywood reveals, *Scroll.in*, 21 August 2014. Available at http://scroll.in/article/674409/though-some-are-embarrassed-by-its-explicitness-maharashtras-traditional-lavani-dance-is-thriving

Prachi Jawadekar Wagh. The return of Lavni, *Livemint*, 15 January 2010. Available at http://www.livemint.com/Leisure/k3oIQBwZwEDmhLz3Rm-d1KK/The-return-of-Lavni.html

Learn more about Jasma, Meghmaya and the Bhavai

Anthropological Survey of India (2002). *People of India: Gujarat, Volume XXII*. Popular Prakashan: Mumbai.

https://www.youtube.com/watch?v=h5HBh0d0W_g BhavniBhavai with subtitles

http://sax.pomona.edu/bhavai/music/bhungal.html

B. Ray (ed.) (2009). *History of Science, Philosophy and Culture in Indian Civilization, Vol. XIV, Part 4*. Pearson Longman: Delhi.

R. M. Perez (2004). *Kings and Untouchables: A Study of the Caste System in Western India*. Chronicle Books: New Delhi.

A Place to Remember

Learn more about Savitribai Phule, Mahatma Jyotiba Phule and Rajarshi Shahu Maharaj

Mukesh Manas, Savitri Phule: first woman teacher of India, 28 January 2012. Available at http://mukeshmanas.blogspot.in/2012/01/savitribai-phule-first-woman-teacher-of.html

Suchismita Pai, TBI Heroes: Savitribai, The mother of modern girls' education in India, *The Better India*, 15 October 2013. Available at http://www.thebetterindia.com/8464/tbi-heroes-savitribai-the-mother-of-modern-girls-education/

Vinay Dabholkar, Jyotiba & Savitri Phule's girl school (1851): A radical innovation, *Catalign Innovation Consulting*, 21 June 2010. Available at http://www.catalign.in/2010/06/jyotiba-savitri-phules-girl-school-1851.html

S. A. Raman (2009). Women in India: A Social and Cultural History (2 volumes) Praeger. Excerpt available at https://books.google.co.in/books?id=KwKrCQAAQBAJ&pg=RA1-PA138&dq=savitribai+phule&hl=en&sa=X&ved=0CEYQ6AEwCWoVChMI6uijgYveyAIVgamUCh1uBgqp#v=onepage&q=savitribai%20phule&f=false

B. R. Mani & P. Sardar (eds) (2008). *A Forgotten Liberator: The Life and Struggle of Savitribai Phule*. Mountain Peak Publishers.

D. Keer (1964). *Mahatma Jotirao Phooley: Father of the Indian Social Revolution*. Popular Prakashan: Bombay.

J. Pawar (Trans.) (2013). *Rajshri Shahu Chhatrapati: A Social Revolutionary King*. Maharashtra Itihas Prabodhini: Kolhapur.

Waman Meshram, Short history of reservation, *Bharat Mukti Morcha Blog*, 24 June 2012. Available at http://bharatmukti.blogspot.in/2012/06/short-history-of-reservation.html

Glossary

Family and Relationships

Atiya: Aunt, father's sister

Bade papa: Uncle, father's elder brother

Behen: Sister

Bhai: Brother

Bua: Aunt, father's sister

Chacha: Uncle, father's younger brother

Chachi: Aunt, wife of father's younger brother

Dada: Paternal grandfather

Dadi: Paternal grandmother

Ma: Mother

Mama: Uncle, mother's brother

Mausi: Aunt, mother's sister

Nana: Maternal grandfather

Nani: Maternal grandmother

Phuphi: Aunt, father's sister

Other Words

aakrosh: Anger

ada: Coquetry

akhadas: Training centres

antayaja: Literally last born; a term initially used by Gandhi to write about the 'Untouchables'

avarna: Literally people without a varna (referring to Dalits)

ayah: Nurse

adhishikshaks: Assistant teachers

baal mela: Children's fair

badi: Big

badhai: Congratulations

bajaa wala: Member of the local village orchestra in Orissa

bakshis: Tip

baithak: Lounge

banjar: Fallow land

basti: Colony

bhang: Hemp

bhoj: Food

bhandara: Community feasts

bindi: Literally point or dot; refers to a coloured dot worn on the centre of the forehead, originally by Hindus and Jains in India

chania choli: Traditional dress worn by women in West India, notably the state of Gujarat. Consists of a blouse and flared skirt.

chaprasi: Peon

charpai: Cot

chattai: Reed mats

choti: Small

chowkidaar: Guard

daan: Charity

dalal: Pimp; Middleman

dastaan: Story

Devadasi: Literally, 'servants of the Goddess'; refers to women who are sexually exploited after being dedicated to the Goddess Yellamma in many states of India.

dhanda: Trade

dharamshala: Resthouse for tourists or pilgrims

dhol: Musical instrument, drum

dhoti: Loincloth

diya: Oil lamps

fakir: Mendicant/beggar

gaali: Expletive

gamcha: Towel

Ganeshotsav: Ganesh festival

gavaiya: Singer

ghee ki roti: Indian bread with ghee

ghungroo: A musical anklet made of tiny, closely spaced bells. It is often worn by dancers in India.

guru: Teacher

Ghumantu jaati: Travelling tribes or nomads

halwa: Pudding

Harijans: Literally the people of God; the name given by Mahatma Gandhi to refer to people from the 'Untouchable' communities.

hunar: Talent/skill

imli: Tamarind

jaat: Caste

jaati bhai: Literally caste brothers; refers to other villagers

jatra: Festival

jhootan: Leftovers

kala: Art

kalakaar: Artist

karambhoomi: Place of work

karamchari: Employees

karyakarta: Worker

katha: Story

khaini: Chewing tobacco

khana: Food

khaprail: Terracotta tiles

Kolhapuri chappals: Slippers made in Kolhapur, Maharashtra

kotha: Brothel

kuch accha: Something nice

kumkum: A red/vermillion powder used by Hindu women on their forehead to mark their marital status.

lipi: Script

mahaul: Atmosphere/environment

maidan: Field

mandali: Group; often referring to groups of artists

mangalsutra: A neckpiece, often worn by married women in Hinduism to show their marital status.

mashaals: Torch

mela: Fair

mohallas: Localities

morcha: Rally

mukhiya: Head of Village Panchayat

mulnivasis: Original inhabitants/indigenous people

nagma: Melody or tune

naik: Leader (generally of a Banjara colony)

naqqarchi: One who plays the naqqara

natak: Plays

natakshalas: Theatres

nautankis: Street plays

nauwari: 9 yard saree

nayak: Narrator or leader

nitya sumangali: A woman eternally free from widowhood.

paal: Temporary hut

padyatra: Foot march

palak poori: Spinach bread fried in oil

pallu: Edge of a saree

panchama: Refers to the fifth varna or people who were outside the varna system or avarna

Pathan suit: Traditional (North) Indian dress that comprises of a long (often knee length) top worn with loose trousers

pitara: Bag or box

pucca: Paved or permanent

pujari: Priest

purusha: Literally man. According to the Rig Veda, the Purusha was a being with a thousand eyes, thousand feet and thousand heads.

rampatars: Literally 'the vessel of Lord Ram'; refers to the cups kept outside the house for Dalits.

roti: Indian bread made from wheat

rotlas: Thick Indian bread made from bajra

saajinde: Instrumentalists

saaz: Instruments

safai karamchari: Cleaner

salaam: Salute or salutation

salwar suit: Traditional (North) Indian dress that comprises of a long (often knee length) top worn with loose trousers.

shagird: Apprentice

seth: Merchant

shishya: Student

sindoor: Vermillion line often put by married Hindu women in their hair to display their marital status.

subedar: Army officer

sutradhar: Narrator

taali: A mangalsutra tied by the groom around the bride's neck in South Indian weddings.

tabeez: Talisman

tanda: Colony; group of Lambada houses

tari: Local alcohol

tel ki roti: Indian bread with oil

thekedaar: Middleman or commissioning agent

trishul: Trident

vanachara: Forest wanderer

vanijyakara: Merchant

vichaar ghostis: Brainstorming sessions

virasaat: Heritage

varna vyavastha: Caste system

varna: A Sanskrit word meaning class, order or colour. It refers to the social classes in Brahmanical texts. It is believed that there were four varnas or social classes in the Hindu society.

veshas: Playlets or stand-alone scenes from a drama

watan: Home

zamindar: Landlord

About the Author

Gunjan Veda is a story teller, a public policy and international development strategist and a gender policy specialist. A social entrepreneur, she is deeply interested in working with humanitarian aid and development assistance programmes, globally, to create innovative solutions ensuring access to rights and resources for vulnerable populations. She has a Master's degree in Public Administration from Harvard University, and a Master's degree in International Relations from the University of Warwick. She was formerly a policymaker with the Government of India with the Health, Nutrition and Gender portfolios. An avid cultural enthusiast and traveller, Gunjan loves interacting with people, learning about fast disappearing cultural forms and sharing nuggets about people and polity, art and artists through powerful stories. She is happiest when surrounded by a mound of books and some cheery birdsong!

Extolled for his extraordinary courage, Bhagat Singh is one of our most venerated freedom fighters. He is valourised for his martyrdom, and rightly so, but in the ensuing enthusiam, most of us forget his contributions as an intellectual and a thinker. In the current political climate, when it has become routine to appropriate Bhagat Singh as a nationalist icon, not much is known about his nationalist vision. This book provides a corrective to this by bringing together a majority of Bhagat Singh's writings, some of which were hitherto unavailable in English.

A collection that brings together Bhagat Singh's seminal writings

For special offers on this and other books from SAGE, write to marketing@sagepub.in

Explore our range at
www.sagepub.in

PAPERBACK
9789352808373

Behind the seemingly ordinary life of a practising architect lies a whole host of non-professional impulses that give shape to buildings. *Stories of Storeys: Art, Architecture and the City* is about these impulses and conditions—social, literate, personal and political—which are expressed, but often ignored in architecture. Bhatia looks at the ordinary, physical, visible and tactile involvement of our urban environment and the way it affects, communicates with, or influences us.

An all-inclusive sociology of architecture through the eyes of a renowned architect

For special offers on this and other books from SAGE, write to marketing@sagepub.in

Explore our range at
www.sagepub.in

PAPERBACK
9789353280802